"Despite the flurry of books on Celtic spirituality in recent years, very little has seen print that combines a solid foundation in Celtic tradition and scholarship with practical guidance for those who hope to follow a living Celtic spiritual path in today's world. Brendan Cathbad Myers' *The Mysteries of Druidry* fills that void admirably, with a clear, accessible, and forthright exploration of Celtic tradition as the foundation of a personal path of mystical transformation that's profoundly relevant to the problems and possibilities of the modern world. This is a book I would be delighted to recommend to my students, to members of my Druid order, and to anyone interested in Celtic spirituality as a living path for today."

—*John Michael Greer*

Grand Archdruid, Ancient Order of Druids in America

Author, The New Encyclopedia of the Occult *and* The Druidry Handbook

"Brendan Myers has created a powerful, passionate book of Celtic spirituality for today's seeker. Informed by his research and scholarship, but also by the poetry in his soul, Myers' book lays out the basis for a compelling, even life-changing path. It's not an easy path—the aspiring Druid finds that true spirituality requires hard work, learning, facing difficult truths, and getting along with others. The intelligent reader will find it far more rewarding than the supermarket sorcery so common in today's Pagan writings."

—*Jane Raeburn*

Author, Celtic Wicca

"*The Mysteries of Druidry* is an exemplary look at one man's approach to Druidism, with excellent food for thought and suggestions for group ritual and personal practice. Brendan's questions and discussions lay a firm foundation for all those seeking to explore the many forms of Druidism for themselves. His personal stories of working with and discovering the spirits of the land are inspiring and useful guides to the readers."

—*Erynn Laurie, Author,* A Circle of Stones,

Co-founder of the Inis Glas Hedge School

"In *The Mysteries of Druidry*, Brendan Myers provides us with his heart knowledge of the Druid Mysteries from his own personal experiences. He also presents us with today's accepted academic wisdom about the Druids (a form of knowledge that is from the head or mind). To complete the triad of knowledge, Myers also teaches us the Druidic technique of Peaceful Abiding which opens one's self to the musical embrace of Nature. He illustrates other Druidic techniques to self knowledge and awareness that are known as the Way of the Warrior, Touching the Earth, and Parting the Mists. The many pathways from initiation to understanding are beautifully described in a series of shared experiences that take us on journeys through land, fire, and water and into Otherworldly realms of spiritual revelation. *The Mysteries of Druidry* is itself a journey well worth taking for any student or teacher of Druidry. Brendan Myers has in this seminal work on Druidry effectively revealed much about the Druid Way that was once hidden. The Ogham would describe this book as the "little cage" (Nature's Place for Peaceful Abiding) which is also known by some as the Circle of Revelation. *The Mysteries of Druidry* is a book that should be an essential part of the library of any seeker of the Druid Way."

—Searles O'Dubhain, Founder of the Summerlands
*Website (*www.summerlands.com*), Ogham Seer and Druid Author*

"Druidry, which tends to be re-invented from scratch every time a new group claims the term as a self-description, has all too often merely reflected the unexamined tastes and prejudices of its diverse practitioners. It is refreshing, in that light, to see Brendan Myers approach the subject with genuine intellectual rigour, yet without abjuring the passion and inspiration such a path requires. He isn't afraid to ask hard questions, and to develop the answers as fully and richly as possible. Even if every reader will not agree with all of his conclusions, his work provides a solid base from which future discussions of the topic can proceed."

—Alexei Kondratiev,
author of The Apple Branch *and* Celtic Ritual

the Mysteries of
DRUIDRY

celtic mysticism, theory & practice

the Mysteries of

DRUIDRY

celtic mysticism,
theory & practice

BRENDAN CATHBAD MYERS, PH.D.
FOREWORD BY ISAAC BONEWITS, FOUNDER of ADF

New Page Books
a division of The Career Press
Franklin Lakes, NJ

THE MYSTERIES OF DRUIDRY
EDITED BY AND TYPESET BY KATE HENCHES
Cover design by Mary Langer and Jane Brideson
Printed in the U.S.A. by Book-mart Press

To order this title, please call toll-free 1-800-CAREER-1 (NJ and Canada: 201-848-0310) to order using VISA or MasterCard, or for further information on books from Career Press.

The Career Press, Inc., 3 Tice Road, PO Box 687,
Franklin Lakes, NJ 07417
www.careerpress.com
www.newpagebooks.com

Library of Congress Cataloging-in-Publication Data

Myers, Brendan Cathbad, 1974-
    The mysteries of Druidry : Celtic mysticism, theory, and practice / by Brendan Cathbad Myers.
        p. cm.
    Includes bibliographical references and index.
    ISBN-13: 978-1-56414-878-0 (pbk.)
    ISBN-10: 1-56414-878-5 (pbk.)
        1. Druids and Druidism. 2. Spiritual life. I. Title.

BL910.M94 2006
299′.16--dc22

                                                                        2005056736

Dedication

This book is dedicated
with love to
Teampall Na Calleach,
An Mhí.

Acknowledgments

The themes and ideas of the present book had been stirring in my mind for many years, even while engaged in other writing projects. But I did not sit down to write in earnest until October of 2003, just after I was brought to visit the royal Hill of Uisneach for the first time. Some of the ideas and meditations which appear in this book came to me in dreams on the nights that followed. Then I collected together notes and letters that I had already written, made many trips to the library in search of research resources, and began preparing new material. Almost precisely one year later, the first complete draft was done.

Some parts of this book are based on the practices of a Celtic clan from Canada which I have been part of for many years. I thank the many members of that clann (they know who they are), but especially Matthew Clooney who stayed in touch with me the most since leaving Canada to live in Ireland. Among other friends, I must thank Maureen Conklin for her valuable comments and corrections, Jane Brideson, for her wonderful artwork, and Isaac Bonewits for his help with understanding the publishing industry.

Among my friends in Ireland, I must thank Gayleen Jacobs and family, Gina McGarry, Adge, Fergal Gallagher, Sylvia Socci, Eoghain Hamilton, Laura McTaggart, and the people of An Conradh Draoithe na h-Éireann. Their friendship, hospitality, and conversation are deeply appreciated, and, while writing this book, I often imagined I was writing for them. For very special thanks, I must name three people without whom this book might never have been written. Without the friendship of Janet Farrar and Gavin Bone, adjusting to life in Ireland would have been very much harder for me, and without the use of their library, this little book would have turned out very differently. I must also give special thanks to Anja Zimmer. Her enthusiasm and confidence in me, and her love, was enormously uplifting. Finally, special thanks go to Bella and Nelix, two of Janet's cats, who sat on my lap while I was writing the first few chapters of this book. They probably believe themselves to be co-authors.

I regret that the present work must be so short. Mysticism is far deeper, more profound, more complicated, and yet more simple than any one book can tell. If this small offering to the world is regarded favorable by the "intimates of the spirit" for whom it is written, then I shall deem it a success.

Contents

Foreword

Ah, the ancient Druids of Ireland—those wise poets wandering through the Celtic mists, performing great acts of magic with nothing but a golden sickle and a sprig of mistletoe, designing huge stone circles with which to predict eclipses and solstices, while teaching their students the mysteries of the pentagram and the five elements it represents...

All of which, however inspiring and romantic, happens to be nonsense, as Brendan "Cathbad" Myers has been telling people online for many years. Now, for the first time in print, he reveals what Paleopagan Irish Druids really believed in this marvelous work of scholarship and heart.

Myers is both an Irishman and a neo-pagan Druid, and, like most modern Druids, he feels a commitment to truth more than to romantic nostalgia for a golden age that never was. He balances this with a love of the old gods and a deep respect for the power of inspiration in spiritual growth.

It takes a lot of patience to learn how to listen to trees, for they speak vvveeerrryyy ssslllooowwwlllyyy. Fortunately, Cathbad has that patience. He has been traveling around the Celtic Isles for many years, soaking up the essence of their sacred landscapes and learning the stories that inhabit them. He shares those stories in this fascinating book that will appeal to everyone who has ever wondered what ancient Druidism was all about.

Readers will learn about the world of Tir Na n-Og, the Sacred Truth, the Mist of Manannan, the Great Marriage, and the Quest of the Hero. These stories revealed spiritual truths to the ancient peoples of Celtic Ireland and continue to speak to modern peoples as well, whether self-identified as Celtic or not, for the core of Celtic Druidry is the relationship between people and the sacred landscapes which surround them everywhere. Now, when the Earth Mother is under assault by all the forces of modern technology and human greed, is when we need new versions of ancient Earth-centered belief systems to restore respect for the sacredness of the physical world around us.

Those new belief systems must be rooted in scholarly, political, economic, artistic, and intuitive truths if they are to become both healthy and effective—something that Cathbad knows all too well. As he puts it, "A spiritual seeker is not an anachronism, nor is she a child. She does not wish to live in the past, nor in a fantasy world. She is a hero, on a journey across the ninth wave of the sea, and she wishes to live in the here and now."

Let Cathbad be your guide along that spiritual journey and, whether you decide to live a Druidic life or not, you will still have a marvelous trip.

Isaac Bonewits

Introduction:

The Call of the Morrigan

This book is meant to be read by candlelight. Go to a silent place, or as quiet a place as you can find. Seat yourself near a window with an interesting view, and open the curtains. Disable the ringer on your telephone. Have something to drink at hand. Arrange a pillow to support your neck and head. Take a moment to feel your breath. When you are still and at rest, the ceremony will begin.

Many ages ago, perhaps only a few short years after the world was made, a young lad named Setanta set out on a journey. He decided that the farm where he lived as a child with his mother and his cousins was too small, and that the world must have more in it to see. His father, who was always away on travels of his own, belonged to a special army that recruited only from the noble clans. Setanta decided it was time to take up his birthright, follow in his father's footsteps, and join the Boy's Troop of the Red Branch Knights.

For someone walking alone, at that time in the age of the world, the roads and spaces between settlements were always wild and dark. The distance from Dundalk to Emain Macha was long and dangerous. Setanta had to be wary of wild animals, brigands, and the elements. He played with his hurley and slither (a stick and "ball" used in the ancient game of hurling) to occupy his mind during the long days of tedious walking. At night he slept in the rough on a bed of leaves and mosses, a stone for his pillow, and his cloak for a blanket. And all along the road, the shadow of a crow followed him, far away enough to be unobtrusive, but close enough to be a constant presence.

On the third morning, he emerged from his sleeping-hole at the side of the road to find a woman standing over him. She seemed much taller than any adult he had ever seen before, and darker. But perhaps that was an effect of the light, for the sun was rising behind her, and shadows fell before her. Her wild red hair and dark green cloak with black feathers seemed to be stirring in a light breeze that he could not feel. A golden torc, the sign of a sovereign, was around her neck. In one hand she carried a spear with a bright spear-tip as long as a sword, and in the other she held a stout wooden shield with metallic reinforcements designed in an intricate knotwork pattern. Her face was hard to see, with the sun behind her head, but there was a strange warmth glowing from it. She was beautiful, but she had the kind of beauty one sometimes finds in thunderstorms and wild tempestuous seas.

"Do not be afraid," she said to him. "I am a great queen of this island, and I have been watching you for a long time. I am here to tell you your destiny."

She sat down on the ground, closer to the boy's level, and spoke further. "If you want it, you can have a long and happy life, with a good home, a wife, and children who will love you well, and when you die you will be old, healthy, well-loved, and happy." The boy thought about this future prospect, intrigued but also bemused.

"But there is another life for you," continued the magical woman. "You could become a great hero, and live a life of adventure, passion, and danger. If you choose this life, you will create a great name for yourself, and the poets and storytellers shall be telling your tale in this land forever, but you shall die very young."

The woman stood again, and thrust the rim of the shield into the ground, just within his reach of his right hand, and then thrust the blunt end of the spear into the ground to his left. "I offer you a choice today," she said to him. "The choice you make will transform your future irreversibly. Which kind of life do you choose to live?"

And without hesitation Setanta made his choice.

This moment, which I have here rendered from a traditional Irish story taught to me as a child, is the most important and definitive moment in the whole body of Celtic mythology and mysticism. There are several other versions of it. For instance, one has Setanta demand weapons from the king when he overhears the Druid, Cathbad, foretell that if anyone takes up arms on that day, "his name would endure in Ireland as a word signifying mighty acts, and stories about him would last forever." Setanta, overhearing this, went to King Conchobar Mac Nessa, and demanded to be granted arms, saying that Cathbad instructed him to do so. When Cathbad is brought to verify if this is true, he says, "Well, this day has this merit: he who arms for the first time today will achieve fame and greatness. But his life is short." Setanta says of this that it is a fair bargain: "If I achieve fame I am content, though I had only one day on earth."[1] And indeed this is what happened to him: he grew up to become Cú Chullain, the greatest warrior in the whole body of Celtic mythology.

One could read this as simply the classic example of the forthright self-assertiveness of a Celtic warrior: to be boastful and proud, to seek fame and glory. Yet I read it as one of the most important moments in all of Celtic mythology. It is the existential, ethical moment when the central character of the story is called upon to choose his future, and in so doing choose how he shall live and what person he will become. This is, I claim, the very image of the situation of someone who wishes to understand the meaning and purpose of her life, to take her life into her own hands, and make something of it. This desire, when pursued as a distinctly religious and spiritual activity, is part of what we normally call *Mysticism*.

Mysticism is the practice of obtaining direct personal connection or unity with the divine forces of the universe. The benefit of its practice is a better knowledge of the world, one's sense of purpose and place within it, and indeed better knowledge of who you are. This latter knowledge is most important. For the first basic teaching of any mature mystery tradition is *know yourself*. The phrase was written over the entrance to the Oracle of Delphi. The philosopher Schopenhauer said it forms the basis and beginning-place of all knowledge of anything. It cannot be overstated what a curious and wonderful phenomena the self actually is. The exploration and discovery of its wondrous heights and dark depths, its relations to other great immensities of the world, and especially the way the quest itself tends to transform the seeker, is that which we dignify with the name of Mysticism. And it is one of the oldest, most unique, most profound, and most rewarding, of all human endeavours.

What, then, is distinctive about *Celtic* Mysticism? As we find it both in ancient literature and in modern revival, it is a romanticism characterized by the near-worship of art and music, of warrior prowess, and the wildness of nature. Through these things the presence of an underlying animating energy seems to appear. This presence is best seen in the descriptions of the Celtic Otherworld, which in Irish is called *Tir Na n-Og*, and translated into English means "Land of Youth." The image of the Druid is an image of mystery and power infused with the presence of this extraordinary realm. Nearly all of the most beautiful and inspiring stories in Celtic mythology involve some relation with Tir Na n-Og (perhaps a journey there, or a meeting with one of its inhabitants). It is a land touched with a certain mysterious quality, in which every hill, stream, tree, lake, and valley has a story, and a voice with which to tell it. It is a place where so many of the things in the ordinary world, which are undertaken with sombre seriousness, are performed with a certain earnest playfulness. The heroes of Celtic renown lack inhibition and restraint and yet also lack the tainting effects of ego. They can engage in erotic lovemaking and bloodthirsty violence without losing their innocence. It is a world where some of the qualities which we prize in ourselves most—beauty, honor, adventurousness, and wonder—become the qualities of the gods themselves. But the important detail about the Celtic Otherworld is that it is all around us. It is not in some separate and distant realm which we can only barely glimpse in rare moments, and fully visit only after we die. It is already spread out on the surface of the Earth. It is easier to see in some special parts of the world, such as the sacred sites of Ireland and the Celtic lands, but to someone who forges and tempers her mind and spirit, it is revealed everywhere. It is everywhere because we carry it with us wherever we go.

The world of Tir Na n-Og is but one distinctive feature of Celtic mysticism, and in this book I will describe many more. There is also the Sacred Truth, the Mist of Manannan, the Great Marriage, and others. The story of Cú Chullain which I have already introduced embodies another one: the Quest of the Hero. The discussion of these mysteries will be followed by a longer discussion of the practical exercises and techniques that can help people seek out and discover them. In the pre-Christian era of Celtic culture, such practices were, for the most part, the province of a professional caste of specialists called *Druids*. Druids were one of the greatest orders of magic-makers and wisdom-keepers in the whole of the ancient world. Their knowledge and magical skill brought them close to a special spiritual realm which was at the same time the natural world: the hills and valleys, oceans and lakes, mountains and forests, of the Celtic lands. They emerged from the ancient Celtic tribes, at a time when people lived a little closer to nature than we do. By the light of the storyteller's fire, and with the play of the harp, the Druids dreamed magic for their people. In the deep woods they would gather, bringing together their mysticism and philosophy, their insight and learning. Their spirit emerged from the tides of the sea, the light of the sun, the wind in the Oak, the cry of the deer. In this way, they created an institution that inspired, frightened, and uplifted their world.

In this book, I emphasize the path of the Druid. There are of course other paths: that of the courageous and honorable Warrior, or the creative and evocative Bard, just to name two more. This book is for those who are exploring the spirituality of the Celts. It is for those who have Celtic ancestors, or who wish they did. It is for those who enjoy learning about the ancient Celts, their beliefs and practices, and have a desire to emulate them in a manner valid for themselves and for this century. It aims to describe some of the ideas and practices which come from Celtic tradition that may benefit the world again. The challenge presented to Setanta by the goddess Morrigan is one small example of a theme embodied in Celtic mythology that is readily applicable to the unique problems and uncertainties of our time. Every new innovation or invention in cultural life generally arises as a response to the challenge of a particular crisis. Nearly every country in the world today has the same problem with war, oppression, and corruption at high levels as any past empire has had. In this respect our time of crisis is neither different nor worse than any other in history. Yet one major crisis of our time, climate change and global warming, is truly unprecedented. There have been other environmental upheavals in history. Indeed environmental destruction tends to be one of the warning-signs that a civilization is on a path toward collapse. But our environmental crisis is the first one to threaten the planet as a whole. Christian ethics may be too narrowly focused on the needs of man to properly understand our spiritual relationship with the Earth. The recent emergence of the notion of environmental "stewardship," while promising, has almost nothing in the Bible to support it. And it will always be overshadowed by the grant of dominion over the Earth which God supposedly gave to Adam. Druidry can fill this need for environmental consciousness more directly. It is a spirituality of dwelling in and with the land, sea, and sky. The needs of humanity are not ignored, for it is a spirituality of tribe and family, of personal empowerment, and of social justice. But it places humanity in the wider setting of the whole of the world, disallowing any image of man as the ruler and master of the world. The Celtic spiritual devotee is not a lord of the land, but is the lover of the land. And as we shall see, Druidry is a spirituality that celebrates the beauty and divinity of love.

The time is ripe, then, for a revival of the spiritual traditions of the Earth. Unlike any other spirituality in the world, the traditions of the Earth directly and unequivocally address the environmental connectivity that is threatened by pollution, resource destruction, mass extinctions, and global warming. This is not because of a commandment from a transcendent, distant God who is separated from the world, nor because the beauties and immensities of the world are somehow exemplary of the glory of that distant God. Rather, the wisdom of the Earth allows the seeker to acknowledge and enjoy the world's beauties and immensities as sacred experiences in their own right. And this is precisely what someone on the Celtic spiritual path, having declared his or her destiny as Setanta did, is on track to discover. At the core of the Druidic mysteries is not an aspiration to transcend the world, but an aspiration at once more complex and also more simple. Druidry seeks to recognize the sacredness already immanent within the material world, and at the same time render the world sacred by an act of will. The only leap of transcendence which the seeker must perform is the transcendence of certain everyday attitudes that prevent her from recognizing and recreating the world as a sacred world.

Most spiritual traditions around the world make a statement about the condition of a human being before he or she answers a spiritual calling. This statement is meant to help the potential seeker understand why the path is important, by promising some kind of "salvation," a solution to the problems and challenges of life. Christianity's "original sin" is an example of this, as is the condition of "Samsara" described by Buddhism and Hinduism. I describe the original situation of humanity in the form of the Morrigan's Challenge to Setanta because it expresses the seriousness of the imperative to "know yourself" in an especially dramatic way. The Goddess, who points a spear at one's heart, is the important detail of the picture. It brings to the foreground our transience and our mortality. For, in a way, the Morrigan was asking

Setanta what circumstances he would prefer for his own death. Yet the Challenge also dramatizes the artistic and playful element in this choice as well. For if one chooses the way Setanta did, then one will have chosen adventurously, that is to say, for the sake of the adventure that shall become one's life. A divinity offers the choice because the right choice, while it does not afford an escape from death, affords the possibility of a kind of immortality. Setanta was promised that one choice would result with the story of his life being told in Ireland forever, and that is, after all, one form of immortality. Death becomes part of the adventure, part of the story that lives forever. The Goddess, pointing the spear to your heart, represents the urgency, the necessity, and the importance of the choice as thrust upon you by special and even archetypal circumstances. She holds you at the point of a weapon when she offers this choice because when you are thrust into such transformative circumstances, the failure or the refusal to choose at all is more deadly than to choose poorly.

However, the Morrigan is not a goddess of death, although she does kill from time to time. Nor is she precisely a goddess of war, although she favors warriors and is popularly known as a warrior's goddess. She is more properly a goddess of sovereignty, the sponsor of those who wield power. In her capacity as the divine spouse of mortal kings through the rite of the "Great Marriage," it could be said that she sponsors those who wield political power, the power of lawmakers and commanders, and, indeed, the power of life and death. On a private level, the Morrigan challenges us to wield such power over one's own life. In the story of Cú Chullain, it was the deity herself who appeared to the hero and forced him to make his choice. In today's world the Challenge tends to appear in the form of events that seem to go beyond one's ability to understand, or which threaten one's life with potential hardship and oppression, like social upheavals, wars, natural disasters, criminal activity, extraordinary injuries or disease afflictions, and death. In such situations, people sometimes turn inward, in search of an explanation for why it is happening, and in search of sufficient courage and hope to survive it. As the great philosopher Hegel said, the owl of the goddess Minerva spreads her wings at the fall of night. It is in these extraordinary times of crisis that one can imagine the voice of the Morrigan, as if speaking through the terror and the confusion, not to placate or to console, but to strengthen and encourage. The Morrigan does *not* come to make you "feel better" for she is not a healer, or at any rate not the kind of healer we would find familiar. Nor does she come to tell you what to do, for she is not a

lawgiver. She comes to revive your strength when you feel weak, to reveal your courage when you feel powerless, to tell your story when you feel forgotten. But after that, it is up to you to use your strength, to do something courageous, and to create a memorable story.

Why should we be so interested in reviving the spirituality of a culture that has practically disappeared? Why revive the customs of a time before "progressive-thinking" people discovered monotheism, humanism, scientific method, and nationalism? All that remains of the original Celtic world is some archaeological treasures and monuments, some literary fragments, a language that is dying, and a few scattered pieces of folk memory. Celtic society in Europe was destroyed by several dramatic military defeats: for instance, the Gaulish hero Vercingetorix, leader of the Arverni who united most of the tribes of Gaul, was defeated by Julius Caesar at the Battle of Alesia (52 B.C.). Boudicca, the warrior-queen of the Iceni tribe, united most of the British tribes to oppose the Romans, but was eventually defeated as well (A.D. 62). The great flowering of Celtic Christianity, which preserved much of the older pre-Christian Celtic ideas, was "officially" erased by the vote of the Roman bishops at the Synod of Whitby (A.D. 663). The last remnant of a Gaelic political order in Ireland was defeated at the Battle of the Boyne (1690). And Scottish traditional language and culture was nearly destroyed by the Highland Clearances (1785-1850). Why is there such an extraordinary interest in the spiritual ideas and practices of a society which, according to most of the history books, all but vanished many hundreds or even thousands of years ago? Is it mere escapism? Is it a kind of cultural malaise that can see little good in one's own society and so prefers to imagine another one? Is it a desire for a life of fantasy and magic which modern civilization does not easily accommodate? The answer may well be "yes," even if we may not want to admit it. Yet there are positive reasons as well.

Here is one. The Celtic spirit has not completely and totally disappeared, despite the various ways in which it has been forgotten or repressed over time. It lives on, and its various new shapes and disguises are all around us. Its popularity can be seen by the success of dance shows, films, and in the multitude of Celtic music concerts and reenactment heritage festivals that have emerged in the last 10 years alone. For many people, a reemergence of Celtic values and spirituality is happening as well. The enduring spirituality of Celtic mysticism is an important part of the religious and cultural inheritance of all humanity. As such, it can never truly be eradicated from the face of the Earth, but will persevere by changing form, travelling from one place to another, or by disguising itself under the mask of another tradition. Many pieces of the Celtic spirit can be found in the tales and legends of King Arthur and the Knights of the Round Table, just to pick one example. Arthur's primary court advisor, the magician Merlin, possesses many of the personal traits, social functions, and magical powers of the ancient Druids. The behavior of one of the most memorable antagonists in Arthurian myth, the "witch" Morganna le Fey, resembles that of the Celtic world's proudest queens and goddesses. Morganna's feminine wisdom and magic is rejected by Arthur in favor of Christianity. Yet he and his knights quest after the Holy Grail, a magical artifact attributed to Christ's Last Supper but is otherwise exactly the same as the many magic cups and cauldrons of the Celtic goddesses who came before. Some of Shakespeare's plays, such as *The Tempest*, *As You Like It*, and especially "That Scottish Play," *Macbeth*, contain Celtic themes and images in abundance. Tolkien's *Lord of the Rings* has Druidic characters, Gandalf and Saruman, and even a race of near-immortal beings, the Elves, whose grace, wisdom, and beauty strongly resembles the race of Celtic gods, the Tuatha de Dannan. That resemblance was Tolkein's intention. Yet it is in music, more than in literature, where I think Celtic feelings find their most perfect expression. There are literally hundreds of popular groups and individuals making the intricate Celtic "trad" sound, and merging it with contemporary rhythms such as rock, jazz, and even techno. In the early 20th century, a massive rescue effort was made for a dying Celtic music tradition by performers like Planxty, the Chieftains, the Dubliners, and the Clancy Brothers. And now, in part thanks to them, more recent Irish and British bands such as the Corrs, Kíla, Runrig, and others can perform modern Celtic music to international acclaim. The music of The Waterboys and Jethro Tull, especially albums like *Fisherman's Blues*, *Room to Roam*, and *Songs from the Wood* links the Celtic spirit of adventure and raggle-taggle fun together with the peace and wisdom of sacred places, and the simple dignity of rural life. The Scottish fiddle tune tradition was preserved in Nova Scotia, and the Irish in Newfoundland and Quebec, and now Canadian performers such as Ashley MacIsaac, Slainte Mhaith, Great Big Sea, and Natalie McMaster have made Canada the world's most prolific producer of Celtic music. Bill Monroe, the creator of country bluegrass music in America, regularly asserted that bluegrass was based on "the ancient tones" of Scottish and Irish traditional music. Thus the Celtic spirit was never conquered, and indeed continues to thrive all around us.

Another reason for the revival of interest in Celtic Mysticism has to do with a particular experience people have of the land. One of the most well-known aspects of Celtic mysticism is the relationship that its practitioners seek to create with the Earth and the physical environment. To a Celt, the world of nature is a sacred world, as it is the sustainer of life and the progenitor of beauty. This is also a relationship with what can be called the "psychic" environment, the magical energy that people sometimes feel in stones, trees, animals, and the weather. One can doubt whether this energy is real, but one should not doubt that people are having these strange mystical experiences. In Ireland, where I live, the revival of Druidry has been driven by the (re)discovery that one can experience this energy in the stone circles, passage mounds, holy wells, and other ancient monuments of the country. Many people are attracted to Celtic Mysticism because they find the experience of this energy appealing and empowering, and want to know more about it. The belief in the existence of this energy is but one way of interpreting *the experience of the sacred*, which is central to any form of Mysticism, and which to my mind is what really matters. The experience of the sacred is available to anyone who adopts what I shall call "the spiritual attitude," which, as I shall describe, is a special way of looking at the world.

To those seeking a spiritual life, Celtic Mysticism is therefore a natural place to turn. Some see in it a way to reconnect, or "ground" themselves in history, or to improve their understanding of their origins and ancestors (if they are of Celtic descent). Some are attracted by the relationship with the natural world that a Druid cultivates, or by the artistic and magical methods used to build that relationship. To those who feel alienated or harmed by Christianity, yet who still believe religion has a place in their lives, Celtic spirituality is a viable, healthy alternative. Finally, there are those who choose Celtic spirituality over other forms of neo-paganism, or over other "alternative" religions imported from other parts of the world, such as Hinduism and Buddhism. Perhaps a reason for this is because Druidism is indigenous to Europe. It was created and developed by Europeans, and while there were influences from other parts of the world, the Druidic spirituality is unique and native to the western world. There are also special variations of Druidic thought and practice that are unique to each of the Celtic nations. Some of these continue to exist as folk traditions and so the revival of Druidry has a familiarity about it which other spiritual traditions may not have. Celtic spirituality can be *our* spirituality, the spirituality of our own culture and people, perhaps more so than other traditions.

To properly understand this spirituality, I felt I had to travel to the places where it all began. Like the young Setanta, I left my home and native land to chase a Celtic dream. This book is a product of that adventure, and a small way of sharing some of it with the world. For four wonderful years I lived in Ireland, met its people, visited its sacred sites, and sought the goddess in her ancient homeland. Yet my mind kept going back to the time when my father taught to me the story of Setanta and the Morrigan as a children's bedside tale. I began to wonder how I would choose if a great queen of old Ireland appeared to me today. It is not hard for me to visualize how the meeting might go. Recently She has added some of the modern symbols of power, especially women's power, to her traditional appearance. She has a tailor-made coat, high heel boots, and a few tattoos. She is a modern woman. Yet she still has her earthy green and black colors, a gold royal torc about her neck, her fierce red hair, as always, and her spear. I know that, before she leaves, she will take it up and tell me to choose my future. But first I pour out a glass of mead and we sit by the fireplace to drink, and talk of heavy things. I describe to her what life is like for mere mortals today, and how our lives seem inevitably bounded by things like the progress of technology, the global market, the environmental crisis, and the war against terrorism. In return she tells me of the things she sees from the divine perspective: time and space, cosmology and divinity, love and death, magic and power, personal identity and human destiny. All these things and heavier things still play themselves out like characters on the stage of our dialogue.

Imagine, if you will, that I am an ambassador from this goddess, describing in this book the conversation we had when she appeared to me in my study. Imagine how you would answer her challenge if she appeared to you.

ULSTER

Emain Macha

CONNACHT

Newgrange

Cruachan MIDE

Tara

Uisneach

Clonmacnoise *Hill of Allen*

LEINSTER

Poulnabrone *Brigid's Well*

Dind Rig

Cnoc Aine

MUNSTER

Paps of Anu

Skellig Michael

Ireland

One:
Questions and Answers

Throughout these regions, as people gradually became more civilized, study of praiseworthy doctrines grew, introduced by the Bards, [Vates], and Druids. The Bards sang the praiseworthy deeds of famous men to the melodious strains of the lyre. The [Vates] endeavored to explain the sublime mysteries of nature. Between them were the Druids, an intimate fellowship of a greater ability who followed the doctrine of Pythagoras. They rose above the rest by seeking the unseen, making little of human mortality, as they believed in the immortality of the soul.

—Ammianus Marcellinus,
circa, A.D. 330-395

In this chapter I shall describe some of the factual information with which the reader may gain a general idea of the character, archaeology, literature, and mythology of the Celtic people through history until today. How much do we know about the ancient Celtic people, and their mysterious priesthood, the Druids? How much do we know about who they were and what they did, and how much of this can be carried forward into today?

1. Who were the Celts?

The Celts were an indigenous people of Europe, whose heroic culture dominated Europe for centuries. Historically, they were almost a nation. They did not have a single central government, but they occupied a distinct territory. They were not genetically distinct from other European populations at the time, but they had their own language. They lived in many tribes which were politically autonomous from each other. Yet they had an intertribal institution, the Druids, who could operate across tribal boundaries—evidence of highly advanced social organization.

The traditional Celtic nations, which are the territories where a Celtic language was once spoken, are:

- *Alba*, Scotland
- *Breizh,* Brittany, northwestern France
- *Gaul*, what is now France, Belgium, and parts of Germany and middle Europe

- *Cymru,* Wales
- *Éire,* Ireland, the "Isle of the Blest"
- *Galatia,* in what is now Turkey
- *Kernow,* Cornwall and parts of England's "West Country"
- *Mannin,* the Isle of Man, in the Irish Sea
- *Britain*, what is now England, the "Island of the Mighty"

Parts of what is now northern Spain also hosted Celtic tribes, and some mythologies assert that Celts from that area colonized Britain and Ireland. Celtic culture was a tribal society, meaning the basic social and political unit was the extended family and not the individual. They had Iron-age technology at the height of their achievement, and lived in settled farmstead communities. The Celtic people migrated from the ancient Indo-European homelands in Eastern Europe to cover most of Western Europe. It is possible to trace the migration routes by examining the artifacts they left behind. Two classes of Celtic artifacts, La Tene and Halstadd, are named for towns in which artifacts from each period were discovered: Halstadd is in the Salzkammergut in Austria, and La Tene is in Switzerland. Switzerland was once the territory of a Gaulish Celtic tribe called the Helvetians, who fought against Julius Caesar's armies in 58 B.C. The official name of Switzerland is still "Confoederatio Helvetica" (Latin for "the Helvetian Confederation"). The Celts of Galatia, in what is now Turkey,

were visited by Paul of Tarsus around A.D. 40; his letter to them has a permanent place in the Christian Bible. The Celts of Scotland came from Irish colonists, called Scots, and also an indigenous and possibly pre-Celtic people known as Picts, who dominated Scotland until united with the Scots of Dalriada by Kenneth Mac Alpine in A.D. 843. Unfortunately, very little about the Picts is known. Even their name is the word the Romans used for them and not the name they used for themselves. They were called "Picti," meaning "painted people," because Pictish warriors used to paint themselves for battle with a blue pigment from the woad plant mixed with semen.

There was a class system in old Celtic society, which had the ruling warrior-aristocracy on the top, followed by the professional classes which included Druids, bards, poets, lawyers, historians, and so on. Next on the ladder were landlords, followed by free workers, followed by bonded workers. There were also provisions for outcast groups. Celtic law included ways for anyone, including bonded workers, to move up or down the social hierarchy; what rights and responsibilities were due to each of them, and what kind of punishment they would recieve based on the status of their victims, and their own status. More was expected from those who had more. An old Celtic proverb goes: "A man is better than his birth."

The main sources of information are the reports of Roman historians, such data as archaeological remains can provide, and mythological literature recorded by monks in the eighth through 12th century. Also, although this is a weaker source, analogies can be drawn between the Celts and similar Indo-European cultures from the same time in history, such as the Vikings, the Greeks, and the Hindus. Had the ancient Celtic religion survived history, I suspect that it would resemble modern Hinduism, with its many diverse forms of expression.

Archaeology is an excellent resource for the study of Celtic history. Scientists have uncovered the remains of votive offerings to the Gods in lake bottoms, bogs, and "votive pits" (a narrow hole dug deep in the ground in which offerings are buried), which tell us about Celtic religion. There are also the remains of Celtic fortresses, habitations, temples, jewelry, and tools. These remains speak to us not of events and individuals in Celtic history. They reveal what life was like, what their technological capability was, what food they ate, what crafts and trades they practiced, what products they made and traded (which in turn tells us about their economy), where they traveled, and how they got there. These facts about Celtic social life are an important element for understanding Druidism, because it is necessary to understand the whole culture in which Druidism was situated.

One of the problems with studying Druidism historically is that the Druids were the subject of a number of persecutions and conquests, not only by the Romans, but also by Norsemen, Normans, Saxons, and Christians. Much Druidic wisdom was censored, evolved into something unrecognizable, or just plain lost. It is true, however, that the Romans never invaded Ireland, so that country became a haven for Druidic learning for a while. A modern person seeking the Druid's path must attempt to reconstruct the wisdom based on some or all of the sources discussed here. Yet in doing so, one discovers that, despite the enormous amount of cultural data presumed lost, the truly Celtic disposition of the sources remains strong and clear.

2. What is the history of the Celtic people?

In general, it is believed by historians that the Celtic people originated in a common Indo-European homeland somewhere in Eastern Europe and migrated westward. The increasing sophistication, social-stratification, state-building, and so forth, of central Europe gave rise to the periods that that scholars call proto-Celtic and Celtic, or Hallstat 800-500 B.C.E. and La Tene 500-100 B.C.E. The spread of Celtic culture to the British Isles and to the Atlantic seaboard of Europe took place around 900 B.C.E.

Here is a brief, and certainly not complete, timeline of the history of the Celtic people, focusing on the time period which is relevant to this project, and the islands of Britain and Ireland.

Time	People	Events
Up to 4000 B.C.E.	Mesolithic (Middle Stone Age)	
4000 to 1800 B.C.E.	Neolithic (Late Stone Age)	
(3500 B.C.E.)		
1800 to 1600 B.C.E.	The Bronze Age	
1000 B.C.E. to Christian era	The Iron Age	
900 to 500 B.C.E.	Halstatt	
Circa 600 B.C.E.		Greeks establish treading colony at Messalia (now Marseilles, France to trade with Gaul.
500 to 15 B.C.E.		"Heroic Age." Most of the events described in the Celtic mythologies take place in this period.
Circa 450 B.C.E.		Celtic people reach Spain.
Circa 400 B.C.E.		Celts cross the Alps into Italy. Within 10 years, they sack Rome itself.
279 B.C.E.		Celts invade Greece, through Macedonia, and plunder the Temple of Delphi.
270 B.C.E.		Celts establish Galatia in Asia Minor.
154 and 125 B.C.E.		Celts sack Massalia. Roman armies raise the seige both times.
82 B.C.E.		Romans defeat Celts in Italy.

Time	People	Events
55 and 54 B.C.E.		Julius Caesar attempts to invade Britain twice.
52 B.C.E.		Julius Caesar defeats Gaulish chieftain Vercingetorix at Alesia, and imprisons him.
C.E. (A.D.) 41 to 60		Queen Cartimandua rules the Brigantia tribe of Britain.
C.E. 43-409	Romani-British period	Rome dominates most of Britain.
C.E. 61		Druidic santuary at Anglesey (Wales) destroyed by Romans. Boudicca begins her rebellion.
C.E. 120		Construction of Hadrian's Wall begins.
Mid 3rd century		Saxons begin raiding east coast of Britain.
Mid 4th century		Cormac Mac Art rules Ireland at Tara.
C.E. 409-600	"Dark Age" Britain	Romans withdraw from Britain.
C.E. 425		Vortigern takes power in Britain and holds off Saxon advances.
C.E. 432		Patrick begins his mission to bring Christianity to Ireland.
Circa C.E. 450		Anglo-Saxon invasion of Britain; British refugees settle in Armorica and Brittany (France).
C.E. 454		Arturus (Arthur) is crowned King of Britain.

Time	People	Events
Circa AD 500		Arthur defeats Saxons at battle of Mount Baden.
Circa AD 500		Formation of Kingdom of Dalriada in south-west Scotland.
Circa AD 537		Arthur is killed at battle of Camlann.
C.E. 563		Columbia establishes monastery at Isle of Iona.
C.E. 663	The "Middle" Ages	Synod of Whitby: The Celtic church joins the Roman church of Mainland Europe.
Circa C.E. 790		Begining of colonization and raiding of British Isles by Vikings.
C.E. 843		Kenneth Mac Alpine unites the Scots of Dalriada and the Picts.
C.E. 1014		Battle of Clontarf: Vikings expelled from Ireland by Brian Boru. They withdraw from Celtic nations everywhere soon after.

3. What is the nature of Celtic Mythology?

In my opinion, the best source for knowledge of Celtic Mysticism is mythology. There we can read of what the Druids did, how they behaved, and what some of them said and taught. They are represented there not as a class, as the Roman writings represent them, but as actual human beings with their own biographies, interests, successes, families, friends, and even failings. The whole range of human emotion and experience is represented here: victory and tragedy, love and romance, violence and death, and even humor and play. Through it all, the presence of magic and wonder is apparent, as if driving the events toward inevitable conclusions both tragic and profound. Celtic mythology is one of the great treasures of European literature.

In Ireland, there are four main groups of stories. The first is the cycle of the Invasion Races, which describes the pseudo-historical tribes who colonized Ireland. It starts with Partholon and his race; and followed by the Nemedians; the Tuatha de Dannan, the only race described by the narrator as gods; and the Milesians, from whom we mortals are descended. Each race fights battles with a tribe of monsters called the Fomorians, until the Tuatha de Dannan finally defeat them. The great tragedies of the Children of Lyr and of the Sons of Uisneach are included here. The second group of Irish myths is the Ulster Cycle, which includes the story of Cú Chullain's birth and boyhood deeds, the tragic romance of Deirdre and Naoise, and the War of the Bull between the armies of Maeve of Cruachan and the province of Ulster. The third group is the Fianna Cycle, which centers mainly around Fionn MacCumhall and the members of his warrior band. They fight various battles against foreign invaders and against other Celtic tribes, and along the way encounter various magical beings and enchantments. The elopement of Dairmud and Grainne is included here. The final group of Irish myths is the Cycle of Kings, which details the life stories of various kings of Tara.

In Wales, the primary myths are contained in a medieval manuscript called The Mabinogion; the stories are of 12th century origin and the characters behave very much like people of that time, but there are numerous clear reflections of the Welsh pagan past. The Mabinogion comprises 11 stories in all, of which the interconnected Four Branches are the most important. The first is the story of Pwyll, lord of a land called Dyfed (south-western Wales), who trades places with Arawn, the lord of the Underworld, to help save Arawn's kingdom. The second is the story of Bran who takes an army to Ireland to avenge his sister Branwen, but on his return trip gets lost in the Otherworld and only seven men, bearing the still-living severed head of Bran, survive. The third branch is the story of Manawydan, a fallen king who restores his wasteland kingdom to glory again by overthrowing the magical forces responsible for his downfall. The final branch of the Mabinogion concerns the goddess Don, her family, and the birth of a hero-god Lleu who overcomes a curse placed on him by his mother (to have no name, no weapon, and no wife) with the help of his sorcerer uncle Gwydion. Lleu's romance with Bloduedd, the "flower-face" woman, is included here. She was created for him by the wizard-king Math ap Mathonwy, but ultimately fell in love with another man. As a result Lleu nearly died but was restored to life through a shamanic transformation.

The stories of King Arthur, the Knights of the Round Table and the Quest for the Holy Grail deserve to be included here as well. This body of mythology is a product of 11th century Norman-French culture, fused with historical memories of an actual 3rd-century British king named Arthur, yet contains many concepts and images which hearken back to earlier Celtic times. Many modern Druids treat them as having spiritual and theological importance. The conception of Arthur and his ascension to power; the wounded Fischer King whose rules over a wasteland; the Holy Grail which heals him; the Perilous Bridge; the romance of Lancelot and Guinevere; the romance of Tristan and Iseuld; the contest between Gawain and the Green Knight; and the last battle between Arthur and his illegitimate son by his half-sister Morganna, are some of the most important tales here. Interestingly, many of them have parallels in Welsh and Irish mythology.

4. Who were the Druids?

In ancient times, the Druids were members of a professional class in which their society's religious and spiritual life was embodied. They were the philosophers, scientists, theologians, and intellectuals of their culture, and the holders of the philosophical, scientific, and religious knowledge of their age. The nearest modern equivalent, then, would be professors in universities or colleges, medical doctors, lawyers and judges, school teachers, and so on. One could say that such people are the real "Druids" of our time. The ancient Druids brought all of these practices together into a single structure, unified by religious commitment. If you imagine what it would be like if your doctor, lawyer, or teacher was also a priest, and the hospital, law court, and college was also a temple, then you have an idea what Druidry was like for ancient Celtic people.

The Roman historians wrote the only first-hand accounts of ancient Druidry that we have. Even though they are usually understood as "hostile witnesses," they were often impressed by the Druids' philosophical wisdom, and their grasp of mathematical, scientific, and astronomical knowledge. Posidonius wanted to fit the Druids into his own Stoic philosophy. Tacitus tried to cast the old Celts in the role of the innocent and wise noble savage, uncorrupted by civilization and close to nature. Diogenes placed the Druids together with the ancient world's wisest philosophers, alongside the Magi of Persia (who allegedly invented magic), the Chaldeans (the priesthood of the Babylonians) and the Gymnosophists (a Hindu sect which preceded the Yogis). Strabo recorded how the intellectual caste of the Celts was subdivided into three distinct sub-castes, each with their own particular specialization:

> *Among all the tribes, generally speaking, there are three classes of men held in special honor; the bárdoi, the*

ováteis, and the druídai. The bárdoi are singers and poets; the ováteis are interpreters of sacrifice and natural philosophers; while the druídai, in addition to the science of nature, study also moral philosophy.[1]

In this note about the Druids as philosophers of nature and of ethics, we have almost universal agreement among ancient commentators. The eminent scholar Fergus Kelly wrote that a Druid was a "priest, prophet, astrologer, and teacher of the sons of nobles." More recently, the American scholar Paul Lonigan narrowed down the list of what Druids do, as follows:

- astrologers and prophets, interpreters of lucky and unlucky days
- conjurers, diviners, necromancers
- guardians of *sencha* (ancient tradition), law, and genealogy
- an institution both national and international
- law interpreters and advisors
- peacemakers
- philosophers
- physicians
- protectors against evil
- sacrificers
- shapechangers
- speakers of divine language
- subsumers and consecrators of the land
- teachers
- tree-diviners
- warriors

To become a Druid, students assembled in large groups for instruction and training. An Irish epic called the *Táin Bo Cuailnge* describes the druid Cathbad teaching 100 students in something like a college. As the story says, "Cathbad the druid was staying with his son, Conchobar Mac Nessa. He had 100 studious men learning druid lore from him—that was always the number that Cathbad taught."[2] Apprentice Druids on the continent of Europe would study for a period of as much as 20 years: although this fact comes to us in only one literary source: Julius Caesar's *De Bello Gallico* ("The War in Gaul"). The exact quote is: "Reports say that in the schools of the Druids, they learn by heart a great number of verses, and therefore some persons remain 20 years under training."[3] The mythologies describe Druids who were capable of many magical powers such as divination and prophesy, control of the weather, healing, levitation, and shape-changing themselves into the forms of animals or other people. But a Druid was not, strictly speaking, exclusively a mystic or a magician. He or she was mainly an important public leader. Her divination skills and magical sight were required for many essential social and political purposes, such as advising the tribal leaders as they make policy, settling disputes and legal claims, and announcing the beginning of agricultural seasons such as planting, harvesting, and hunting. Druids were responsible for providing a system of justice, and apparently they possessed many of the same powers of investigation, mediation, conflict-resolution, and even sentencing that today's court judges have. It also appears that they were able to magically oppose criminal activity by, for example, performing magical spells intended to return stolen property, or to reveal the thief's identity in a dream. In times of war a Druid's magical skills were needed to learn about the enemy's movements and plans, to magically empower the warriors, and also to call environmental powers to the aid of the tribe. Alternatively, the Druids could put an end to an unjust war by walking into the center of the battlefield and telling everyone to go home. As reported by Julius Caesar, who observed Druids in action first-hand,

> They are believed to be the most just of men, and are therefore entrusted with the decision of cases affecting either individuals or the public; indeed in former times they arbitrated in war and brought to a standstill the opponents when about to draw up in a line of battle; and murder cases have mostly been entrusted to their decision.[4]

On the other hand, an Irish text states that "...defeat against odds, and setting territories at war, confer status on a Druid."[5] The general point here is that a Druid's status and powers are inextricably connected to a human community. Indeed the Druid's social standing was so important that at any assembly, the chiefs and kings could not speak until the Druids had spoken first.

Druidic wisdom clearly had enormous importance in the politics of Celtic society.

What did they believe? The very origin of the word *Druid* gives us a clue. It comes from an ancient Celtic word for an oak tree, *druis*, and we find it in the root of other words such as endurance and durability. The implication is that Druidic knowledge "endures." The Irish word for magic is *Draoicht*, which literally means "what Druids do." This connection reveals a little more about who they were and what their place in society was. Interestingly, the word *dryad*, most well-known today as the name for an ever-young, ever-beautiful female tree spirit of fantasy, may actually have come from *dryas*, the word used by Continental Celts for a female druid.[6] The Irish word for a female Druid is *bandraoi*, literally "woman Druid." We know quite a bit about their religious beliefs and practices, in broad strokes but not in fine details. We don't know the script of their ceremonies but we have a fairly good idea of what myths, beliefs, and principles their ceremonies were designed to affirm and re-enact. The ancient Druids used fire in their rituals, divined the future by watching the flight of birds and the movements of clouds, contacted their gods in sanctuaries deep in forests, and were therefore associated with trees. We know they regarded the head as the seat of the soul. We know that they believed in the immortality of the soul. We know they believed in the existence of an Otherworld where souls travel after death, and we know they believed that it is possible to communicate with the beings who dwell there. And we know that at least on the continent of Europe, Druids had ceremonies of animal and sometimes human sacrifice. With the information we have, we can say that a Druid is a *professional invigilator of living spiritual mysteries as expressed by Celtic cultural forms*. The strength of this definition is that it can identify both ancient and modern Druids at the same time. It is a theoretical, analytic definition which may require some explanation.

A Druid is a "professional" because Druidry requires the application of skill and knowledge in the service of certain social responsibilities. A Druid's responsibilities are to the world as well, for as the ancient Druids said, "We created the world," and without Druids to bring about the renewal of the seasons with their rituals, the world might end. So say the legends. Contemporary Druids have similar responsibilities to the world, for our Earth and its people, animals, and environments suffer so terribly and so needlessly. An "invigilator" is a person who keeps a vigil, which means being watchful and mindful and attentive over something. The word encompasses a range of ideas, including steward, investigator, watcher, even knower. So to say that a Druid is an invigilator is to say that a Druid is watchful and mindful of something. The "living spiritual mysteries" are that which Druids are watchful and mindful of (and what they are, we shall see in the chapters to come).

Finally, the "Celtic cultural forms" are the poetry, art, archaeology, literature, mythology, language, and folklore of the Celtic people, ancient and modern. These elements distinguish Druids from the religious specialists of other cultures, while allowing for some overlap with other cultures who emerged from similar origins and who have similar practices.

5. Who were the Bards and Poets?

The popular image we have of Bards is, as you might expect, not quite like the historical reality. Bards were considered cheap entertainers, outclassed by the *fili*, the poets. The poets had far more respect because they had tougher responsibilities: in addition to musicianship and poetic composition, they were responsible for memorizing the histories and genealogies (very important to ensure the continuity of a political dynasty's power) and were also capable of magic. The poets were very close to the Druids in that respect, and the mythologies describe many Druids who were poets as well. The difference here between bards and poets is rather like the difference in medieval times between minstrels and troubadors. Minstrels were travelling musicians whose usual repertoire consisted in praise for the military exploits of their employers, or of the military life in general, and also in comic entertainment such as juggling acts, clowning, and even toilet humor. Troubadors, on the other hand, performed music and poetry on more sophisticated themes, especially on the theme of romantic love, and generally performed for a more educated audience.

A Druidic-poet was expected to be able to perform what were called the "three noble strains," which was music to inspire laughter, tears, or sleep. Poets and Bards were guaranteed to receive special hospitality wherever they went, and be free from insult, among other rights. A breach of these rights would allow them to compose a satire-poem that would tarnish the offender's reputation for generations to come. In Ireland, Bards and Poets survived up until at least the 17th century. Some of the ancient Druids found that they were able to survive by becoming travelling poets. We also have a record of an edict by Queen Elisabeth the 1st of England outlawing the "poets and lewd rhymers" of Ireland. They were providing a national communications network for the Gaelic nobles, and they had a habit of portraying the English nobles in a very bad light.

The last of Ireland's great Bards in the old Gaelic tradition was a harper named Turlough O'Carolan, who lived in the 1700s. He was blind from the age of 18, due to smallpox, and was apprenticed to a harper so he could still earn a livelihood. One night, apparently after an evening of very heavy drinking, he fell asleep on the walk home between the hills of Si Beag and Si Mor (in Ireland's county Leitrim). These two hills are also the location of two underground faerie forts: one rules the surrounding territory from Bealtaine to Samhain, the other rules from Samhain to Beltaine. During the night he was able to hear the music of the faerie hosts in his sleep, and the music continued to reverberate in his head for most of the rest of his life. The music he composed thereafter we can say is actual faerie music, or inspired by faerie music. It has become a standard part the repertoire of nearly every traditional Irish musician today. O'Carolan's "planxties," for instance, were tunes composed in honor of families who gave him room and board as he travelled around Ireland. And in old Gaelic fashion, O'Carolan would recite a *glam* (a curse or a satire) on someone who refused to offer him hospitality. One of them, in loose English translation, ran like this:

> *Alas! As Hell's gates are kept*
> *by O'Flynn!*
> *So surely the dog would let*
> *no one in.*

The life of O'Carolan, then, we can take as a fine example of the Bardic life in a Celtic society, as near as we are able to tell.

The Bards and Poets fill a special social function not filled by others. They are the *keepers and transmitters of culture*. A community has a history, and by taking part in community one takes part in its history as well. The history of one's community is an inheritance which forms a large part of one's social identity. Indeed every role one plays as a member of a community, be it a family role, an occupational or professional role, or even the spiritual path one commits to, also has a history. Insofar as I take on these roles I take on their history as well. Even original composition, when it is clearly a part of a living tradition, serves to keep and to transmit culture, and so help people know who they are. The songs, stories, histories, genealogies, and so on which forms a Bard's repertoire embodies the very past which informs everyone's present social identity and relations, being either a commemoration of certain people or events, whether historical or mythological. Through original composition on those events, and on events as they happen, the bard brings the community forward into the future. Her repertoire expresses the values and shared cultural commitments that in large measure makes a community what it is.

6. Who were the Warriors?

It is difficult to describe the life of an Iron Age Celtic warrior to 20th century people living in modern western societies, because there is very little that is comparable. A young boy in Celtic society was "initiated" into manhood when an elder of the tribe gave him his first weapons. Roman writers frequently said that all grown Celtic men were "mad for war," and that they were constantly preparing themselves for the next cattle raid, the next border incursion, or the next territorial conquest. They would drink heavily (Romans used to mix water in their wine, whereas Celts drank their wine "straight") and would boast about what great fighters they were and what great deeds they would do at the next battle. An insult against their honor might trigger a sword fight. These warriors were rough, dangerous, bombastic, and proud young men, assured of their greatness and the greatness of their tribe. The nearest modern day equivalent would be the typical British football hooligan.

However, the energy and recklessness of the ancient Celtic warrior was also tempered by allegiances to tribes and territories, and to high-minded notions of honor, reliability, trustworthiness, and fair play. These allegiances are more important to a Celtic warrior than how deadly and dangerous a fighter she is. The custom of fosterage, in which a child would be raised by another family for half of his childhood, created strong and complex bonds of solidarity. This enabled fighters to share in each other's honor. They made it important for each fighter to uphold his own honor lest he bring shame upon his friends and family. Warriors such as Asterix and Obelix, although they are cartoon characters, exemplify this spirit very well. Among the members of an Irish mythological army called the Red Branch Knights, it was important that only honorable noblemen can be members, and that they commit themselves to the protection of the province of Ulster, whatever their personal allegiances and prejudices might be. It was also important for warriors to have a sense of dry humor. At the end of the Battle of Clontarf, when the Irish king Brian Boru expelled the Vikings from Ireland, one Viking warrior was found not fleeing to the ships with the others, but instead nonchalantly tying up the straps of his shoes. When questioned by an Irish captain by the name of Kerthialfad, the warrior said, "I live in Iceland, and would not be able to get home tonight." Kerthialfad spared him.

A custom known as the "single combat" enabled Celts to earn personal glory on the battlefield and also keep the number of casualties down. The two fighting sides would line up and challenge each other with noise, taunts, threats, boasts, and curses. It is probable that each tribe had its own battle-chant, connected with a choreography of threatening gestures, rather like the way the Maori tribes of New Zealand have a battle chant called the Haka. (Even today, the "All Blacks," New Zealand's national rugby team, chant the Haka before every game.) At some point during all of this mad shouting, a single fighter would step forward and challenge the best fighter of the other side to a one-on-one combat, often to the death. The outcome of the entire battle, then, would be decided on the outcome of these warrior line-ups and single combats. This enabled conflicts to be resolved with a minimum of bloodshed.

One group of Celtic warriors worth special mention is the *Fianna*, a class of outlaw warriors, typically adolescents and young adults. Fianna may spend their time living off the land, traveling, cattle raiding, and experiencing some freedom. There was also a mystical dimension to them. Many Fianna bands required their members to learn music and poetry. And Fianna legends are filled with magical hunting expeditions, in which white animals with red ears lead hunters on a wild chase through unknown territory, after which they emerge in the Otherworld, in the presence of the gods.

Hunting was part of the life of the Celtic warrior, for hunting was an important source of their food. Yet the prey that the hunter follows is also a guide and a pathfinder in the Otherworld, in a manner reminiscent of the "totem animals" used by shaman as they travel through the spirit world. The Welsh story of Pwyll, Prince of Dyfed, for example, brings Pwyll into the presence of Arawn, lord of Annwn (a Welsh word for the Otherworld) while the two of them were hunting after the same stag. Most societies across the world that have hunted for their food have developed rituals to affirm and strengthen that brotherhood with the animals they hunt, and to bring the hunted animals back again. It is very difficult to convey this idea when the animals we eat are captive, fed with hormones and genetically selected, and the preservative-laden meat we purchase bears little resemblance to the animal it came from. It is sometimes believed that the hunted animal chooses the hunter, and allows itself to be caught and killed. But it does not make it easy for the hunter, so that the hunter is not allowed to forget the danger involved, and not allowed to be casual about bringing death to other beings. After all, the same death will some day come to him in return. If a hunter caught something, it might be because the quarry found him worthy. The hunter's honorable character is thus one of the things he needs to be a successful hunter. In this way the relationship between predator and prey is not one of competition nor antagonism, but of love and kinship.

I am happy to be friends with several people both in Ireland and in other countries who are part time battle reenactors. They "perform" at festivals and public events, using actual (blunted) steel weapons, not padded plastic tubes, to make their fighting skills as authentic, and as disciplined, as possible. Most of the ones I have met also take their role as warriors to heart in other parts of their lives. They are prepared for action at almost any time, yet they are also judicial and prudent in the actions they choose. They do not go out of their way to court danger. They don't even like to draw attention to themselves. When called upon, they do no more and no less than what needs to be done. What distinguishes a warrior is *not* his or her ability to obstruct or harm people, even if a righteous cause can be said to justify the action. Rather, *a warrior is someone willing to risk danger and suffer harm, or even death, in the service of a righteous cause.* Thus, warriors are not just soldiers,

police men, or firemen; they are also women's shelter workers, food bank volunteers, ambulance attendants, and third-world relief workers. They are in the fight for social justice, human rights, and environmental protection. I spent many years on this path myself, first as an environmentalist and then as a labor union activist. Many people follow the warrior path without knowing it.

7. Can Women become Druids, Bards, or Warriors?

Yes. The mythologies describe many women who were powerful warriors, excellent poets, and wise Druids. In fact Celtic women enjoyed more freedom and rights than women in most other cultures of the same time in history. They had the right to enter battle, own and inherit property, trace her kinship through her mother's family line, and to choose and divorce her husband. The Irish hero Cú Chullain was trained by a land-owning warrior queen named Scathach, for whom the Scottish island of Skye is named. The Welsh heroine Bloduedd can be seen as a positive role-model for women: although she was magically created to be Lleu's wife she made her own choice to love another man. Similarly the Irish beauty Deirdre, betrothed before birth to Conchobor, chose to love Naoise and preferred to flee the country than marry a man she did not love. The enormously popular novel, *The Mists of Avalon*, re-presented some of the Arthurian stories from the point of view of the lead female characters, and interpreted them as representing a conflict between the falling world of the Earth Goddess and the rising world of Christianity. Morganna le Fey, traditionally cast as an evil witch, is presented (quite appropriately, I believe) as a priestess of the Pagan order trying as best she can to hold on to her Goddess, and to her independence. Mogh Roith, who was one of the greatest Irish Druids, was taught by a female Druid named Banbhuana, the daughter of Deargdhualach. Similarly, Irish women have a heroine in Queen Maeve of Cruachan, who led an army against the province of Ulster, all to establish her equality in her marriage. Queen Maeve employed the services of a Druidess named Fedelm, who had a gift for prophesy and who was asked by Maeve to predict the outcome of the war she was launching against Ulster. Fedelm predicted (correctly, as it turned out) that Maeve would be defeated.

Women were also permitted to become warriors. Fionn Mac Cumhall, from the Irish Fianna myths, was raised by two Druidesses who lived in the Slieve Bloom hills (county Laois). A woman named Asa (Irish for "Gentle") became Fianna and took the name Ni-Asa ("Not Gentle"). Her name was shortened to "Nessa," when she became mother to King Conchobar. Her influence was such that her son kept her name instead of his father's name, thus: "Conchobar Mac Nessa," or "Connor, son of Nessa." Historical British tribal queens like Boudicca led rebellions of united Celtic tribes against the Romans.

Thus there is no good reason to believe that Druidism was strictly and unilaterally patriarchal in ancient times, and modern Druidism certainly is not patriarchal. A great many women who feel themselves disempowered or damaged by Christianity often find in Druidry a more welcoming and inclusive spiritual home.

8. What are the Celtic holy days?

There are eight major festivals in all, and they are used by pagans from nearly all traditions with few shades of variation in meaning. Some are still commemorated to this day as secular festivals by people in modern Celtic countries, with bonfires, costuming, special meals, and wild parties. Four are connected to solar observations: they are the solstices and equinoxes. The other four are called "fire festivals" or "cross quarter" days and they are located on the calendar between the solar days. There is almost nothing in the literary record or in the mythologies to indicate that the Celts celebrated the solar festivals. Even the Coligny Calendar, the most important ancient calendar to have survived to our time, indicates only one special day by name: the date of Samos, the new year, around the same time as the Irish festival of Samhain. In the archaeology of the Neolithic time, the reverse is true: there is nearly no evidence for the fire festivals but abundant evidence for the astronomical days, mainly in the form of solar alignments in stone circles and other monuments. Modern Druids, of course, celebrate all eight. Although each of them deserves a whole book of its own,[7] it is enough for the present purpose to introduce the four "fire festivals":

- *Samhain* (pronounced SOW-win) The word literally means "end of summer," and in modern Irish it is the standard word for the month of November. Games, feasts, and bonfires were held in honor of the dead, and it was believed the faeries and spirits would hold revels of their own, and sometimes invite mortals to join them. The historian Ronald Hutton has suggested that the burning of bonfires on this day is not a continuity of an ancient custom, and that there are reasons to doubt that Samhain was the Celtic New Year. However he did observe that the date has always been regarded as related to supernatural powers, and that costuming, feasting, and trickery has always been among its traditions.[8] This festival has become the primary New Year's festival on the Celtic calendar and the main occasion for confronting death and the supernatural.

    On this day it was thought that the boundary between this world and the Otherworld is weakest, and so passage between the worlds is smoother, making the night more dangerous. Festivities to honor, to banish, and indeed to make fun of these powers would have helped people psychologically prepare themselves for the hardships of the coming winter.

- *Imbolc* (pronounced IM-volk) The Return of Light. In Ireland and Britain, the ewes (female sheep) begin lactating around this time of year, and spring flowers start to bloom, which are the signs that spring is coming. Perhaps divinations were cast to determine when spring would come. (Groundhog Day may have evolved from this practice.) Imbolc celebrates the coming springtime and preparations for the planting season are begun. In Anglo-Saxon and Wiccan culture, Imbolc is sometimes called Candlemas. Imbolc was sacred to the Goddess Brigid, and the rituals on this day tended to center upon the home and family.

- *Beltaine* (pronounced Bay-AL-tin-yuh). This was a day of fertility and life, often the choice day for marriages. This is the beginning of the summer half of the year, and the mid point of the seasonal cycle. Fairs, dances, and divination games to determine the identity of future marriage partners were held at this time of year. It has become the primary festival of beauty, fertility, frivolous fun, sexual play and romantic lovemaking. The Tuatha de Dannan are said to have landed in Ireland on this day, and it is also on this day when Nemed lit the first fire in Ireland, on the Hill of Uisneach, in present-day county Westmeath.

- *Lughnasad* (pronounced Loo-NA-sa) The Feast of Lugh. The essential harvest festival, to give thanks to the Earth for Her bounty. The name is a reference to the Irish god Lugh of the Long Hand, son of the Sun, who defeated Balor in the Battle of Maigh Tuireadh and won the knowledge of animal husbandry for His people on this day. Lugh is said to have instituted athletic games for this festival in honor of his foster-mother Taltiu who died in the battle against Balor. Accordingly, Lughnasad festivals in Celtic times were characterized by sporting competitions. It marks the end of the supplies from the previous year and the beginning of the current harvest.

When should these festivals be celebrated? In the case of the four astronomical days, there can be only one day, and indeed only one moment. The other four days were mainly agricultural festivals. Not only did they last for several days, sometimes even weeks, but it was also the case that they were celebrated when certain environmental observations were made: the blossoming of certain flowers and trees, the availability of certain harvest crops, the behavior of certain animals. We have, then, four festivals of the Sun, located on fixed dates, and four festivals of the Earth, which are more flexible.

Just to make things easier, here are calendar dates and astrological occasions on which the eight festivals could be fixed, to space them all apart evenly and symmetrically. We can now see the complete mandala of the wheel of the Year:

- Samhain ("Halloween"), 1st November, or 15 degrees Scorpio
  Celtic New Year: a feast of the dead and of passage to and from the Otherworld.
- Midwinter Solstice, 21st December, or zero degrees Capricorn
  The shortest day of the year; the death and rebirth of the Sun.
- Imbolc ("Brigid's Day" or "Candlemas"), 1st February, or 15 degrees Aquarius

The first signs of the end of winter.

- ☉ Spring Equinox, 23rd March, or zero degrees Aries

  The equal balance of night and day, with the day increasing.

- ☉ Beltaine ("May Day"), 1st May, or 15 degrees Taurus

  A festival of spring fertility, of marriages, and of the transfer from the dark half of the year, that began at Samhain, to the bright half.

- ☉ Midsummer Solstice, 21st June, or zero degrees Cancer

  The longest day of the year, and the height of the strength of the sun.

- ☉ Lughnasad ("Lammas"), 1st August, or 15 degrees Leo

  The beginning of the harvest, and the usual time for harvesting grain crops.

- ☉ Autumn Equinox, 23rd September, or zero degrees Libra

  The feast of the harvest of fruit and berries; the equal balance of night and day with the night increasing.

9. What gods did the Celtic people worship?

The Celtic people believed in a variety of gods and goddesses, and not every Celtic nation had exactly the same pantheon. The archaeological record in Gaul reveals 374 god-names, many of which were gods of particular tribes or localities. Sometimes the same god was known by different names, and many of the names were deemed too holy to pronounce aloud (thus the common oath: "I swear by the god my tribe swears by"). This taboo may also have been intended to prevent your enemies from invoking your own gods against you.

It is important to remember that in the pre-Christian times, the people believed in complex and imperfect gods who, like human beings, had personalities, interests, and feelings. A religious professional would be required to know these things in order to work with them and avoid angering them, thereby risking the welfare of the tribe. Because the Celtic Gods are similar to humans in disposition and temperament, they are so much more accessible and easier to understand. The idea that the gods might be makers of morality and judges of humanity is a foreign idea to most ancient European cultures. Some of the gods are simply the beings who live in and with natural forces, landmarks, special places, weather events, animals, trees, and so on, and who are controllers of their movements and dispositions. Others are the deities of particular tribes or nations, who sponsor that tribe and support it in various ways. A tribal deity may be seen as a distant divine ancestor, who confers special benefits upon the best of his mortal descendants. As a general rule, although there are exceptions, male deities look after human social affairs, and female deities dwell in landforms and the forces of nature. Each tribe had its own small group of local gods, although there were a few "rock-star" deities embodied in the landscape of whole continents, or who were the progenitors and sponsors of whole nations.

In the chapters to follow, I will discuss some gods in detail, as the discourse requires. Here, I will briefly mention a few of them, which will give an impression of the diversity in the Celtic pantheon as well as some of the commonalties among the different Celtic nations.

From Ireland:

- *Lugh Lamh-Fada*, the "Long Handed" or "Many Talented," a god of the sun, of military victory, and of the harvest
- *Manannan*, the god of the sea, and of passage to the Otherworld
- *Morrigan*, a goddess of the Earth, and of sovereignty
- *Dagda*, another god of the sun, and of tribal leadership
- *Brighid*, a goddess of healing, midwifery, blacksmithing, poetry, and fire
- *Diancecht*, a god of medicine and physicians
- *Ogma*, a god of writing, knowledge, wisdom, and public speaking
- *Angus*, son of the Dagda, god of youth, beauty, and love

From Wales:

- *Arawn*, lord of the Annwyn, the Otherworldly realm of ancestors

- *Pwyll*, lord of the kingdom of Davyd, and husband of Rhiannon
- *Arianhrod*: She is the Goddess of Caer Arianhrod, sometimes identified with the constellation Coronea Borealis, which is where the souls of slain heroes go
- *Rhiannon*, goddess of sovereignty associated with horses and the Underworld
- *Cerridwen*, mother of the poet Taliesson, goddess of wisdom and old age
- *Lyr*, god of the sea

From Gaul (including some equivalent Roman deities according to Julius Caesar):

- *Lugh* (Mercury), a god of the sun
- *Belinus* (Apollo)
- *Taranis* (Mars) a thunder god
- *Teutatis* (Jupiter) a "father" god
- *Brigid* (Minerva)
- *Cernunnos* (Dispater) a god of animals, hunting, fertility, and death
- *Epona*, a goddess of horses and of motherhood

10. Did the Druids practice human or animal sacrifice?

For those who want to believe the answer is yes, there is plenty of literary and archaeological evidence to justify the belief. For those who want to believe the answer is no, there are plenty of other ways to interpret the evidence.

The Romans recorded that the Druids executed criminals and prisoners of war in religious ceremonies. This was no different than elsewhere in the ancient world. Julius Caesar wrote that such victims were tied into huge man-shaped effigies made of wicker and burned alive. The ancient historian Livy reported that when an army of Celtic Gauls attacked and defeated a Roman army commander named Postumius, they killed him and made a chalice from his skull. Some accounts describe one person's life being sacrificed so that a terminally ill noble would survive, thus indicating a belief in a cosmic balance of forces.

It is fashionable among some contemporary Druids to claim that Julius Caesar's account of the Wicker Man is mere propaganda, designed to stir up support for his war in Gaul. Less easy to dismiss is the image on the inside of the Gundestrup Cauldron, which has a panel depicting a man about to stab a bull through the throat with a sword. This artifact corroborates Roman and Greek literary accounts of the "Bull Feast" in which animal sacrifice was a necessary part of the ceremony of inaugurating kings. Less easy to dismiss again is Ann Ross' account of the "Lindow Man," the bog body discovered in England, near the border of Wales on 1st August 1984. He had been simultaneously strangled, drowned, and clubbed. The absence of any signs of struggle on the body seems to indicate that he did not resist the sacrifice but rather agreed to it willingly. His last meal included a bit of burned bread (possibly the equivalent of "pulling the short straw"). All of these facts, among others, according to Ross, provide strong evidence that the Lindow Man was a Druid who agreed to be sacrificed in an (unsuccessful) attempt to prevent Roman armies from invading Britain.[9] There are numerous other bog bodies discovered all over Europe, killed in similar ways and with evidence similarly pointing to a willing victim. Celtic scholar Miranda Green has described how the selected "victim" would be treated like a king for as much as a full year before the sacrifice. He would be given all the best food and clothing, for instance, or permission to have sex with anyone he wanted. This may have been intended as an incentive for volunteers, or perhaps the result of a belief that high-status victims were more valuable than low status victims. If the latter is true, then it would be necessary to make the victim a temporary king to maximize the magic of the sacrifice.

In the last decade of the 19th century, the Scottish-born anthropologist James Frazer published *The Golden Bough*. This was the first major work of comparative mythology, the first to list the "laws of magic" as occultists know them today, and the first to suggest that the purpose of myth was not only to explain the world but also to effect change. Myth, to his mind, was tied to ritual: people connected with the gods and with the sacred powers of the world by re-enacting their mythologies in ceremonial dramas. The book is most well-known for the description of the ritual sacrifice of society's highest ranking member: the king. In his account, the murder of the king was a widespread custom. His idea was that the king was a sacred figure, the embodiment of a god, whose personal qualities were connected to the condition of the territory he ruled. In Frazer's words:

> ...*the king's life or spirit is so sympathetically bound up with the prosperity of the whole country, that if he fell ill or grew senile the cattle would sicken and cease to multiply, the crops would rot in the fields, and men would perish of widespread disease. Hence, in their opinion, the only way of averting these calamities is to put the king to death while he is still hale and hearty, in order that the divine spirit which he has inherited from his predecessors may be transmitted in turn by him to his successor while it is still in full vigor and has not yet been impaired by the weakness of disease and old age.*[10]

As we can see, this death had a practical ritual purpose tied to the community's desire for survival. It was intended to achieve a renewal of the world, in particular the revival of plant life, in order to prevent starvation. Some Sacred Kings were killed automatically after a certain amount of time (on Frazer's account, usually seven years), others were subject to challenges on regular occasions like annual festivals, still others were in perpetual danger from those who might kill him to take his place at any time. Some Sacred Kings were ordinary members of the community who temporarily substituted for the king after losing a bet, for instance by drawing a burned piece of bread from a basket. And some Sacred Kings were effigies or animals, so that no human being had to be killed. The spirit of the sacrificed king was then "reborn" in the fertility of the plants and crops. Frazer had effectively shown that the death and resurrection of a god was a rather commonplace belief in the ancient world, and not something accomplished only by Christ. Frazer emphasizes that it was also accomplished by the Greek hero Adonis, for instance. It may be that the Celts accepted Christianity so readily because the idea of a sacrificed and resurrected deity was already familiar to them.

However, there is a great deal of controversy about this. Many of the details of Frazer's work were disputed, and various inconsistencies led scholars to reject his account by at least the 1950s if not earlier, at least insofar as it was claimed to be a factual account. His ideas about the logic of magic, and of the connection between mythology and ritual, remain respected. The bog bodies like the Lindow Man could have been convicted criminals or prisoners of war rather than willing victims. Finally, there is no evidence of human sacrifice in Ireland, though there is evidence of animal sacrifice there. And there is no evidence of the sacrifice of women, anywhere in Celtic world.

To understand this phenomenon, it is important not to assume that ancient people held the same values that we do today. To the Celts, death was not the frightening, final thing it is to most of us born in the 20th century. It was a Druidic doctrine that the soul is immortal and that death is part of the cycle of someone's existence. It follows that human sacrifice may not have been so repugnant to ancient people. Indeed a certain amount of violence may have been part of the meaning of the sacred—the violence of the warrior on the battlefield, the animals in the forest, the hunters who chase them, and the thunderstorm in the sky. Certainly, there were other forms of punishment in Celtic law deemed worse than death, such as banishment. If Julius Caesar had lied about the Wicker Man in order to fuel his propaganda effort, he would have been quickly exposed by other eyewitnesses and his credibility would have been ruined. If ancient cultures killed people for religious purposes, it would have been a very special and powerful ritual, performed only in times of serious need.

We today regard death as a negative thing, or even as an annoying interruption of the status-quo, if we acknowledge it at all. But Death is one of the most important facts and mysteries of human life. How we acknowledge this mystery, or how we fail to acknowledge it, tends to reveal our deepest spiritual commitments and our most strongly-held values. I think it cannot be denied that ancient Pagan societies had this dark side, the transformation of murder into one of their most important ritual dramatizations of myth and meaning. But it would be wrong to paint Druidry as nothing more than an elaborate death-cult. Obviously, there are no modern Druids who continue the practice of human sacrifice today.

11. What Celtic temples and sacred places exist?

There are literally thousands of stone forts, earthwork rings, holy wells, stone circles, and other monuments scattered all over Europe. Unfortunately the majority of them are in ruins today, either through age and disuse or else from deliberate destruction. Still others have been "converted" to serve Christianity. The site of Gaul's central Druidic stronghold, in what was then the territory of the Carnutes tribe, is presently the site of Chartres Cathedral. Another class of sacred places are those constructed by the pre-Celtic Neolithic people, which because of their monumental size remain numerous and reasonably intact to this day. The two most well known Irish sites of this kind are Tara and Newgrange.

Newgrange has many names: Cashel Aengus, Brugh Na Boinne, or the Wonder Hill. It is what archaeologists call a "passage grave" or "passage mound." It is a large circular man-made mound of earth surrounded by a ring of kerbstones. A single (known) passage opens from its southeast face that leads into the mound to a central chamber. The passage is angled so carefully that direct sunlight can enter as far as the central chamber, some 80 feet inside the monument, only at sunrise on midwinter morning. Within a few miles from Newgrange are several other passage mounds, including Knowth, which has two passages aligned to sunrise and sunset on the equinoxes. Other famous passage mounds include the Loughcrew Complex, elsewhere in Ireland, and Maes Howe in Scotland which also admits sunlight only on Midwinter morning.

The Hill of Tara is one of my favorite places in Ireland. Its serene grassy fields, great earthwork circles, and the extraordinary view over the countryside make it easy to feel like a king. It was, indeed, the seat of the national kings of Ireland. It is a low hill with gently sloping sides, and features a large concentration of earthwork circles and avenues. The largest earthwork enclosure, *Rath na Rí* (Fort

The Lia Fáil, on the hill of Tara

of the King) is more than 100 meters in diameter, and inside it are two smaller earthwork circles and a passage mound. There are also six holy wells surrounding the hill, a massive royal avenue now known as the "Banquet Hall," and numerous satellite mounds and enclosures.

Tara is also the home of the *Lia Fáil*, (Stone of Destiny), the upright standing stone on which Ireland's kings were ceremonially confirmed. It presently stands in the Rath of the Assemblies, one of the two earthwork enclosures inside Rath na Rí. One of the translations of the name Tara is *spectacle* or *wide view*, because it affords an excellent view over the landscape of Ireland. Tara has been the center of religious and political power in Ireland for approximately 4,000 years, and nearly 500 kings are buried in its vicinity. Its importance obtains even in the modern period. For instance, thousands of people attended a meeting called by Daniel O'Connell in 1843 to support his demand that the Act of Union with Great Britain should be repealed. And in 1916, the Declaration of the Republic was read out on Tara before it was read out on

O'Connell Street, in Dublin. Some of Ireland's most noteworthy public figures in the late 19th to early 20th century, including Arthur Griffith, Maude Gonne, W.B. Yeats, George Moore, and Douglass Hyde, all protected Tara from being excavated by the British Isrealite Association by standing in the way of the bulldozers. The British Isrealites were looking for the Arc of the Covenant, which they believed was buried under the earthwork circle now known as the Rath of the Synods. Although the hill is presently threatened by nearby motorway construction and the possibility of intrusive tourist "development," it remains one of the jewels of the Irish landscape.

12. What is Celtic spirituality like today?

The revival of Celtic spirituality in the modern period begins with the Renaissance in England. Classical thought was being re-introduced into European universities, and there was an interest in what theological ideas God had revealed to humanity prior to, and "in preparation for," Christianity. British intellectuals sought sources indigenous to Britain and Ireland, and discovered the caste of the Druids. The Druids, as portrayed in various Roman historical accounts and fragments of Bardic poetry, had an image and reputation as sorcerer-priests and possessors of divine knowledge which still commanded respect. They saw in the Druids parallels to the spiritual philosophy of ancient Greek figures like Pythagoras and Plato. A study of Britain's stone age monuments was carried out, most notably by the 18th century antiquarian John Aubrey who was the first to interpret Stonehenge as a Druidic temple. These ideas were further developed by other antiquarian scholars at the time, such as John Toland and William Stukeley. Theologically, these men were Deists: they believed that God created the world, set its laws in motion, and then generally left it alone but gave evidence of his presence in the order of nature and the cosmos. Many were also Pantheists: they believed that God was everywhere, within and part of the world of nature, rather than separate from it in a transcendent realm. They believed that the geometrical proportions and astronomical alignments of Stonehenge and other monuments was proof that ancient people were Deists and Pantheists, too. They may have been first to claim that the diameter of Stonehenge's measurements are the same as the width of the Great Pyramid of Giza and the alleged width of Solomon's Temple in Jerusalem (outer ring: 316 feet or 200 cubits; inner ring 96 feet or 60 cubits). Other British stone circles, such as Stanton Drew, had the same measurements as well. Toland, who was born in the northern Irish city of Derry (Londonderry as he would have called it), founded in 1717 a Druidic group called the Universal Druid Bond, in a London pub called the Apple Tree Tavern (an auspicious name!).[11] Britain's largest Druidic organization, the Order of Bards,

Ovates, and Druids, grew from this organization, and Toland and Stukeley were its first and second Chosen Chiefs. This form of Druidry is now usually called "Revival" Druidry, "Theosophical" Druidry, or more simply, "meso-Druidry." Incidentally, The Apple Tree Tavern, in London's Covent Garden, was one of four pubs which early Freemasons used as meeting places, and 1717 was the same year the Grand Lodge of London was created.[12] Stukeley became a Fellow of the Royal Society in 1717, a Freemason in 1720, and Chief of the Order of Druids two years later. There was a lot of crossover membership between Druids, Freemasons, Rosicrucians, and similar groups during this period.

The intention of the early modern Druids was apparently to create a spiritual movement that would be genuinely British, owing nothing to Christianity yet compatible with it. It was to be practiced as a supplement to whatever religion one already professed. It had two main sources of inspiration. One was a "sacred geometry" or "geomancy" in which the divine plan of God was revealed in the mathematical proportions of astronomical bodies, living plants and animals, and the structure of ancient megaliths. The other main inspirational source was the mythology of King Arthur. Arthur is treated a bit like a saviour-deity in his own right, who will come again to restore peace, beauty, and justice to the world. Revival Druidry has a history spanning almost 300 years, and it has produced

its own art, literature, and architecture. For example, the Circus and the Royal Crescent of the city of Bath, England, is a Druidic sun and moon. It was designed by architect John Wood, a Mason who was obsessed with Druids, and incorporates the sacred measurement of 96 feet. The poetry of William Blake is another example—he was, so they say, Chosen Chief of the British Druids from 1799 to 1827. Blake's religious views were profound—they expressed a Gnostic monotheism with a profound confidence in human goodness. Although he called himself a Christian, his religious views were quite radical, in that they were spiritual yet humanist, and also deeply anti-authoritarian. His vision of a "New Jerusalem," a society structured like a kind of egalitarian Gnostic theocracy, is described with megalithic architecture.

A book called "The Barddas" was part of the literature of the Revival, and was alleged to contain ancient Bardic and Druidic knowledge from Wales. It was written by an 18th century stonemason and neo-Platonist named Edward Williams. In order to give his work some public attention, he used a Welsh-sounding pen name, Iolo Morganwyg. He also claimed that the book was based on an ancient text which he never showed to anyone. The ideas and teachings embodied in the Barddas are products of the modern Druidic revival and not the ancient Celtic age. But they display an extraordinary originality, having philosophical and artistic merit that one would be wrong to deny. By the way, "secret documents" are time-honored propaganda devices. When Geoffrey of Monmouth wrote the first comprehensive written account of the life of King Arthur in the 12th century, he claimed his story was based on a secret document given to him by his uncle. And in the 20th century, the author of a popular book on Merlin's lessons to the child Arthur also claimed to possess a secret text, the "Book of Pferyllt." I personally have no opinion whether any "secret documents" actually exist, although I am inclined to believe they do not.

Ireland produced a "Druidic" literature of its own in the late 19th and early 20th centuries. The Irish Literary Revival which, while not a neo-Druidic movement, included authors who were deeply interested in Celtic myth and magic. W.B. Yeats, George "A.E." Russell, Lady Augusta Gregory, and Ella Young all made collections of folk storytelling, and produced some of the finest original poetry and prose the world has ever known. Two novels, *Cuchullain of Muirthemney* and *Gods and Fighting Men* produced in 1902 and 1904, written by Lady Augusta Gregory, are excellent source texts for the study of Celtic spirituality, as they integrate the original texts with the oral folklore available at the time into an original and beautiful synthesis. These books were accused of being neo-pagan by some of her critics (and this appears to be the first use of the word in the 20th century).

Yeats and Russell were both, for a short while, members of an occult society called the Golden Dawn, and both were interested in reshaping its theology and rituals into a uniquely Irish form, based on Irish mythology. What has come to be called the "Faerie Faith" was, in part, their creation. Yeats and Gregory both published collections of folk storytelling, and Russell was the anonymous mystic interviewed by the folklorist W.Y. Evans-Wentz in *The Fairy Faith in Celtic Countries*. They believed that a kind of pristine spirituality could be found in the folk practices and even superstitions of ordinary country people, uncorrupted by priests, church hierarchies, or intellectual theology. Its scripture was folk memory—and seeing how industrialization was making Britain and Ireland more and more urbanized, collections of folk storytelling and traditional practices were considered enormously valuable. Faerie Faith believers were (or are) ordinary people, but for whom the world is also populated by faerie beings, ghosts, prophetic signs, and the like. They might know a magical cure or two, or could predict the weather, or could tell when someone far away was in danger or about to die. In every other respect, such a person was likely to be an ordinary member of the community, even a devout Christian. Instead of priests and ministers, the Faerie Faith has "wise women," "cunning men," and "faerie doctors;" individuals who have experienced the faeries and possess the knowledge and skills to see them, identify their handiwork, and solve any problems caused by disturbing or angering them. An example of such a person is Biddy Early, the famous wise woman from county Clare, Ireland. She had a little glass bottle which she always kept close to her, with which she could see the future or see far distant places.

In the mid 20th century there emerged an "eclectic" Celtic Mysticism, which grew within the New Age movement and in the neo-pagan Witchcraft movement. These movements made it possible to break from Christianity more radically than ever before. We know that Druidry influenced both of them. For instance, Ross Nichols (Chief of the British Druids from 1964-1975) gave to Gerald Gardner, the founder of Wicca, the idea of restoring the eight-fold Celtic festival calendar now known as the "Wheel of the Year." For Eclecticism, what matters is not the connection to the historic past but the connection to Tir Na n-Og, the dreamlike Otherworld described in Celtic mythology, and the use of imaginative creativity to create that connection. It adopted the Faerie Faith, as well as some ideas imported from astrology and occultism through association with the astronomical alignments of ancient monuments. It declared its belief in a monotheistic principle of being, "the Light," which would bring contentment and personal empowerment. It also rejected the spoken word and any "book knowledge" as valid ways to understand the Light, and took pure inner experience as its main source of inspiration instead.

As if in reaction to this, there also emerged a "neo" Druidry, also called Reconstructionist Druidism. In the eyes of both meso-Druids and neo-Druids, the Eclectics lacked connection to tradition and the past, and sometimes also to reality. In my own experience, New-Age Druids speak and behave as if they believe that faeries, ghosts, earth-energies, and spirit guides are more real than shopping malls, landfill sites, or tax inspectors. But in the eyes of neo-Druids, the meso-Druids lacked an appropriate relation to history as well. Neo-Druidry sought an "authentic" spirituality through a re-enactment of what Iron Age Celtic religious custom was actually like, as much as was possible using available historical information, and as much as the law would allow. (So human sacrifice was of course right out!) Books like James Frazer's *The Golden Bough* and Robert Graves' *The White Goddess*, enormously influential on the Celtic revival when first published, were regarded as untrustworthy. The neo-Druids refused to accept that any direct ancient survival of original Celtic beliefs existed, which many Revival Druids wanted to believe. They also refused to accept any "secret documents," because they knew from Roman historical accounts that the Druids taught their doctrines by word of mouth and never wrote anything down. Instead they thought that Druidry had to be "reconstructed" from historical, archaeological, and literary accounts. They encouraged polytheism, the worship of many distinct gods and goddesses, instead of deist monotheism, and claimed that the gods are immanent (part of the world) rather than transcendent (separate from the world). They emphasized that the spiritual importance of nature was not its geometry but its beauty. And they took a great interest in the language, storytelling, and native practices of ordinary people, which the 18th century revivalists never did. The most prolific Reconstructionist Druidic groups that currently exist are American, such as Arn Draoicht Fein ("Our Own Druidism"), the Henge of Keltria, and their offshoots. The figure most responsible for the rise of this kind of Druidry in America is Isaac Bonewits, an occultist and author who founded Arn Draiocht Fein and a number of other groups. He is also well known for earning a Bachelor's degree in Magic from the University of California. (Afterward, the embarrassed university disallowed the granting of degrees in magic from then on.) Most British groups, including OBOD, were perfectly happy to accept many of the insights of neo-Druidry, such as the need to respect actual Celtic traditions. Indeed they already professed the (poly)theological principle of immanence. However, they kept to their own roots and continued to use the *Barddas* and other "unhistorical" texts as inspirational sources.

The Reconstructionists were worried about a peculiar problem which is in part academic but is also a problem of spiritual identity. I would like to call it the "problem of history." Like any revival movement, the revival of Celtic Mysticism was subject to the needs, wishes, beliefs, and desires of the people who revive it. Therefore concessions are made to accommodate their way of life, and of course their preconceptions. The problem was essentially this: the more concessions we make for our own time and our own beliefs, the more we weaken the ties with the past, and so the less justification there is for calling our revival genuinely "Celtic". The neo-Druids had charged the meso-Druids of having no historical basis whatever, and denied their claim to be "real" Druids. But the neo-Druids quickly found their own connections to history were similarly shaky. Ancient Celtic warriors were head hunters, for instance, and nobody wanted to revive that! So the problem became: What is to be revived, and what left behind? It cannot be denied that history and the past figures into all of our present day identities, and so cannot be ignored by someone seeking to "know herself." That very connection to the past was precisely what both kinds of modern Druids were seeking. But where the meso-Druids of the 18th and 19th centuries sought confirmations of what they already believed, the neo-Druids of the 20th century wanted something new and different. They wanted to re-create the beliefs and customs of the Celtic heroic age. For they thought that only a careful study of history would give their religion legitimacy in their own eyes and, potentially, in the eyes of the wider society. I find no fault in this aim in itself. However some critics observed, quite rightly in many cases, that they were hiding a resentment for real or imagined deficiencies in their own society, or even in themselves, and that they were looking for ways to feel empowered, or even to feel superior.

Every form of modern Druidry and Celtic Mysticism seems to be driven by a quest for spiritual identity, which is one form of the impulse to "know yourself." Some people find that by identifying themselves as Celts, as envisaged by historical discovery or even imaginative fantasy, they will "know themselves." And every form of Druidry has its strengths and faults. I am not convinced that Reconstructionism is the complete answer to the problem of history and the need for spiritual identity. One should not fuss too much about the placement of knives and forks on a table when what really matters is how tasty and healthy the food is. However I am not convinced that New-Age Eclecticism is the way to go either. People need roots and traditions, which only a connection to family, society, and history can provide. To my mind, *what matters most is the pursuit of a worthwhile life*. With this aim in mind, we can bring the insights of all the different kinds of Druidry together, and use them to create a grounded spirituality linked to nature which is appropriate for our own needs and our own time. A spiritual seeker is not an anachronism, nor is she a child. She does not wish to live in the past, nor in a fantasy world. She is a hero, on a journey across the ninth wave of the sea, and she wishes to live in the here and now.

It seems to me that some kind of fusion or synthesis between the early Renaissance druids, the modern neo-Druids, and also a level of Eclecticism, may be emerging. It is my hope that modern Druids will some day become the philosopher-mystics of the modern Celtic community, as their counterparts were for the ancient Celtic world. It may be many decades before this happens. Indeed it may be a long time before all the different types of Druids can sit at the same table and acknowledge each other as Druids. But there are encouraging signs. For instance, it was through the cooperation of several British Druidic groups that Stonehenge became open to the general public on summer solstice morning. An impromptu festival now takes place there at that time every year, attended by thousands of people. In Ireland, Druids are involved in the community summer solstice festival on the Hill of Tara every year, and in the Samhain bonfire festival on the nearby Hill of Ward.

An enthusiasm for history and historical re-enactment can and should be a part of the revival of Druidry today. It can be loads of fun! And it can help to bring history and mythology to life, and so make the origins of our traditions real to us. Similarly, a capacity for imagination and creativity should be part of one's path as well. Without it, we may not be able to change our lives for the better, for we may not be able to see how things might be made different than they are. Whatever Druidry we eventually settle upon, it will be shaped by our own intentions and interpretations, and so it will inevitably be different than ancient Druidry. Yet the connection to the past cannot be ignored: what we inherit from history and tradition is a large part of who and what we are today. What, then, is the solution to the problem of history? The answer is: we should revive that which will help bring out the best in us. And the Celtic tradition provides many images of greatness we can strive to embody in our lives: gods and goddesses, mythological heroes, historical figures, and so on. How much eclectic invention and borrowing should be allowed? Again, the answer is, as much as will help us to become the best human beings we can be. What matters here is the degree to which Celtic tradition and imagination promotes human excellence and flourishing. What matters is how the adventure of self-discovery lifts up our lives, and gives us peace, confidence, courage, and happiness. Where the tradition seems incomplete or incoherent, and where imaginative creativity seems disconnected from reality, we may always refer back to the eternal mysteries as revealed to us through honest and open perception of the world, coupled with clear thinking and right intentions.

While there is no doubt that the standards of living and the lifestyles we lead have changed incredibly since the age of the Celts, and even within each of our lifetimes, the human needs for understanding, communication, companionship, and even empowerment have not changed. To questions about human life, the solution is not more right nor wrong just because it is old or new. A revival of the spirituality of the Earth could be a healing force in the world in this life and time. Celtic spirituality today is not a retreat from the world into an illusory garden of delight where problems need not be faced. Rather, it is an affirmation of our needs in this life, and an energetic attempt to take power over them. It is a reaffirmation of the sacredness of the land, sea, and sky. It is a reclaiming of the sacredness of the feminine, the Goddess, whose place in western culture has always been ambivalent, uncertain, downplayed, or even ignored. And it is a recelebration of ourselves as participants in the ongoing and never-ending creation of the world.

Two:
Nine Druidic Mysteries

Great indeed was the strength and power of that Meadhbh over the men of Ireland, for it was she who would not allow a king in Tara unless he had her as wife.
—from the *Annals of the Four Masters.*

The first Druids to set foot on Ireland were members of the tribe of Partholon, and their names were Fis, Eolas, and Fochmarc. In English these names mean Wisdom, Knowledge, and Enquiry. The intellectual, philosophical, and mystical character of the Druids is established immediately. But what, we may ask, is Druidic wisdom? What knowledge did they seek, and how did they seek it?

1. The Mist of Manannan

The landscape of Britain and Ireland has been farmed and worked over by humankind for thousands of years. Its hills, valleys, fields, earthworks, and archaeological remains are a testament to the continuity of human culture and history throughout all that time. The climate is very mild and wet, and so days of heavy rain and fog are rather common. Some of its regions, like the many bogs, and the stone fields of Connemara and the Burren,

appear positively barren and desolate. And yet there is a quality about the land which continues to attract one's attention. Just when you think you have seen all there is to see, some new surprise catches your eyes and you have to look again. The patchwork fields with their thick leafy hedgerows, or dry stone walls, harbor a timeless, ethereal, and indeed comforting quality. The horizon is never far away, and the clouds close to the Earth, making the land seem closer, more intimate. It gives the impression that the next valley, the next field, the next hill, just beyond the horizon, will be a different kind of place. When the sky is clear and the sun able to shine in his full glory, the landscape becomes transformed into a magnificent garden, and every green growing thing seems to sing. In Ireland it is easy to drift into a condition of vision. I walked along the north edge of Galway Bay one evening in autumn. It had been raining in the afternoon but was then clearing and the sun was going down. In the far distance I could see one of the Arran Islands. As I looked across the bay to Black Head, the sunlight appeared under the clouds, shining the water-washed stones of the Burren, and reflecting the sunset's reds and oranges on to the clouds from below.

And as the sun sank under the sea, the sky and the water took on the same shade of deep blue, with a reddish band on the horizon. The coast of the Burren across the bay was a black silhouette which seemed to hang in space. I felt as if I was looking into the Otherworld. And I felt very much at ease, at home, at peace. This is the environment in which the ancient Celtic people developed the mythology, the storytelling, the music, and the wisdom which has come to us today as the tradition of Celtic Mysticism.

In Britain and Ireland, atmospheric conditions created by the unique combination of cool northern air and warm ocean currents from the tropics create extraordinary light effects in the sky and on the landscape. So far as I know, there isn't a sky like it anywhere else in the world. Much of Ireland and north-western Europe in general was, in ancient times, inhospitable bogland, hard to exploit for resources and nearly impossible to farm, and full of strange fogs, gasses, and fires which made the land mysterious and dangerous. Great wooden roads and stone causeways needed to be built just to enter them safely. The Corlea Trackway, in county Longford, Ireland, is an example of one. It must have been very natural, then, for ancient Celtic people to consider the mists and clouds that constantly surrounded them as in some way connected to the great mysteries of the world. Mists are described in the mythologies as the hiding-places of the gods, the barriers between this world and the Otherworld, and yet also the means of transport to the Otherworld as well. The magical mist from the Otherworld is named for the God of the Sea, Manannan, who is also a God of

passages to and from the Otherworld. It is a fog which the Gods conjure in order to hide their comings and goings. When the Tuatha de Dannan landed in Ireland, they burned their ships. The smoke covered the whole country for three days. Then when the Milesians arrived, the Tuatha de Dannan raised another magical mist to prevent them from landing their ships. The Mist is that which makes it hard to see into the Otherworld, and yet it is also the vehicle to take us there.

Another term used in Irish sources for this mist is *féth fiadha*, which means "the art of resembling." It appears in mythology as a magical skill possessed by immortal deities as well as by mortal Druids. The Tuatha de Dannans hide their comings and goings and their dwelling-places in it. And Druids could sometimes raise the fog on their own in order to reach the inhabitants of the Otherworld. It is possible, then, that the technique of féth fiadha was actually a theatrical illusion designed to impress gullible audiences. The Druids may have used the fire of special kinds of wood, adding certain herbs or oils, to create different kinds of smoke for rituals, for battle, or for hiding their movements.

In the mythologies, when a figure from the Otherworld is about to appear, a mist or a fog normally surrounds the area. Then the Druids are called upon to interpret the origin and meaning of the fog and to communicate with the beings who raised it. An early Irish legal text says that one of the professional responsibilities of a Druid was to "perform the féth fiadha or the divination." This may relate to the idea that the mist is a medium for obtaining knowledge from the Otherworld. A prayer called "Fath-Fith" existed in the Hebrides of

Scotland, and was recorded by Alexander Carmichael in his study of the folk prayers of the people living in that area. It was connected to a form of divination which could be performed on the morning of one of the fire-festivals, or on the morning of the first Monday after a festival. The person seeking knowledge would walk three times, sunwise, around the fire, and then stand in the door-frame of his house, his hands on the door-posts, looking out. He would then recite this incantation:

Fath-fith

Will I make on thee,

By Mary of the augury,

By Bride of the corslet,

From sheep, from rain,

From goat, from buck,

From fox, from wolf,

From sow, from boar,

From dog, from cat,

From hipped-bear,

From wilderness-dog,

From watchful scan,

From cow, from horse,

From bull, from heifer,

From daughter, from son,

From the birds of the air,

From the creeping things of the earth,

From the fishes of the sea,

From the imps of the storm.[1]

Each of these different animals, people, and imagined creatures is something that a subsistence farmer or fisherman (the sort of person Carmichael was interviewing) could expect to see at any time when looking out of her door. Yet the ritual and the special time of year in which it was performed encourages a slightly changed frame of mind. The things which he might see as he looks out the door become messages from "God" or "the saints," revealing the hidden order that sustains the world. As a form of divination, the idea appears to be that when the Fath-Fith incantation was recited, then the appearance of one or more of the beings described in the incantation would have a corresponding occult meaning which would answer the question. Note the invocation of two saints, Mary and Bride, in the first lines, and the reference to the creatures of the air, earth, and sea in the last lines. This may be a subtle remnant of belief in the goddesses of the land (Mary may stand for Danu, and Bride for Brigid), and of the "three realms" of land, sea, and sky which together comprised the shape of Celtic cosmology.

I regard the Mist as the Druidic near-equivalent of the Hindu principle "The Veil of Maya." This analogy suggests that to achieve access to the Otherworld, and the knowledge that can be gained there, it is necessary to think and feel differently. As described by the Eastern traditions, the Veil of Maya is the intellectual separation of things into separate classes and categories, which sometimes clouds our powers of perception. To part the mist is to dissolve, at least partially, the boundaries of some of our intellectual categories, and experience the world as a perceptual unity. The analogy with the Celtic traditions is in the use of "threshold places" for magic. Shorelines, riversides, doorways, bridges, dawns and twilights, and so on, and especially holy days because they stand between seasons, are places neither at sea nor on land, neither inside nor out, neither night nor day, neither the previous day nor the next. Thus they are the time and place preferred for the Fath-Fith divination. The indefinite-ness of certain times and places apparently gives them magical potency. Perhaps it is the inapplicability of intellectual categories to those places which weakens the boundary between this world and the Otherworld. The boundaries between categories of thinking do exist (we invented them) and they have great usefulness, especially for practical tasks. Yet the mist surrounds us at places where these categories and divisions do not seem to apply very easily. The Mist of Manannan, in this way, can be seen as what it feels like for someone standing in a place that is neither one place nor another, neither day nor night, neither sea nor land, neither one world nor the other. It is what it feels like to be stepping into a realm of magic. The dissolution of these boundaries is a step towards the recognition of primordial unity.

Normally, the process of learning to perceive this primordial unity requires nothing more, and nothing less, than *a change of attitude*. An attitude is a way of being in the world. It is a mental and emotional window through which we interpret and understand everything we see and experience. An attitude is also a kind of activity, and a way of behaving more or less consistently across time. In our routine of ordinary life, we live in terms of what might be called "everyday attitudes" or "ordinary habits." When we approach the world this way, we tend to see things and think about things in terms of their separation from other things, in terms of their familiarity or predictability, and in terms of what we might be able to do with them. Under the everyday attitude, we tend to understand and categorize things in terms of our *intentions*. An intention is some purpose we

are aiming at, or some goal we are striving to achieve with some action or group of actions taken together. For instance, if my intention is to prepare a meal, a knife would appear to me as useful, but if my intention is to have a bath, the knife appears as not-useful. Likewise, a knife in my kitchen drawer appears to me as safe, but in the hands of a mugger it appears dangerous. Most of the time one's intentions are directed at ordinary, practical tasks, with the aim of producing some kind of result. If my intention is to have a drink with a friend, a wooden table appears to me as a useful place on which to set my glass. If my intention is to heat my home and I haven't paid the gas bill recently, the same table appears to me as a useful source of firewood. We construct the world with intentions.

It is this "everyday" attitude which enables us to read bus time tables, prepare meals, have conversations, build houses, and do all the things involved in having and sustaining ordinary life. In terms of the everyday attitude, the impulse to "Know Yourself," is a plain absurdity. To someone who asks who I am, I can easily reply with just my name, my job, my various family relationships, and so on. At the level of the everyday attitude, selfhood does not appear as a question at all. It appears as an obvious given. Yet this ordinary attitude to things tends to obscure certain spiritual possibilities. Eastern Mysticism is fairly clear on this point. One of its dominant themes is that the pursuit of material wealth, social prestige, political or economic power, and so on, is fundamentally contrary to the pursuit of spiritual attainments.

So if an attitude is a group of intentionalities, and the everyday attitude is the practical, ordinary intentionalities, we can say that with a spiritual attitude we suspend the practical intentions and adopt spiritual intentions. We suspend all of the intentionalities that are aimed towards producing material results. This is the first step in the process of parting the Mist of Manannan. When adopting a spiritual intention, one looks upon the world without a practical project, thus rendering the categories of useful and not-useful redundant. In this respect it may appear as if the spiritual attitude encourages idleness. But this is far from the truth. For the spiritual attitude is still an intentionality, and so it is still an activity, and still requires work, passion, will, and initiative. In the spiritual attitude, the mind is both receptive and active at the same time. The spiritual attitude consists in looking at the world in such a way as to bring out the spiritual qualities of things. Such qualities do not generally have to do with usefulness. They tend to be in the object's ability to function as a symbol for a spiritual mystery, used for instance in ceremonies, or act as a conduit for the experience of the sacred. The spectacles of the sacred reveal the relations of meaning and value in life. These relations are usually described as *correspondences*, of which the well known mantra "as above, so below" is the general formula. So we can say that the spiritual attitude is the group of intentionalities which seek out the spiritual correspondences of things: their capacity to serve as either a symbol or even as the presence of a spiritual power.

We find this represented in the various ways the Otherworld appears to the characters of Celtic mythology: for instance in the story of the Voyage of Bran, the sea-god Manannan approaches the sailors in a chariot that drives across the sea as if the sea was solid ground. Manannan recites this poem of invitation to him:

> It is what Bran thinks, he is going in his curragh over the wonderful, beautiful clear sea; but to me, from far off in my chariot, it is a flowery plain he is riding on.

> What is a clear sea to the good boat Bran is in, is a happy plain with many flowers to me in my two-wheeled chariot.

> It is what Bran sees, many waves beating across the clear sea; it is what I myself see, red flowers without any fault.

> The sea-horses [wave crests] are bright in summer-time, as far as Bran's eyes can reach; there is a wood of beautiful acorns under the head of your little boat.

> A wood with blossom and fruit that has the smell of wine; a wood without fault, without withering, with leaves the color of gold.

> Let Bran row on steadily, it is not far to the Land of Women; before the setting of the sun you will reach Emhain, of many-colored hospitality.[2]

Manannan's spiritual perception enabled him to see the ocean as a flowery meadow on which he could drive his chariot. This does not mean that adopting the spiritual attitude will allow you to walk on water! The point here is that spirituality has its foundation in the way we see the world, and the way we see ourselves in it. The spiritual attitude reveals to us the world in a different light, an Otherworldly light.

2. Earth and Sky

There are several ways in which the presence of the spirit is revealed in Celtic mythology, and the most important of them, surprisingly, is a *political* category. In Irish, the word for this concept is *flaith*, which in English means "sovereignty." The basic idea is that the ruler of a territory is magically connected to the landscape. Traditionally, once a candidate for leadership of the tribe passed all the tests (elections, chariot races, or even Druidic prophesy!), then in the ceremony of his inauguration magical forces would have been called upon to ensure that he would be a good king. Special speeches on the qualities of the just king, such as the *Testament of Morann*, would have been recited as part of the ceremony. As recorded by the ancient historian Geraldus Cambriensis in the *Topographica Hibernica*, the ceremony for inaugurating the king of Ulster involved three acts. In the first, the king-to-be showed himself to his people, naked, in an arena near Emain Macha, the royal fort. He would slowly turn around in a circle, so the people could see and know who he is, and so he could demonstrate that he had no blemishes. In the second, he had to embrace and kiss a white mare, which represented the Goddess of Sovereignty. This mare was then taken away and killed. The king's third act was to bathe in its blood and dress in its skin. This may seem very macabre to us, and to those involved in the animal rights movement it must appear horrifying. To the ancient Celts, the horse represented the goddess of the sovereignty of the land. So this ceremony was, to them, a powerful representation of the new king's authority, responsibility, and connection with the goddess. It elevated him from being an ordinary mortal to being something half way between humanity and divinity.

The principle at work here is called the *Heiros Gamos*, in classical literature; or in English, the *Great Marriage*. It is the idea that there is a special, magical connectivity between the human tribe, as represented by its chief (who for this purpose is sometimes called a Sacred King), and the goddess of the land the tribe lives on. This connectivity is presented as a marriage bond, a sexual and familial bond made magical. Because of this connection, and this is the clever part, the physical health and vitality, the brightness of his intellect, the honor and charisma of his character, or the lack thereof, would arouse the approval or disapproval of the goddess, and that would manifest as fertility or barrenness in the land itself. Human morality and environmental health are intimately linked. The principle of the Great Marriage is, in my view, the best evidence of an ancient Druidic "land-ethic" or "environmentalism." Here is how a 7th-century wisdom text called the *Testament of Morann* describes that relation.

> *Let him preserve truth [Fírinne], it will preserve him.*
>
> *Let him raise truth, it will raise him.*
>
> *Let him exalt mercy, it will exalt him.*
>
> *Let him care for his tribes, they will care for him.*
>
> *Let him help his tribes, they will help him.*
>
> *Let him soothe his tribes, they will soothe him.*

Tell him, it is through the truth of the ruler that plagues and great lightnings are kept from the people.

It is through the truth of the ruler that he judges great tribes [and] great riches.

It is through the truth of the ruler that he secures peace, tranquillity, joy, ease, [and] comfort.

It is through the truth of the ruler that he dispatches (great) battalions to the borders of hostile neighbors.

It is through the truth of the ruler that every heir plants his house-post in his fair inheritance.

It is through the truth of the ruler that abundances of great tree-fruit of the great wood are tasted.

It is through the truth of the ruler that milk-yields of great cattle are maintained.

It is through the truth of the ruler that there is abundance of every high, tall corn.

It is through the truth of the ruler that abundance of fish swim in streams.

It is through the truth of the ruler that fair children are well begotten.[3]

We have seen that the ruler must be without physical blemishes, or else he would be unable to please his goddess. In this text, it is emphasized that the ruler must be without blemishes of *character*. He must embody all the qualities which are considered noble and exalted among human qualities, both aesthetic and moral. The personal example the leader sets for others, and the way he runs his administration, may mutually reflect the character of the society he leads. Note also that

the relationship between the ruler and the goddess is obtained through a category of knowledge: "truth." The Irish word being translated here is *fírinne*, which can also be translated as "justice." The overall point here is that a king is magically ordained by the goddess, and regarded as embodying the presence of the god, and so he is no longer an ordinary man. He becomes a man who exists halfway in the spirit world as well. He is thus magically and ceremonially compelled to exercise the wisdom and justice that his new authority requires. This does not mean he can rule by unquestionable "divine right," nor does it mean he cannot be deposed. The chief earns his position not because he occupies a special office, from which he is, himself, theoretically separated. He earns it with of the force of his character.

There are many instances of the Great Marriage in mythology. In the Irish story of the Second Battle of Maigh Tuireadh, we have a Celtic example, in which the Dagda makes love with the Morrigan.

The Dagdha had a tryst arranged within a year at the Samhain of the battle, at Gleann Éadain, and the (river) Uineas of the Connachta roars to the south of it. He saw a woman at a weir in the Uineas, washing, with her second foot at Alladh Eacha at the south of the water and the other foot at Lios Conduibh at the north of the water. Nine loosened tresses were on her head, The Dagdha addressed her, and they copulated. The name of the place since then is "the Lying of the Couple." The woman mentioned here is the Mor-Rioghain.[4]

Dagdha belongs to the tribe of the gods, the Tuatha de Dannan, and so his lovemaking with the Morrigan secured her favor for Dagda and his tribe, ensuring victory for the Tuatha de Dannan over the Fomhoire. The Morrigan's name in Irish was originally *Mór-Ríoghain* ("great queen" or "phantom queen"). She is a goddess

On top of the Paps of Anu.

the goddess of the sovereignty of Tara whose name is commemorated in one of the ring-forts there. Meadhbh is also the Queen of Connaught in the story of the *Táin Bo Cuailnge*, although she is not described as a goddess in that story. This Meadhbh

of war. It is clear in the story that the Tuatha de Dannan were victorious because they earned her favor. Yet she is also a goddess of the earth, of sex and fertility, and of the sovereignty of the land. Some scholars think that her name may be linguistically connected to *Danu*, the mother of the gods, for whom the Tuatha de Dannan are named, and who is also identified with the landscape of Ireland, especially with rivers. Both Danu and the Morrigan have hills named after their breasts: the Paps of Anu, along the Cork and Kerry border, and the Paps of the Morrigan, in county Meath, near Newgrange.

Morrigan is also identical with Meadhbh,

had a voracious appetite for sex, and it is said she required seven men each night if her husband Ailell was not available. The Morrigan's name reappears in the Arthurian legends as Morganna le Fey, in Welsh mythology as Rhiannon, and among the Continental Gauls as Rigantona. Interestingly, both the Irish and the Welsh "Great Queens" have power over ravens and crows, and are associated with horses. The Irish Morrigan has the power to transform into a crow, and that is how she first approached Cú Chullain. And it is while riding "a slow horse that cannot be overtaken" that the Welsh hero Pwyll first encounters Rhiannon. Her earliest artistic representations may have been the giant horses carved into the chalk hillsides of southern England, like the Uffington White Horse. Her

Stone with Sheila-na-gig, Hill of Tara.

earliest human-shaped representations may be the image called a "Sheila-na-gig," which depicts a woman pulling open her own reproductive organs. This image is usually found as an architectural ornament in many of the same contexts as the Green Man, although there is a stone on Tara which has an ancient, heavily weather-beaten carving that resembles her.

Morrigan is thus a natural match for the Dagda, whose name means "the good god." He is associated with the sun, for he has sun-related titles like *Áncheann* ("glowing head"), *Aedh álainn* ("beautiful fire"), and *Eochaidh*, ("horseman"; continental Celts sometimes depicted their sun-gods riding on a horse). Dagda is also a primordial ancestor figure. Julius Caesar wrote that the Celts all claimed to be descended from the god of the underworld, whom they called *Dis Pater* ("the father god"). In his words, "The Gauls all assert their descent from Dis Pater and say that it is the Druidic belief. For this reason they count periods of time not by the number of days but by the number of nights; and in reckoning birthdays and the new moon and new year their unit of reckoning is the night followed by the day."[5] The Dagda has just such a title of his own: *Ollathair* ("father of all"). He possesses a great club, the *Lorg an Daghda*, which has a "rough" end that can kill with a mere touch, and a "smooth" end which revives the dead. He also possesses a special cauldron, the *Coire an Dagda*, from which no assembly ever went unsatisfied.

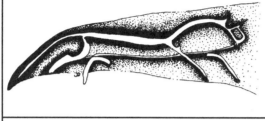

The Uffington White Horse

Dagda is a primordial father-god who continues to provide for his descendants. And like the Morrigan, Dagda has a powerful sex drive. Dagda's club is undeniably phallic. And the Morrigan agrees to a tryst with him quite readily.

The Great Marriage is an instance of the ancient idea that the cosmos is configured by the interaction of two primordial forces or events, in this case represented as sky and earth, male and female, tribe and land. Strabo recorded a Druidic belief that "men's souls and the universe are indestructible, though at times fire and water may prevail." In fire and water we have the primordial pair represented as impersonal elements. We find the water in the rivers and well springs which goddesses of the land are often associated with. The goddess Boann, for instance, is identified with the river Boyne which flows through Meath close to both Tara and Newgrange, and Dagda made a tryst with her to gain possession of Newgrange. Danu is a river goddess whose name appears in the Danube river of central Europe, among others. Tribal gods, as we have seen, are associated with the fire of the sun.

We find the principle of the Great Marriage in the life of Cartimandua, a Celtic queen of the Brigantia tribe of Britain in the first century. Cartimandua was seen as the living embodiment of the goddess Brighid, for whom the tribe was named, and her husband Venutius could co-rule with her because he was married to her. So when she divorced Venutius, her second husband Vellocatus, who was Venutius' arms bearer, became the new king. (Venutius started a civil war on this account, but Cartimandua won in the end, with help from Roman auxiliaries.) We also find the Great Marriage in other cultures, for instance in *The Odyssey,* when Demeter lies on the seeded Earth with Iasion. It is in a creation story described in an ancient Hindu holy text, the *Bhradaranyaka Upanisad*. This text describes a primordial being who splits into male and female halves, which chase each other and mate to give birth to everything in the world. Blake expressed it his poem, "The Marriage of Heaven and Hell." There used to be a custom in Europe in which young couples on certain special days of the year would go into the fields and forests to make love. Some scholars of mythology and anthropology like James Frazer and Mircea Eliade believed this was a re-enactment of the Great Marriage of earth and sky, and a throwback to the time when the act was believed to sympathetically encourage the crops to grow. They found it to be a common theme all over the ancient world. It is reproduced in the inauguration of kings, as it is in wedding ceremonies and New Year celebrations. As Eliade says,

> It is on New Year's day that Ishtar lies with Tammuz, and the king reproduces this mythical heirogamy by consummating ritual union with the goddess (i.e. with the heirodule [priestess] who represents her on earth) in a secret chamber of the temple, where the nuptial bed of the goddess stands. The divine union assures terrestrial fecundity; when Ninlil lies with Enlil, rain begins to fall.[6]

We could say, then, that Druidry represents certain agricultural facts in human terms, to emphasize our environmental connectivity. The great lesson here is that the forces which make possible the regeneration of life in the environment are also at work within the human body, mind, and spirit, and so there is continuity between the environment and ourselves. Moreover, the regeneration of plant life in the spring is an image of immanent divinity we may aspire to embody in our lives. For the relation between these two forces is not that of moral conflict: no question of good and evil is suggested here. Their relationship is a human relationship made divine: the relation of love. The love of the Dagda and the Morrigan for each other makes possible the defeat of evil and the regeneration of the world. It is an idea which, as an object of spiritual contemplation, can be internalized into our own lives. Every woman has, within her, the presence of the Goddess of Sovereignty, and every man has within him the stature of a Sacred King. The Great Marriage is the very ground of cosmic unity obtained through the interaction of two principles of cosmic order. To the ancient Celts, as to the other ancient cultures who perceived the same idea, this discovery must have been an astounding spiritual breakthrough.

3. The Three Realms

The "duality" of the principle of the Great Marriage implies a third principle between them. For instance, a child may be born from the union: the Irish god of youth and love, Aengus Og, is the child of Dagda and Boann. In Wales, the divine child is called Mabon Ap Modron, meaning "The Son of the Mother." This child acts as a messenger bringing to us the good news of the consummation of the Great Marriage, and the promise of a bountiful future.

Entrance to Newgrange.

The third principle may also be the mortal realm, where we live, and where the divine realms of seeded Earth and shining Sky meet each other. There is a famous symbol carved in the passage wall of the most famous Neolithic passage mound in the world, Newgrange, which is illuminated when the moment of the Great Marriage between earth and sky takes place inside its central chamber. Brugh Na Boinne, better known as Newgrange, is more than 5,000 years old, and it is the greatest artistic, engineering, and spiritual achievement of the mysterious Neolithic culture that built it. It was seamlessly weaved into the mythology of the Celtic-speaking people of Ireland: it is the birth place of heroes, including Cú Chullain, the dwelling place of gods including Dagda and his son Angus, and the burial place of kings. The goddess of the nearby river Boyne, whose name is Boann, is a Goddess of Sovereignty. The male characters mate with her to acquire possession of the mound, just as the kings of Tara must mate with the Morrigan to acquire rulership over Ireland.

The main feature of the monument, which makes it so important, is that the long passage is aligned such that sunlight enters the central chamber on only one day a year: the morning of 21st December, Midwinter's day, the shortest day and the longest night of the year. Here we have the Great Marriage played out as an astronomical event. The sun penetrates the inner womb of the mound, giving birth to the new sun and fertilizing the Earth for the coming year. The "three" which come together at Newgrange are the realm of Heaven, Earth, and Underworld. The sunlight from the sky, the landscape on which the mound is built, and the darkness of the Underworld in the mound's inner chamber are all brought together on that magic morning. Mircea Eliade is credited with articulating for the first time the importance of the centre in mythology: as he says, these three realms all align themselves together at the centre, along a vertical axis, making communication and travel between them possible. "Hell, the center of the earth, and the "gate" of the sky are, then, situated on the same axis, and it is along this axis that passage from one cosmic region to another was effected."[7]

The "third" principle, understood this way, is the triplicity of "realms" or "worlds." In the system of the Barddas, created in the 18th century by Iolo Morganwyg and still used by most British Druid orders today, these realms are arranged as concentric circles, and they are called:

- ☘ *Annwn*, (pronounced "AH-noo-in"), the cthonic (Underworld) realm of the dead, ruled by the god Arawn who is the god of the dead and is the divine father of the human race. It is located either beneath the surface of the sea and/or at the center of the cosmos. Outside and/or above it is:

- ☘ *Abred*, ("EH-breth"), the terrestrial realm where we live as mortal human beings. We migrated here from Annwn, on our way to:

- ☘ *Gwynfyd*, ("GOO-in-fith"), the celestial realm of spirits and divinities above us and/or on the outer edge of the circle, which is humanity's proper home. Within, or even further beyond, the realm of Gwynfyd is *Ceugant*, ("COY-gant"), the inaccessible and mysterious dwelling place of God.

The Barddas describes the spiritual journey of the soul as a migration from Annwn, the Underworld, to Abred where it experiences life as every kind of living creature from fungus and insects to plants and animals, and then finally becomes human. As humans we can advance to Gwynfyd and become divine, or return to a "pre-human" form and try again. Iolo may have gotten the idea from Julius Caesar's note that the Celts of Gaul claimed that they came from the Underworld and were descended from Dis Pater, the god of the dead. These three realms correspond with the physical environment: the sky above, the land on which we stand, and the sea below. The sky and the sun is the celestial realm because, obviously, it is "above" us; in Celtic mythology, the gods arrive in Ireland in ships that fly through the air. The sea was in Celtic myth often associated with the Underworld and with passages to and from Tir Na n-Og: a story of an Otherworld adventure is called an *imramma*, meaning "sea journey." Taliesin, a shamanic poet of Wales, described crossing the sea to reach Annwyn. In ancient Ireland, one had to cross the water of the river Boyne to reach Newgrange from Tara. The land, then, remains in the cosmology as the world we inhabit. The scientific principle of evolution tells the same story of spiritual migration in its own way: our pre-human ancestors emerged from the sea, evolved into human form on the land, and now with our airplanes and spacecraft we take can take flight to the sky.

When the three realms align together, such as in the chamber of Newgrange on Midwinter morning, time itself is renewed, and life is empowered to continue by the increasing energy of the sun. This is not a once-and-for-all event, but is rather an *annual* event. It is essentially a repetition of the original act of creation, which makes creation an ongoing, continuous process.

4. The Four Quarters

From Midwinter until Midsummer, the newly reborn sun's highest daily position rises higher and the total daylight time increases. Time itself takes on the form of a circle, with four special stations for the solstices and equinoxes along its circumference, and also for the four places on the horizon. These four places are: the sunrise position in the east, the sunset position in the west, the top of the sun's arc in the south, and the bottom of the sun's arc, under the horizon, in the north. (In the southern hemisphere, north and south are of course reversed.) Perhaps that is why the interior chamber of Newgrange, and of so many other similar chambered cairns like it in Ireland, has a cross-shaped layout. Newgrange is just the most famous because of its age—it is older than the Pyramids in Egypt!—and the mathematical precision of its design, and the enigmatic shapes and figures carved on to its stones. Typically there is a long and narrow passage from the entrance to the center, where the ceiling is much higher and where three small recessed chambers form a little cross. Knowth, Fourknocks, Carrowkeel, and Loughcrew all have the same general pattern, as do other passage mounds in Scotland and other Celtic countries. The architecture thus configures a circle of time with four stations, two solstices and two equinoxes, and the correspondence of these stations to points on the circle of the horizon, the north, south, east, and west. Time takes the form of an equal-armed cross within a circle, a Celtic cross.

The Celtic Cross is famous as a symbol of Celtic Christianity. Massive and beautifully carved stone crosses with a circle around the intersection are featured at monasteries and churches around the country. Even today the Celtic Cross is a preferred shape for a grave marker for Irish Catholics. They can be found all over the world where Irish people settled. Will it surprise the reader to learn that this symbol is repeated in the Earth's atmosphere as well? On days when the conditions are right, the sun can create a gigantic cross in the sky. When the sun's angle is just right, and when there is the right kind of moisture in the air, the light creates a vertical line above and below the sun, and also two rainbow-colored flashes called "sun dogs" directly to the left and right. It is rare for both of these effects to appear at the same time. I have seen both together only once in my life.

The idea that the physical world is divided into four territorial realms in each of the cardinal directions, intersecting at a "fifth province" which constitutes the center, is an ancient idea. Almost every other culture in the world at one time or another shared it. This may be because of the way our bodies are shaped. Because our eyes are at the front of our heads, and not on the sides as it is in other animals such as horses, birds, and rabbits, all of our perceptions are automatically structured into space-relations of front and back, left side, and right side. A natural fourfold correspondence already obtains in everything we see. The equal-armed cross in a circle represents this. Another cross is formed by the vertical dimension of the upright tree, mountain, or human being, intersecting the horizontal dimension of the horizon, or the human being's outstretched arms. The symbol works simply because it has its foundation in the way we exist in the world. Similarly, the four cardinal directions are founded on the "stations of the sun." The east-west axis is given by the sun's rising and setting positions. The north-south axis is given by the positions in the sky where the sun reaches its daily height, the south, and where it does not ever go, the north. Vertical lines reach upward and recall our relationship to the spiritual realms of sun, moon, and stars; horizontal lines recall the horizon of the Earth and the transient, death-shadowed condition of embodied being. The fifth point, the intersection, is where both of these conditions of our existence unite. As a symbol of centeredness, groundedness, and relation to space and time, the cross is older by centuries than the Roman cross of Christianity. The many cross shapes on the sides of Ogham stones around Ireland, which were probably inscribed there by early Christians to "de-paganize" them, still call to mind this natural symbol of the intersection of space and time, spiritual and temporal, above and below.

As mentioned, the Island of Ireland is divided into four traditional provinces. For Druids, this traditional division also corresponds to four directions of four social functions. A story called "The Settling of the Manor House At Tara" gives us the following:

The East an t-Oirthear	The South an deisceart	The West an t-Iarrthar	The North an tuaisceart
Leinster	Munster	Connaught	Ulster
Dind Ríg, co. Carlow	Cnoc Áine co. Limerick	Cruachan Ai co. Roscommon	Emain Macha co. Armagh
Laborers and farmers	Craftsmen and artisans	Druids, poets, and musicians	Warriors
Production of food and material wealth	Music, artistry, and craftmanship	Learning and education	Battle and protection
The rising sun	The midday sun	The setting sun	Darkness

The threefold "vertical" division of Sky, Land, and Sea, which roughly corresponds to Heaven, Earth, and Underworld, is intersected with a fourfold "horizontal" division of the Earth, the realm where we live, corresponding to the four cardinal directions. In the case of Ireland, the fourfold division also corresponds to the four traditional provinces of the island.

The arrangement of the universe into these realms effectively creates a mandala. A mandala is a diagram space and time, in the shape of a combination of concentric circles and radial lines. Its geometry is balanced by equal and repetitive divisions, usually numbering some multiple of three or four. And it always has a center, an undivided "world axis," which unites them all. The description of the world in Celtic tradition is the description of a mandala. The "Four Green Fields" are the four provinces of Ireland, arranged in a mandala pattern: Leinster, Munster, Connaught, and Ulster are corresponded with cardinal directions and social functions.

5. The Center

A mandala must have a center. Newgrange serves that purpose, although Irish mythology describes several others. The story of the arrival of the gods to Ireland describes a purely mythological center called The Well of Wisdom. It has five streams flowing from it, one for each province of Ireland (including Meath), or perhaps for each of the five physical senses. Nine hazel trees grow in a circle around it; nine was always a number associated with magic and the divine. Salmon swim up and down the streams, eating the hazelnuts. All who drink of the well, or eat the nuts, or

the salmon-meat, gain all the knowledge and wisdom of all things. Its additional power, to restore life to the dead, a power also borne by other wells in Irish mythology, is activated by four ritual operators who stand around it. Diancecht and his three children, chanting over the Well of Healing, in the story of the battle of Maigh Tuireadh are an example of this, as are the four teachers of wisdom from the four cities from whence the Gods came and brought their treasures. The Well exists at the center of Tir Na n-Og, the Irish Otherworld. This center is thus everywhere and nowhere—we carry it within us wherever we go.

The mythologies describe two more important centers: a "royal" site for political purposes, which is the Hill of Tara, and a "religious" center on the hill of Uisneach, in present day county Westmeath. These centers may well have had international importance even in ancient times: for instance, archaeologists discovered fragments of Phoenician fabric at Uisneach. Standing on the summit of Tara is another important center: a phallic standing stone called the Lia Fáil. Its name comes from an Indo-European language root meaning "to be strong," and to the word *flaith*, meaning "sovereignty." It is also related to the word *fodhla*, one of the ancient names for Ireland. The tradition surrounding it holds that it has the power to cry out when someone who is destined to be a True King of Ireland treads upon it. This stone was brought to Ireland by the Gods, and still stands on the summit of the Hill of Tara, the ancient and traditional seat of the High Kings. I first visited Tara in the year 2002. When I touched it for the first time a strong sense of its dignity and serenity came to me, as if the stone had endured with patience the mad vicissitudes of human history that fumbled all around it. I felt as if the stone's mere presence was a kind of signpost, saying "This is where we came from, this is who we are." The mandala of Celtic cosmology can now be completed with the addition of the center and the outside, thus:

The Center *an Lár*	The Outside *an Taobh Amuigh*
Sovereignty	Primordial chaos
An Mhí The province of Meath ("The Middle")	*An Farriage Mhor* The ocean
Hill of Tara and hill of Uisneach; the Well of Wisdom; the Lia Fáil.	The Rest of the World
The King.	Foreigners, transient laborers, banished criminals, and slaves.

The Lia Fáil's legendary function connects the Great Marriage, as an object which has the magical property of responding to the Truth of nearby mortals. It is the only treasure not identified as the personal property of a God. It has the function of crying out when a true king stands on it. Clearly, then, it is the stone that embodies the union of heaven and earth, tribal chief and land goddess, "above" and "below."

There are other "center" stones in Ireland, such as the massive Stone of the Divisions on the Hill of Uisneach, near Mullingar, in Westmeath, and the lavishly decorated Turoe Stone near Loughcrea, in Galway. Furthermore, the Lia Fáil is one of four special treasures brought to the world by the gods. The others are described in the story of the *Cath Maigh Tuireadh* as follows:

The Tuatha de Dannan were in the northern islands of the world, studying occult lore and sorcery, Druidic arts and witchcraft and magical skill, until they surpassed the sages of the pagan arts. They studied occult lore and secret knowledge and diabolic arts in four cities: Falias, Gorias, Murias, and Findias. From Falias was brought the Stone of Fál which was located in Tara. It used to cry out beneath every king that would take Ireland. From Gorias was brought the spear which Lug had. No battle was ever sustained against it, or against the man who held it in his hand. From Findias was brought the sword of Nuadu. No one ever escaped from it once it was drawn from its deadly sheath, and no one could resist it. From Murias was brought the Dagda's cauldron. No company ever went away from it unsatisfied. There were four Druids in those four cities. Morfesa was in Falias; Esras was in Gorias; Uiscias was in Findias; Semias was in Murias. Those are the four poets from whom the Tuatha De learned occult lore and secret knowledge.[8]

Here the three- and fourfold cosmology is enriched by the addition of four treasures, originating in four cities that are ruled by four druids.

It is a Celtic religious custom from both pagan and Christian times to

Celtic cross slab stone at Clonmacnoise

circumnabulate (walk in a clockwise circle) aroundsacred centers like wells, fires, and mounds. Did ancient Celtic Druids honor the four cardinal directions? For several reasons, I believe that they did. There is the extraordinary evidence of the High Crosses, erected at early Celtic Christian monastic sites which, like the passage mounds and standing stones of their pre-Christian predecessors, served as the anchoring *axis-mundi* of the community's world. The artistic subject-matter of the carved panels on these crosses is unquestionably Christian but the style is in perfect continuity with the art of pagan metalwork and stonework that came

before it. Two cross-slabs discovered at Clonmacnoise, one of the most important early Christian sites in Ireland, have a triskele carved into the center. To me this represents the threefold "vertical" division of sacred space into three realms, brought together with the fourfold "horizontal" division of sacred space into four cardinal quarters. There are also hints in the mythologies that the four directions were part of early Celtic spiritual practice. There are descriptions of Druids performing magical rituals in which four Druids stand in a circle facing something in the center which is being magically empowered for some purpose. In the story of the Battle of Maigh Tuireadh, Diancecht, the god of healing, stood around a holy well with his three children in this way, to empower the well to heal the wounds of anyone placed inside it. The Fomorians found the well and filled it with stones. It is now known as Heapstown Cairn, and is located in county Sligo. The coming of Cormac to the kingship at Tara was prophesized in the dream of a Druid who slept beneath a bull's hide while four Druids chanted magical incantations above him. This is not the same as the "calls to the quarters" performed in the ceremonies of Wiccans and other modern Pagans. It also has nothing to do with the four elements of earth, air, fire, and water, an idea invented by the Greek philosopher Anaximander around 610 B.C. But it is a further repetition of the idea that sacred space and time has four divisions revolving around a center-place. The four divisions certainly correspond to the four cardinal directions. They may possibly relate to other principles as well like social functions, stages of life, and so on, although it may be hard to be precise about these correspondences.

Because of the dominance of Christianity in Western culture, any kind of cross shape, including the ones here discussed, recalls the one on which Christ died. Roman crosses, which are not equal armed but have a long bottom stem, were originally symbols of dominance and oppression: they were the instruments with which the Roman state executed political criminals. Similarly, because of the brutal history of the 20th century, it is impossible to look at a swastika without being reminded of the second world war. Modern pagans should not try to and reclaim the symbol for their own purposes. But equal armed crosses within circles, like these Celtic crosses on the Ogham stones, are crosses of perfect harmony: they have bilateral symmetry on eight different axes. Celtic crosses are thus symbols of unity and peace. Acknowledging this profound message, Druids from most British orders have within their ceremonies declarations of peace announced to the four cardinal directions. For several years now, a Midsummer fire-lighting ceremony at sunset on the Hill of Tara has included a warrior clad in a traditional battle dress of saffron-yellow Irish linen. He holds aloft a half-unsheathed sword at each of the four cardinal quarters in turn, and calls out, "Is it War, or is it Peace?" The assembled crowd answers back, "It is Peace." He sheaths his sword and moves on to the next quarter. In a time when terrorism, xenophobia, religious fanaticism, and war compels millions of people to live in fear of each other, and in fear of foreign nations, this is a radical statement.

6. The Adventure of the Hero

So far we have seen the Mist of Manannan, which is part of the change in attitude and intentionality through which spiritual presences and relations are revealed. The first relation which it reveals to us is the Great Marriage. Exploring that relationship brought out a whole mandala of space and time, enclosing the whole physical, mental, and spiritual cosmos into one schematic of understanding and experience. We have also seen some of the things which stand at the center of this schematic, which enable knowledge of all the realms and worlds within it. But of all the centers of the spiritual world, the most important is the human being herself.

Nearly every religion in the world possesses a story of a creator deity, a founder, or a central hero. In Celtic mythology, there are the Kings of Tara, the heroes of the Red Branch in the Táin Bo Cuailnge, King Arthur and the knights of the Grail Quest from Britain, the Fianna warriors, the Welsh heroes from the Mabinogion, and many more. Their stories tend to follow a particular classical pattern, described by Joseph Campbell as the "Hero's Journey." This is pattern of separation, initiation, and return, as required by some problem in the world which the journey rectifies.

A hero ventures forth from the world of common day into a region of supernatural wonder: fabulous forces are there encountered and a decisive victory is won: the hero comes back from this mysterious adventure with the power to bestow boons on his fellow man... The effect of the successful adventure of the hero is the unlocking and release again of the flow of life into the body of the world. The miracle of this flow may be represented in physical terms as a circulation of food substance, dynamically as a streaming of energy, or spiritually as a manifestation of grace. Such varieties of image alternate easily, representing three degrees of condensation of the one life force.[9]

This is a pattern that exists in nearly all of the world's mythologies. In the story of the Conception of Cú Chullain, the plain of Emain Macha was being laid waste by a flock of birds. This implies the need for a hero to drive off the birds and restore fertility to the land. The heroes of Ulster chase the birds as far south as Newgrange, where they seek shelter for the night. There they discovered Dechtine, pregnant with a child who became Cú Chullain. The father was the god Lugh Lamh-Fada, and Cú Chullain is effectively Lugh's avatar. Newgrange serves as an Otherworld destination, and the treasure is the heroic child.

In various ways, as will be shown in coming chapters, this pattern of storytelling also serves as the template for ritual, especially the rituals of initiation and of spirit-flight meditation. The spiritual attitude requires a partial suspension of one's own intentions in order to allow the sacred presences in the world to reveal themselves to you. In order to know ourselves, we must step out of the familiar home world of the everyday attitude. We must embark upon a heroic journey.

This enables us to look back on the principle of the Sacred King in a slightly new light. For one of the features of the hero of the quest, as indeed one of the qualities bestowed upon someone who becomes a Sacred King, is that he or she is a *magical* being. For instance, after the inauguration ceremony, a Sacred King receives one or more magical obligations and prohibitions called *geasa* (singular: *geis*) which keep him in a ceremonial or ritual state more or less permanently. They also connect him to the larger immensities of fate and destiny because to preserve them was thought to give prosperity and success to his reign, and to break them could be disastrous for both himself and his dynasty. One of the most prominent High Kings of Tara, Conaire Mor, had these geasa upon him:

> You must not go right-handwise around Tara or left-handwise around Breagha; you must not hunt the wild animals of Cernae; you must not venture each ninth night out of Tara; and you must not stay in a house from which firelight can be seen to emerge after sunset or can be seen from outside; and three reds must not precede you to the house of Dearg; and no plunder must be taken in your reign; and a company of one woman or one man must not come to you in your house after sunset; and you must not intervene in a quarrel between two of your servants.[10]

As it is the sacred king's duty to maintain the peace and prosperity of society, and as he is married to the local land Goddess, his life is surrounded and infused with magic. The geasa upon him are there to help him avoid unbalancing that magic, and keep him in a more or less permanent condition of ritual, that is, perpetually in contact with the Otherworld and its magical powers. Great heroes could also be bound by geasa, and so long as the hero observes his geasa he will be successful and victorious. The risk of breaking a geas is great. For some, to break a geas would result in the loss of one's honor and social standing. (Thus it is impossible to use a geas to "curse" or "bind" someone who has no sense of honor.) For others, especially magical people like Druids or kings, to break a geas is to act contrary to the forces of nature, and the result is the person's death, or some social catastrophe. This is in part the price of the hero's victory. Perhaps it is also a sign that ancient Celts were highly superstitious. But it is also a sign that to the Celts the world was full to the brim with magic.

7. Magic and the Experience of the Sacred

The Irish word for magic is "Draiocht;" literally translated, it means "what Druids do." The Irish word "Draoi," which is sometimes translated as "Druid," can also mean a magical person, someone who practices magic. In ancient Celtic society, everyone would have been able to do a little magic, such as by making offerings into lakes, streams, wells, pits, and fires. Indeed, the practice of magic was so widespread among the Celts that the ancient historian Pliny was moved to say, "Britain continues to be spellbound by magic and conducts so much ritual that it would seem that Britain had given magic to the Persians."[11] But the highly specialized or socially important ceremonies would have been in the hands of professionals such as Druids, or public figures such as clann chiefs or the heads of households.

Magic, according to an ordinary definition, is the attempted gain of information or power by psychic or occult methods. On the most popular level, people who believe in magic believe that certain extraordinary effects can be realized by the use of immaterial, mysterious forces which everyone, or almost everyone, has

a hidden ability to sense and to control. On this basic level, people are looking for extra ways to do practical things. They wish to make an illness or injury heal quickly; obtain success in their jobs, in school, in athletics, and even court cases; or remove "bad luck." Some seek to control the behavior of other people as well, from relieving sadness and depression, to finding companionship and love, to "binding" those who are perceived to be harmful to themselves or others. Perhaps modern people seek to become Druids because they want to possess such abilities. Yet people are often seeking something a little deeper, as I shall try to explain.

The most common form of magic described in the mythologies are operations of precognition and prophesy. For example, a female Druid named Fedelm prophesized the outcome of the *Táin Bo Cuailnge* and the victory of Cú Chullain with the memorable poetic statement: "I see it bloody, I see it red." A character named Figol, one of the race of the Tuatha de Dannan, prophesized the outcome of the Battle of Maigh Tuireadh with a magical poem. Even the coming of Saint Patrick was prophesized. The opening of the *Táin Bo Cuailnge* itself begins with an instance of "Raising the Name," a magical "resurrection" of the spirit of a dead person. The bards and historians of Ireland had gathered to settle upon the proper telling of the story. One of them, despondent that no agreement had been reached, left the meeting and went to a hidden, lonely place in a nearby forest, and composed a poem of lamentation addressed to the heroes of the tale. Then he fell asleep. By chance, he found himself sleeping on the grave of Fergus, one of the story's central characters.

In his dream, a mist surrounded the area and from it stepped Fergus himself, who recited the whole of the story as we have it today.

One might notice the association between magic and poetry here. A 7th century text called the *Cauldron of Poesy* describes three cauldrons which are born within the poet, which symbolize his or her progression to enlightenment, and which are "turned" to their proper upright positions by the artistic inspiration of "sorrow and joy." The American Druid Erynn Laurie has interpreted this as akin to the *chakras*, the seven energy-stations in a person's body described by Hindu Mysticism.[12] Aside from prophesy, magical poetry could be used for other purposes. A poet named Cairbre pronounced a magical satire on the miserly and unjust king Bres, which caused blemishes to appear on the king's face, requiring him to abdicate the throne. Similarly, a Druid named Mogh Roith caused the rivers of Munster, which had been dried up by the Druids of King Cormac, to burst their banks. Irish tradition records three particular magical operations which an *Ollamh* (chief poet) was required to know. They have come to be called the Three Illuminations. Their names are, *Imbas forosnaí* ("knowledge which illuminates"), *teinm laída* ("breaking the marrow"), and *díchetal do chennaibh* ("incantation from heads"). They represent abilities which today we would recognize as the psychic abilities of meditation, psychometry, and chanting. All of them were forms of gaining information. The first two, but not the third, required the practitioner to call upon pagan gods and so they were outlawed by Saint Patrick.

It is unclear whether ancient Druids regarded magic as an incidental byproduct of wisdom, or a "skillful means" to gain it. However, because some of the most prominently reported magical operations of Druids have to do with the performance of public functions such as legal judgement or arbitration, I am inclined to believe the latter. That is the first clue that the pursuit of magic disguises the pursuit of something else—in this case, knowledge.

Another clue is in the kind of magic that surrounds sacred kings. The relationship between the king and the Goddess of Sovereignty, as we have seen, is such that the qualities of the land reflect the qualities of the king. In certain wisdom-texts, such as the *Testament of Morann* which I quoted earlier, this relationship has a name: the *Truth*. This is the most important principle of Druidry. Therefore, from this point forward, I shall refer to it as the Sacred Truth. We learn about it from observing certain magical people (Druids, kings, poets, heroes, etc.) who make pronouncements on the way things ought to be, and thereafter the world itself responds by transforming in accord with the pronouncement. In part, the Sacred Truth is a magical word that magical people speak, to which the world responds. For instance, Cormac mac Art halted the slide of the King's house when he spoke the correct judgement of a case which the King had blundered. Amergin calmed a storm with the magical poem, the first line of which is "I invoke the Land of Ireland," and with it secured for his people the right to colonize Ireland. In the story of Manannan's Three Calls to Cormac, a pig is roasted and ready to eat after a truth-story is told for every quarter of it. Mogh Roith burst the dams on the rivers of Munster with a verbal spell. The skill in eloquence and oratory that Druids were famous for possessing also seems to attest to this Sacred Truth. With its songs, chants, spells, anagrams, rhymes, and poetry, Druidry reveals itself to be a religion not of the book, but of the spoken word.

In the spoken word of magical poetry, we find the well-accounted Druidic relationship with trees, animals, plants, ancestors, and the gods. This continues from the Iron Age Celtic period, through Celtic Christianity where it spread from poetry to the intricate knot-work paintings of illuminated manuscripts. Nearly all magical workings described in Celtic mythologies are accompanied by the recitation of a special rhetoric, usually a spontaneously composed magical poem. According to Dáithí Ó h-Ógáin, "Such composition 'without thinking' was regarded in Irish tradition as being the test of a *fiorfhile* ("true poet"), and no doubt it shows an ancient emphasis on the divine source of the druid-poet's power."[13] One text says, "…it is through a poem that he [the druid] does his spells."[14] This was revived in the work of Irish Literary Revival authors, especially W.B. Yeats. He observed that "Poetry in Ireland has always been mysteriously connected with magic."[15] Some of his early works recreated that magic. Poems such as *The Stolen Child* and *The Song of Wandering Angus* have more magic in them than a hundred books of occultism.

It was believed that a Druid could influence the world and bring good or bad fortune by the power of his words. For instance, a Druid could pronounce a satire on someone and if it was justified, it would cause blemishes to appear on the victim's face, for which he would loose honor and respect in the community. This may have been nothing more than the physiological reaction of blushing with shame. But it was also believed that a powerful satire for a serious offence could cause disfigurements, illness, or even death. More positively, it was believed that hearing a member of the Druid-caste recite a traditional mythology or history would grant the listeners a special blessing. It is the truth of the Druid's words which makes them magical. Truthful words arouse the goddess, summon her attention, and call forth her response.

An ancient Druid would have had to learn the traditional poems and songs of magic along with the stories, genealogies, legal precedents, and other narratives which he would have had to know. Note that this magical poem would have been chanted or sung musically, and while it often had to be produced spontaneously, it would have had to conform to one of several traditional poetic meters of Bardic poetry. Therefore someone who spontaneously produces "free form" poetry of the kind that is fashionable these days but lacks narrative and rhythm is *not* performing a Bardic magical *roscann*. But these poetic meters were, as a rule, very simple: for instance, one required the last word of each line to rhyme with the first word of the next line. Admittedly, it requires a certain amount of practice, skill, and talent to produce a spontaneously invented poem within the pattern of a rhyming couplet. However, a friend of mine who practices a Wiccan technique of trance-prophesy assured me that spontaneously produced rhyme is a common occurrence. The single exception to this structured approach to magical sound appears to be the practice of "keening," a deep-throated, high-pitched inarticulate wailing sound that Celtic women used to perform at funerals. Keening is also attributed to a spirit harbinger of death known as the "Ban Shee" (from the Irish words *Bean Sidhe*, "fairy woman").

The relationship between magic and poetry is, to my mind, a signal that Celtic magic has little or nothing to do with exercising power or causing changes in the world. Rather, it has to do with *the cultivation of the sense of wonder*. For such a person, the world is more full of surprise, more full of danger and mystery, more full of beauty and indeed love, than it would otherwise be. That is what I think the pursuit of magic truly involves. And surely the will to create such a world is more important and valuable than the development of any (real or imaginary) psychic powers. The relation between magic and poetry, on one hand, to the Sacred Truth, on the other, suggests that the sense of wonder cultivated by poetry and magic directs itself towards a universal binding principle of knowledge and justice. At the places where our sense of wonder is aroused, where we find beauty and love, there we find the Mist of Manannan, opening the way to the Sacred Truth.

So, when someone asks if magic is real and wants to know if it is possible to predict the future, control the weather, talk to the dead, and so on, the correct answer is that the question is wrong. (At any rate, someone who does not believe in *that* kind of magic is not likely to change his or her mind.) On the other hand, if someone asks if magic is real and wants to know if art, music, and poetry has some hard-to-define quality which makes life more interesting and worthwhile, then the answer is an unqualified yes. When someone asks if magic is real, *what he or she is often really looking for is somewhere to direct his or her sense of wonder.* I believe that whatever else we may believe about magic, we may always direct our sense of wonder to artistic inspiration and creativity. The experience, the process, and the end-products of artistic creation can help induce the spiritual attitude, pierce the Mist of Manannan, and reveal to us the underlying shape of things. Someone wishing to become a Sacred King, in command of his own life, should address himself through poetry to his immortal lover, the Goddess of the land. Through art we find that ordinary things like plants, animals, stones, and even building materials, possess extra properties that enable us to do more with them than we might otherwise do. Through art we meet the faeries, ghosts, spirits, monsters, deities, and other strange creatures of the Hero's Journey, from whom gifts are received or challenges are won. Through art we "come into our own" as magical beings, capable of speaking a creative word of Sacred Truth, and so creating the world.

8. The Otherworld

Each of the forgoing principles can be thought of as a means by which the Otherworld reveals itself. In Irish, the name for the Otherworld is *Tir Na n-Og*, which means "Land of Youth." It is described as a collection of islands in the ocean to the west of Ireland, accessible if one sails past "the ninth wave," which is the horizon, the point at which the solid reliability of the mortal world gives way to the dynamic fluidity of the Otherworld. One may also access the Otherworld by venturing below the surface of the ocean, which is sometimes called "Manannan's Plain." The Otherworld is believed to exist by Celts of all the ancient nations: Julius Caesar reported that the belief in rebirth in an Otherworldly realm gave the Gauls fearlessness in battle, and the same belief allowed people to put off repayments of debt until the afterlife.

The properties of the Otherworld which make it an interesting setting for mythology are so well known they are hardly worth mentioning. It is day there when it is night here; the passage of time flows faster or slower; lakes are islands and the sea is solid ground; if a traveller eats the food he will be unable to leave; and everybody is young and beautiful. In the story of Manannan's Three Calls to Cormac, Tir Na n-Og is described as a land "where there is nothing but truth, and where there is neither age nor withering away, nor heaviness, nor sadness, nor jealousy, nor envy, nor pride." Tir Na n-Og is free from the qualities of *mortality*: old age, suffering, and death. A mortal life is but a day and a night, says the god Aengus Og says, for there is nothing permanent nor enduring here. Faerie abductions seem to remove from this mortal realm the best of our kind, the most innocent, beautiful and saintly, as if to preserve them in the Otherworld, "for the world's more full of weeping than he can understand." It is because mortal life is beset with suffering and sadness, that heroes venture to the Otherworld, and return bearing a treasure

that has the power to bring some relief to human suffering. But sometimes, as in the case of the Voyage of Bran, they return only to say goodbye.

Although we find Tir na n-Og to be a place free from the three qualities of mortality, a complete description has more to it than that. It is also the case that the Otherworld is a realm of *romanticism*. Faerie beauty is almost always fragile, as if lightly touched with peril and sorrow. When Deirdre was conceived, Cathbad the Druid predicted that she would be the most wonderfully beautiful woman in the world, and yet much suffering and death would occur because of her. King Conchobar immediately declared that to prevent all the future bloodshed Deirdre would be raised in secret, and he himself would marry her when she came of age. For no one would dare court a woman already betrothed, before birth, to the king. But in that declaration he set in motion the very events Cathbad foretold. The heroic always appears together with the tragic, and the causes of victory are also the causes of despair. Yet it is through tragedy we come to know ourselves. As Yeats wrote in his autobiography, "We begin to live when we have conceived life as a tragedy."[16] To the Celtic mind, even sorrow is framed with art. Wandering Aengus, who begins his journey with a "fire in his head," spends his whole life searching for the Otherworldly beauty which he met once while young, and he became an old and lonely traveller who even now is still searching.

Casting our gaze wider than Celtic sources, we also find that the Otherworld can occasionally be a world of fear. J.R.R. Tolkien described its dark side, as follows:

> Faërie is a perilous land and in it are pitfalls for the unwary and dungeons for the overbold....The realm of faërie-story is wide and deep and high and filled with many things: all manner of beasts and birds are found there, shoreless seas and stars uncounted; beauty that is an enchantment, and an ever-present peril: both joy and sorrow as sharp as swords.[17]

Tolkien might have added that faerie tales often contain scenes of graphic violence and uninhibited sexuality. Certainly, they are not lacking in sources of fear and danger. Yet in a way, these things confirm the Otherworld's essential romanticism. In Faerie-land, even grotesque and terrible things are *interesting*, perhaps even sublime and beautiful. And they have a story to tell. We sometimes find ourselves repelled yet at the same time fascinated. A place called Fangorn Forest, described in *The Two Towers*, is an Otherworld because it is a realm of magic and wonder, yet it is unlike Ireland's Tir Na n-Og because it is full of danger. It is dark and thick; its old trees twisted and malevolent. Some of them can move their branches and roots like tentacles to trap and kill unwary travellers. This may appear completely unlike Tir Na n-Og as it is popularly characterized. Yet its stewards, the Ents, a race of tree-like creatures, attack and destroy a factory for mass-producing weapons of war. This scene is plainly an indictment of industrialization and a glorification of the magic of nature. In a lecture that Yeats delivered in New York in 1904, he affirmed the same

thing. "Whenever men have tried to imagine a perfect life they have imagined a place where men plough and sow and reap, not a place where there are great wheels turning and great chimneys vomiting smoke."[18]

It cannot be denied that many of the people who are attracted to Celtic Mysticism are seeking an escape from the same soul-crushing commercialism and industrialization also condemned by Yeats and by Tolkien. But one must be wary of trading one kind of oppression for another. It may do no one any good to believe that their "higher self" lives in a fantasy world, far distant from the great turning wheels and smoke-belching chimneys of the mortal world. What, then, is the proper place of the Otherworld in our lives, and what can it mean to seek it? I would like to suggest that the Otherworld, despite its contrast with the mortal world, is still a reflection of it. Like a funhouse mirror, the Mist of Manannan transforms our perceptions to bring different aspects of the world to the foreground of our attention. The three qualities of mortality, which are old age, suffering, and death, are changed into the romantic qualities of the sublime, the strange, and the tragic. This change of perception enables us to see things as they could be or ought to be, and so provides inspiration to us with which we may work to change the real world, the mortal world in which we live.

Like the morning sunlight entering Newgrange every Midwinter, the renewal of time and the physical world obtains as a regular, predictable cycle. In the Quest of the Hero and the Great Marriage, the renewal of human society is made possible through the actions of exceptional individuals who embody humanity's excellences. I have said earlier that the Otherworld is not separate from the mortal world but surrounds us in the world of nature. Here I shall try to explain. In pagan times, people lived in smaller close-knit communities and depended on the availability of plants and animals, certain resources such as stone and various metals, and the vagarities of the weather, just to survive. The idea that humanity can own and control nature can be a major force in human thought only for urban societies, where most if not all of the environment is man-made. To an Iron-age Celt, living in small farming towns surrounded on all sides by fields and forests, the natural assumption was that humanity belonged to the Earth, and that it was necessary to build various bonds and relations with the Earth in order to survive. These bonds were also needed to achieve culture and the many things which, above and beyond survival, make life worth living. These bonds were constituted by the different ways they looked upon the landscape as an Otherworld, the abode of gods, of nature spirits, and of the dead.

We have already seen one of these bonds: the Great Marriage. Another is the practice of constructing burial mounds. Most of the monuments built by our pagan ancestors, including the many passage mounds like Newgrange and portal dolmen such as

Poulnabrone Dolmen

Poulnabrone (co. Clare), were not only timekeeping devices, but also graves. As such they provided a center-place for the community, and a way to think of the dead as still a part of the community. The Celts had a strong belief in the immortality of the soul and so regarded the dead as beings who may still be among them and who could provide knowledge from the Otherworld. By making burial monuments their most important ceremonial structures, they were effectively affirming that the Otherworld was close to them, and indeed easily accessible to them. The passage mounds like Newgrange, with their massive kerb-stones dividing ordinary space from sacred space, were open and easily entered. The portal-dolmen, with their huge cap-stones supported by uprights, was wide open to the elements, and normally built on a small mound where cremated human remains were buried. Its portal served as a gateway to the Otherworld for the spirits of the people buried there. The Hill of Tara, the seat of Ireland's national kings, was also an elaborate cemetery, a complex of temples to the dead. A long structure of two parallel earthwork banks built on a north-south alignment, which is now known as the "Banquet Hall," was originally a ceremonial avenue leading to the mounds and circular enclosures on the top of the hill.

Notches in the banks offer direct views of small satellite burial mounds adjacent to the main enclosures. Visitors would ascend the north slope of the hill, with the mid-day sun in front of them, above the mighty wooden ring-fort of the Hill. This sight, combined with the knowledge that one was approaching the home of the sacred king and the dwelling place of the ancestors, must have made the experience awe-inspiring. Think of this if you ever visit your nation's capital. You will almost always find a war memorial, and timekeeping device like a clock tower or an observatory, near or attached to the most important government buildings. Canada's Peace Tower, Britain's Palace of Westminster, and America's National Mall, all serve to bring past, present, and future together, as do the monuments of Tara and Newgrange.

The landscape, when seen as the home of one's honored ancestors, offers a sense of home and place, and continuity through history, and so creates a sense of belonging and identity. Knowing where one's ancestors are buried means knowing where one comes from and where one belongs. The stories of their lives and actions electrifies the experience of the landscape, creating deeper layers of meaning and significance. The Otherworld, the dwelling place of the gods and spirits and of the dead, was a place that the Celtic people could visit and experience in the real world, not just in their mind through dreams or visions (although they had such practices, as do we). The mythologies state that after the Milesians arrived in Ireland, the Tuatha de Dannans retreated to the hills and lakes, and that Manannan raised a magical mist to hide their dwelling places. The Otherworld is what happens to the mortal world when it is made sacred by mythology and storytelling, by the burial mounds, the sacrifices and ceremonies of cosmic renewal. All of these, in their own way are expressions of Sacred Truth. These various relations are often treated by modern pagans as a relation between us and the gods of nature who give gifts to us (food, building materials, knowledge, and so on) in return for our love and worship. In ancient paganism the human community occasionally had to give back to the gods something more substantial than love and worship. They had to sacrifice tools, objects of art, weapons, food, and on rare occasions, human beings. We know this because archaeologists have found the remains. Wells, lakes, springs, and bogs have preserved swords, gold artifacts, wooden statues, whole chariots with the horses still attached to the reigns, and occasionally whole human bodies. The ancient relationship was thus like a kind of bargain. The gods would give gifts, but the human community had to reciprocate. Ceremonies of cosmic renewal which involve sacrifice were intended to achieve that. They brought to the forefront of the participant's attention the fragility of their place in the world and the need to respect the environmental creatures and forces upon whom they relied. The requirements and taboos surrounding a Sacred King also had this intention. It created, in effect, a mytho-poetic rationale for what we today would call "sustainable development." Their societies could exploit the resources of the world but never to the point of depletion, and never unnecessarily nor disrespectfully. They had to do their part to help take care of the world.

This renewal of the world involved rituals and ceremonies intended to release the energy and presence of the Otherworld. To the ancient pagan mind, the actions which release that Otherworldly energy make possible the turning of the seasons, the return of crops and animals, and indeed the return of justice and order to their societies. It can be translated into the personal spiritual life of the modern seeker. *Mysticism* is a practice of internalizing all of the symbols, metaphors, and narratives so that they become the lenses of the spiritual attitude. These, in turn, animate our perception of the world. It is this world of perception which is created and recreated by spiritual practice. Tir Na n-Og is, therefore, what life feels like for someone who has started a Heroic Quest, parted the Mist of Manannan, and thereby discovered the Fire in the Head and the Well of Wisdom. Such a person is able to perform the Great Marriage, and her actions become expressions of the Sacred Truth. Indeed this is how we may now define a Druid, in a poetic way that complements the analytic definition given in the previous chapter. *A Druid is one who parts the Mist of Manannan, who drinks deeply from the Well of Wisdom, and who speaks the Sacred Truth.* [19] Parting the Mist is the activity of engaging the spiritual attitude, perceiving the hidden symbolic or holistic relations between things, and indeed the original unity of the world. Drinking from the Well of Wisdom is the activity of immersing yourself in the presence of the Otherworld and receiving its gifts. And the Sacred Truth puts these discoveries to work, to make positive, life-affirming changes in one's life and one's world.

9. The Immortality of the Soul

The ancient Druids taught that the soul is immortal. It passes through death to the Otherworld, and may be reborn again. There are many references among classical authors concerning the Druidic doctrine of the immortality of the soul. For example, Pomponius Mela recorded,

> One of their dogmas has come to common knowledge, namely, that souls are eternal and that there is another life in the infernal regions, and this has been permitted manifestly because it makes the multitude readier for war. And it is for this reason too that they burn or bury, with their dead, things appropriate to them in life; and that in times past they even used to defer the completion of business and the payment of debts until their arrival in another world. [20]

This may explain why the victims of human sacrifice, such as Lindow Man, may have been *willing* victims. Diodorus observed the same doctrine, and cited it as the reason why Celtic warriors were often so reckless with their lives in battle. In his words:

> For the belief of Pythagoras is strong among them, that the souls of men are immortal, and that after a definite number of years they live a second life when the soul passes into another body. [21]

What is this soul? What is this "higher self" that survives death and lives forever? The direction to "know yourself" would be a dishonest sham if we refused to acknowledge death. Is the belief in the immortal soul perhaps just a contrivance with which we avoid facing the stark truth of our transience and mortality?

The popular view of the soul is that it is an immaterial essence which survives death and reincarnates as another life form, or travels to an advanced plane of existence. It retains the knowledge and wisdom learned from each incarnation and seeks out further incarnations in order to learn more. Many people believe the soul possesses perfect knowledge of other people's feelings and enough sympathy to make it incapable of disrespecting or harming others. Many also believe that when our lives are not going as well as we might like, it is because the soul has brought us here to learn certain spiritual lessons. Perhaps prior to being born, we actually chose the life we are living now. This can make someone's sufferings and misfortunes seem intelligible and therefore bearable. I am afraid I cannot accept this view. Not because it is necessarily false—there's no way to definitively prove it or deny it. However, in practical terms, it tends to draw one's attention away from the here and now, the present world, and one's embodied life within it. And this seems terribly wrongheaded to me. A person with cancer or arthritis might learn important lessons about perseverance and the value of friendship, but no right minded person would wish that suffering on anyone. Yet the popular view of the soul indirectly does exactly that. I find it impossible to believe that the five billion or more people in this world who live short and brutal lives of poverty, starvation, neglect, exploitation, disease, and death actually *chose* to live that way before they

were born. The very idea is utterly horrifying to me. We may have chosen lives of danger, struggle, difficulty, and risk—indeed I believe that the most worthwhile life must necessarily contain an element of challenge and adventure—but no one would choose the acute suffering and injustice experienced by a third-world famine victim. But if we believe the popular view of the nature of the higher self, we would be committing ourselves to the view that billions of third-world famine victims queued up for their fate before they were born. And this, it seems to me, goes *against* the idea that we possess immortal souls.

I believe in something a little different. To my mind, immortality is essentially a *moral* idea. When you embark on a quest to "know yourself" one of the things that you will discover is an image of yourself that is idealized, which embodies all that is noble, excellent, and divine about human life. Ancient people encountering the same discovery described this image using mythology. It is how they depicted their heroes, the founders of their cultures, and their gods. This image of the self is not an entity that is necessarily separate from the body. It is not what people normally believe about the soul. But it is something we can bring into being in our lives. We can embody it, or fail to embody it, through the attitudes and intentionalities (remember those?) which enable us to see through the Mist into the Otherworld, and achieve excellence and greatness in the things we do. We manifest them, or fail to manifest them, with our thinking, speaking, acting, and living. The "higher self," if I may call it that, is the kind of person you become when your decisions and choices spring from the best part of yourself, the part that most resembles the divine image.

What has this to do with immortality? The aim to know yourself is a temporally continuous, future-directed act, in and through which a kind of immortality is possible. Someone able to achieve spiritual self-knowledge is able to identify with the eternal and timeless powers of the world. These powers are enabled to act in and through her, and she is thus able to share in their immortality. What are those powers? The literary sources describe a few of them. For instance, there is a Triad of Ireland that reads:

> Three candles which illuminate every darkness: truth, nature, knowledge.

Here we have three important philosophical principles brought together. We have seen one of them already: *fírinne*, "truth," which can also be translated as "justice," and which constitutes a ruler's relationship to the land and to the people he or she governs. Here it constitutes the spiritual person's relationship to the whole of her life, the world constructed by her intentions and attitudes. Nature is, of course, the enduring and neverending wheel of life. It is the growth and regeneration cycle of plants, the birth, death, and reproduction of animals, the rising and setting of the sun and moon. Knowledge, the third candle in the triad, endures by passing from one person to the next, from one generation to the next. This is what education, language, and even friendship is about. Knowledge is a Druid's special responsibility. A similar triad was offered by the Celtic hero Oisin, who was asked by Saint Patrick what sustained the Irish people before the coming of Christianity. Oisin answered:

> It is what kept us all through our lifetime: truth that was in our hearts,

and strength in our arms, and fulfilment in our tongues.

The message here is a moral message: the Celtic heroes were sustained by character virtues such as truth, justice, strength, courage, and reliability. This is similar to the description of Druidic teachings recorded by the Roman observer Diogenes Laertius, who wrote:

> [The Druids] make their pronouncements by means of riddles and dark sayings, teaching that the gods must be worshipped and no evil done and manly [honorable] behavior maintained.

The hidden message inside this triad is, again, that a certain standard of excellent character is to be upheld. The overall message is this: By learning of the elements of the world which are eternal (truth, nature, knowledge), through the quest to "know yourself," and then internalizing them into our sense of character and identity, we are able to speak the Sacred Truth of who and what we are. The most well known expression of this truth came from the great poet Amergin, the first mortal to set foot on Ireland, in a declaration of spiritual identity which is known as the *Song of Amergin*:

> *I am the wind on the sea;*
> *I am the wave of the sea;*
> *I am the bull of seven battles;*
> *I am the eagle on the rock;*
> *I am the flash from the sun;*
> *I am the most beautiful of plants;*
> *I am a strong wild boar;*
> *I am a salmon in the water;*
> *I am a lake in the plain;*
> *I am the word of knowledge;*

I am the head of the spear in battle;

I am the god that puts fire in the head;

Who spreads light in the gathering on the hills?

Who can tell the ages of the moon?

Who can tell the place where the sun rests?[22]

On one level this is an example of the aggressive and bombastic pride which was characteristic of the Celtic heroic age. Amergin could be saying he has the same power as all the things listed in the poem. In the context of the story in which this poem appears, Amergin first banished a sea storm which was magically raised against him by the Tuatha de Dannan. He then set foot on Ireland and chanted the poem. It is thus a declaration of the sovereignty of Amergin's people over the land. It is therefore an expression of the Sacred Truth: it is a verbal statement which expresses the speaker's connection with the land. It is the sort of thing that can only be said by someone who has achieved complete self-knowledge. For uses the language of identity ("I am"), not possession ("I have"). It is the rough equivalent of the famous Hindu spiritual motto, *Tat tvam asi*, ("That art thou!"), which uses the same language of identity. Indeed there are several passages in the *Bhagavad Gita* in which the god Krishna announces himself the same way as Amergin, with a confident "I am!"

One may doubt whether this comparative mythology makes a perfect match. But what matters here is the philosophical point. In coming to "know yourself," you will find that the powers and immensities of the world are represented within you. This discovery enables you to identify with them, and say, as did Amergin, "I am." This is the immortality of the "now," the eternity of the moment.

This kind of immortality does not offer immunity from death. Indeed if we denied or ignored our essential mortality then we will not have attained self-knowledge. Yet it offers the possibility that the eternal and timeless realities of the world which one has internalized in one's character may become like one's legacy. Self-knowledge is an achievement that is attainable in the present, yet it is also future-directed for it is temporally continuous. Just as the flowers and birds disappear each winter and return each spring, self-knowledge must be renewed by the spoken word of Sacred Truth. Once attained it has to be attained again, not because it is instantly lost but because to attain it only once is not enough. One must also be able to cultivate it, nurture it and care for it, build on it, and craft it much like one crafts a fine work of art, for the whole of one's life. It is an attainment that can be lost—in this sense, there might be failed human beings— but if gained and lost then it can be gained again. As a temporally-inscribed achievement, the aim of achieving self knowledge is an aim that reaches into the future, past one's mortality, and thus offers one the possibility of immortality.

Three:
Peaceful Abiding

*The sound that the wind
makes is musical,
The voice of the cuckoo above
Caise Con is musical,
The splendor that the sun
makes is beautiful,
From the west the whistling of
the blackbird is musical...*
—*Music of the World*
attributed to Suibne
the Madman, 7th century

The sections which follow are intended to provide an understanding of the foundations of Celtic Mysticism through practice, and to sketch how the theoretical principles described in previous sections can enter the stream of one's life in a direct and tangible way. A practical understanding is appropriate because, as noted, certain mysteries need to be experienced to be properly understood.

1. Setting Out on an Adventure

The world must first be understood and grasped by consciousness before anything else can begin. Therefore the seeker must first learn how to understand and grasp the world before he can express himself in it. Just as one must learn before one may teach, one must be able to see and hear before one may speak. Most of the ancient spiritual traditions of the world had, in their training systems, a time when the students did nothing but sit at the feet of superiors. They would watch the performance of ceremonies, or listen to the teachers read from a holy text, or impart the wisdom of the oral tradition, together with the teacher's own innovations and contributions. The current revival of Druidry does not yet have that kind of a tradition. Even after more than 60 years it is still finding its feet. All of the important trailblazers who have made contributions to the revival have been in the situation of putting together a puzzle without knowing what the final picture should look like, how many pieces there are, or even whether they have of all of them. Today's paganism exists in a social world characterized by suspicion or even distrust of authority figures, and a belief that to "sit at the feat of superiors" is absurd and unjust. This may be because of the many "leaders" who have seriously harmed their followers, by for instance exploiting them for money, sexual favors, psychological power, and so forth. (The very first "Druid" I personally met was such a man. I learned valuable lessons from that experience—but I would not wish that experience on anyone.) Their presence in the community, however rare they may be, justifies the suspicion and distrust of authority many Pagans possess.

We are fortunate, therefore, that in this situation we may still return to the original mysteries and spiritual experiences of the world of nature which inspired our ancestors and predecessors. These cannot be lost to us, so long as there remain open spaces on Earth from which to view the endless depths of the sky, the wide wilderness of the land, and the great pouring sea. For Nature's authority, if it may be called that, is not social or political in character. It is the unignorable fact that we are embodied beings, or in other words, animals, tied to the Earth by gravity and by our biological requirements for food and air. We may think of ourselves as intelligent animals, social animals, spiritual animals, but we are animals nonetheless. Nature's authority is our corporeal groundedness in an embodied world. This is the plain fact of our belonging to the world, living in and with it, and being

inseparable from it. It refers to the powers and potentials of our bodies which are inseparably a part of the world, lived in and with the world, operating or functioning in relation to things in the world, and in various ways are connected to the world. Our groundedness is a fundamental condition of our existence. It cannot be reduced, imagined away, dismissed, ignored, or overthrown, however much we may aspire to transcend it, although we can, and often do, debate the meaning and significance of this fact. Thus to "sit at the feet of the world" does not have to carry the same potentially negative connotation as does sitting at the feet of a human being.

Whatever gaps, inconsistencies, and fragments there are in the historical, literary, and archaeological record of the spiritual heritage of humanity, we may always return to our organs of perception, directed at the world, for guidance. We may always turn to our psychological, emotional, and intellectual endowments of nature, which are the powers of perception, imagination, intuition, and reason. Therefore, this first exercise for cultivating the spiritual life should aid the seeker in regaining the use of her senses and to read and hear the spiritual messages communicated by the sacred world. All spirituality begins with such moments of contact with the sacred world. The first project, therefore, is to seek out that contact. There used to be a custom among the Irish and Scottish in which you had to walk the land, at least once a year, to assert that you owned, and belonged to, the land. For those on a Celtic spiritual path, I propose something similar.

Eachtra—The Adventure. Go to a place that is still untouched wilderness, or to an area with as little evidence of human impact as you can find. Most countries have systems of national parks and conservation areas that allow visitors. Be sure that the place you select is a place where you have never been. Take nothing with you that is electrical, battery-powered, or motorized, except the vehicle which transported you there. Do not take any communication devices, clocks, firearms, cameras, or wristwatches. But do take as much water and safety equipment as you will require for the duration of your stay, which should be not less than three complete revolutions of the sun. Bring food, but not commercial food—bring ordinary bread, cheese, and items high in carbohydrates. Bring paper, pencils, paintbrushes and paints, musical instruments, a diary, or anything else of a private nature. Tell someone where you have gone, in case of an emergency; but otherwise, go alone.

This activity is not the simple holiday it appears to be. One shall quickly find that without the usual distractions of the telephone, the Internet, the radio, or television, the duties of one's occupation, and the like, most people become quickly frustrated, distracted, agitated, or even bored. If you run out of food, you may find yourself forced to forage—and if you don't know what you should be looking for, you could be in trouble. But in this there may be an opportunity. We often find that by going without certain material comforts and conveniences for a while, and by being away from friends and loved ones, we appreciate them better. And the elimination of distractions can lead to an increased sensitivity to the life of the land, and indeed to the life within you. For the best way, and perhaps even the *only* way, to experience the spiritual qualities of stone and soil, tree and flower, bird and beast, sun and sky, is to get close to them. Only then can we understand and experience the beauty, the danger, the mystery, and the life, of the natural world. We are better able to understand the great value of life when we see how fragile it is—how easily it is disturbed and how much work and love must go into its maintenance and protection. After a while we discover, in strange and unexpected ways, that having the right skills and knowledge to work "with" the world, we may survive and flourish with relative ease. In many people this promotes a transformation of perception and attitude, which, if sustained long enough, leads to a transformation of character. For this reason, among others, Thomas Jefferson thought that the life of the small farmer was the most virtuous kind of life. He thought that because the occupation by its nature demanded a closeness to the elements and the land, it would therefore teach virtues like respect, industriousness, patience, and responsibility.

I have often thought that an Eachtra like this would be an excellent "rite of passage" for young people. It may give them a chance to learn the realities and dangers of the natural and human world, and also about their own powers and potentials. This is also a spiritual lesson, for it is a large part of what it means to learn who you are. I consider the time I spent living in Newfoundland, Canada, including two months of winter-camping and hitchhiking across the island, to be my own Eachtra of passage into adulthood. The Eachtra could also be a form of 'therapy' for people addicted to cigarettes, alcohol, junk food, various illegal substances, to television, or to shopping. Removed from the consumerist environment of shopping malls and mass media advertising, we may find addictive desires subsiding, leading to a lessening of stress and anxiety. An Eachtra might help people with anti-social habits such as freeloading, violence, or anger. Someone who is unable to communicate with others except through manipulative "head-games" or through abuse would find himself running out of food. He would find that episodes of rage or self-pity, offerings of empty promises, a feeling of entitlement, and other contrivances to obtain a "free lunch," leave him hungry and shivering in the cold. He would find that patience, perseverance, volunteerism, and group cooperation are the traits needed for success. Nature can be a great teacher in this way.

Ancient Druids sought out seclusion to learn wisdom and to communicate with Otherworldly beings. The practice of setting their holy places in remote forest groves attests to this, as does literary evidence from Roman historians. Pomponius Mela wrote that the Druids have their meeting places "either in a cave or in secluded dales." This practice was continued by Celtic Christians, who constructed their monastic retreats and beehive huts to meditate in peace, closer to the wild of nature, which for many of them was the same as being closer to God. The extraordinary monastery on the summit of Skellig Michael, off the coast of Kerry, is an example of such a place. Skellig Michael is an island of sheer jagged rock that thrusts up from the sea like a broken mountain. There is not a level piece of land on it but for where people have levelled it themselves. The vast ocean surrounding the two bleak Skellig rocks were the closest Irish environment to the lonely deserts described in the Gospels.

I visited the monastery, which is now a heritage site, on a day when thick fog covered the tops of the hills and cliffs of the coast, not high above the sea level at all, and rendered to everything a mysterious and magical quality. Once the boat passed the land, the fog obscured everything. We passed the smaller Skellig without quite knowing that it was there, for all that was present was its phantom shadow and the sound of the sea birds that cover it, their calls and cries echoing in the fog from all directions. Then the boat turned and Skellig Michael appeared before me, leaping from the blue-grey shadow into my consciousness like a sudden chord of music from out of strange silence. As the boat came to the landing place, I heard the strange voices of the sea birds echo-

Monastic cells on Skellig Michael.

ing in the grotto of sky-reaching stones that towered into the low clouds and out of sight. Hundreds of steps carved from the side of the mountain led up the cliffs to the hidden summit, and a mantle of green clover-like foliage and carpeting moss covered the surface of the island along most of the ascent. Skellig Michael felt to me timeless but for the passage of the sun and seasons, placeless but for the distant peaks of the coastal mountains, both of which, on the day I visited, had disappeared in the fog. Time and space felt suspended. Yet the island was full of life with the plants, birds, and the movement of the sea. I understand now why the ancient Celts set their paradise in islands to the west accessible only through shrouds of mist. On such an island, it would be easy to find one's God, but also easy to become consumed by loneliness and so lose one's mind. It is not just the physical tasks of survival, but is also, and primarily, the psychological task of preserving the mind, which the Eachtra presents.

To a pre-industrial society the world of nature was full of dangers, some real, some imagined. To go into that world, for instance to the remote isolation of Skellig Michael, or even only as far as the edge of the circle of light created by a campfire after dark, required a great deal of courage. Human life existed in little havens of safety, in towns, villages, or camps, surrounded by the dark unknown of forests or oceans. Rough winds, wild animals, poisonous plants, and thieves and outlaws, inhabited the wild places of the world, along with the "imagined" monsters of mythology and legendary storytelling. And that is precisely where the Druids built their sanctuaries! They must have understood something which we are only now remembering: that spirituality requires courage and initiative, that fear is to be confronted and not repressed, and that on the path to spiritual knowledge we must seek out, not avoid, what is strange, dark, and dangerous. We who have banished almost all wilderness from the surface of the Earth may find it very hard to appreciate nature the same way ancient people did.

They also understood that spirituality requires solitude. "All religion," wrote the philosopher A.N. Whitehead, "is solitariness." This is because, as he says, all the great spiritual traditions of the world began when the inaugural hero spent time in seclusion and silence. Moses must climb the mountain alone to receive the Ten Commandments. Christ must have his 40 days in the desert. The Prophet Mohammed must also climb a mountain alone to hear the angel dictate to him the Koran. And the Buddha must retreat alone to the forest where, under the Bodhi tree, at the moment of sunrise, he achieved enlightenment. The world of nature is one of the last places where one can have true solitude. In a private room in a city, one can be "alone"; one can even be alone in a crowd. But that is not solitude. City noises, street lights, and just the knowledge that other people are rushing around a few meters beyond one's door, can invade your privacy. The presence of the sacred reveals itself best in secluded and remote places, which is why ancient Druids set their sanctuaries there. Without distractions and interruptions invading one's consciousness, solitude turns one's attention inward. Ultimately to enter a remote place to experience solitude is to enter the depths of one's own mind. This is the deeper reason why entering such places requires courage. Yeats wrote that "Man needs reckless courage to descend into the abyss of himself." Like the wild regions of the world of nature, the abyss of the self is an undiscovered country. But into that abyss we must go. Just as the water of a Holy Well travels for a long time underground, in silence and darkness, before reaching the surface, spiritual insight and inspiration emerges from the silence and darkness of solitude.

The ancient Celts had another practice very much like this as well. It was called the *Fianna*, the name of a social "class" (really an out-class) of warriors living on the fringes of society. The most famous of Fianna band leaders was Fionn mac Cumhal, a man who combines within himself the path of the poet, warrior, and druid. Lady Gregory wrote that he was "a king and a seer and a poet, a Druid and a knowledgeable man" as well as great warrior.[1] With his leadership, the Fianna had a headquarters of sorts on the Hill of Allen (co. Kildare). Joining a band of Fianna was an acceptable way for young people to "drop out" of society for a short time, so that young boys and girls could assert their independence, go a bit wild, get injured perhaps, learn a few hard lessons about survival and life. Then they could establish their place in society as adults. It gave them a chance to grow up. It was not treated as an escape for people who could not handle the difficulties of their life and duties of their station, nor was it mandatory for everyone. Rather it functioned as a kind of proving ground for growing young people, offering them a tough environment for transformation to adulthood. Today's equivalents might be wilderness education programs such as "Outward Bound," the "Brat Camps" for troubled teenagers, or possibly the regular army. Backpacking in a foreign country for a few months can serve this purpose. In the apprenticeship program for training certain kinds of skilled tradesmen such as carpenters, electricians, stonemasons, and so on, there is a middle rank between "master" and "apprentice" called "journeyman." It comes from a medieval tradition in which someone who finished an apprenticeship would then travel from town to town, to learn from other masters and practitioners, and pick up work where he could get it. In Germany, this tradition survives to this day. During this time, the journeyman cannot come within 50 miles of home, possibly for as long as three years.

A long-distance cross-country hiking trek, or a bicycle or canoe journey perhaps, taking days or weeks, might serve as a modern-day version of the Eachtra for spiritual seekers, and indeed a modern day version of the Fianna initiation. Most modern countries have excellent long-distance hiking and bicycling trails which one could follow for this purpose. The West Highland Way in Scotland, for instance, traverses most of the length of the country and includes some of the most scenic mountains and glens. If someone were to spend a certain amount of time in the wild, immersed in the natural world and away from contact with civilization, that might be the simplest and best available equivalent to the mythological trials of Fionn Mac Cumhall's Fianna. The task of a long-distance hike across rough country might test the same physical, mental, and emotional powers of endurance, resourcefulness, and maturity.

2. Touching the Earth

Solitude in the wild as a spiritual experience disconnects you from the usual points of reference with the human social world, such as clocks, calendars, street addresses, telephones, commercials, and the like. It forces a direct encounter with the primordial world of nature and with your self. Without the distractions of advertizing and media culture, one would be forced to encounter one's own thoughts, feelings, intentions, and frustrations. At some point, a new perspective may dawn. The experience of nature as the impersonal and harsh task-master gives way to the experience of nature as a generous provider of gifts, be they material, aesthetic, or spiritual. This is the Mist of Manannan beginning to lift. As soon as one learns how to work with nature, and succeed, nature will appear much more inviting and beautiful. And something similar happens when one learns to work with the hidden resources of will and imagination which exist in the silence and darkness of solitude.

There is a simple form of meditation which can help prepare you for the opening of the Mist. It goes like this:

Peaceful Abiding. Find a place that affords an interesting view of a river, lake, valley, hill, mountain, or other natural landscape. Sit directly on the ground, without anything separating you from the earth other than your clothing. Arrange yourself so that you are comfortable, perhaps by leaning on a tree or a rock.

Listen to the sounds that you hear: birds, water, wind, insects. Acknowledge that you are hearing these sounds.

Feel the sensations that affect you: the temperature of the breeze, the sturdiness of the ground. Acknowledge that you are feeling these sensations.

Smell the texture of the air that comes to you: the pollen of flowers, the algae of lakes and streams, the freshness of the wind. Acknowledge that you are feeling these sensations.

See the things that are before to you: the light of the sun, the shape of the land, the movements of trees and animals. Acknowledge that you are seeing these things.

Take a step back from your perceptions now. As you hear, see, smell, and touch things, think not of the things you are hearing, seeing, smelling, and touching. Think only of the activity of perception. Look only at the light as it comes to you. Look at the contrasts of light and shadow, the colors, the shapes, and the intensities. See them now just as images and patterns of light.

Instead of hearing an animal, an insect, or a water rapid, hear the sound that comes to you. Instead of feeling the ground, or the wind, feel the sensation that touches you. Instead of smelling the trees, grass, and flowers, smell the breath that comes to you.

"Peaceful Abiding" is a form of meditation in which one simply becomes the passive recipient of sensation. Its purpose is to encourage straightforward perceptual openness to the world of nature. It aims for no particular enlightened state nor any elevated level of consciousness or psychic ability, except a change in one's approach towards the world, from the "everyday attitude" to the "spiritual attitude." The only wisdom that this activity provides to the seeker is the knowledge that one has a place in the world. One becomes aware of "being here," and nothing *less*. This wisdom is the starting place for all environmentally-centred spirituality including Celtic Mysticism and Druidry. As strange and silly as it might sound, the first task of the spiritual life is to sit down, shut up, and mind the clouds!

To the mind of a Druid, the world of nature is a world of peace. Despite all of its dangers, the hardships involved in survival, the fear we sometimes experience when thrust unprotected into its midst, the world of nature is essentially characterized by beauty, goodness, fruitfulness, and especially peace. We find this in the words of the Morrigan, the Irish Goddess who is popularly (and wrongfully) known as a goddess of war. At the end of the Second Battle of Maigh Tuireadh, when the race of the Tuatha de Dannan finally defeated the race of monsters known as the Fomhoir, she recited a special magical poem which has come to be known as the "Morrigan's Prophesy."

> *Peace up to the sky!*
> *Sky down to Earth*
> *Earth beneath heaven*
> *Strength to everyone!*[2]

Morrigan has here proclaimed that the defeat of the Fomhoir transformed the world from a condition of misery, turbulence, and war, into a condition of happiness, prosperity, and peace. This peace extends to the whole of the world. It fills everything on the earth, all the way up to the sky. Of course this does not mean that there was never again any bad weather! The peace declared by the Morrigan is the peace of the qualities of character which the Tuatha de Dannan embody: especially hospitality, honor, justice, and truth. As we have seen, the Morrigan is the Goddess to whom mortal kings are ritually married. It is therefore appropriate that she is the one who has declared the peace. For now the Tuatha de Dannan's qualities can manifest themselves in nature, in accord with the principle of the Sacred Truth, the principle of correspondence by which the justice of the ruler manifests itself in the qualities of the environment. With the just and honorable Tuatha de Dannan installed as the new rulers of the land, their justice and honor manifests as fertile crops, favorable weather, calm seas, and the like. Indeed the Morrigan's Prophesy continues on, describing the agricultural abundance and prosperity which the

Stone circle in northern Donegal.

peace now makes possible. Thus, although the world of nature is a world of peace, this is so only when its rulers are just. Indeed, the Morrigan followed her prophesy of peace with another prophesy, describing the corruption and degradation of the world under rulers who are unjust, decadent, and evil.

The simple meditation of Peaceful Abiding can be done nearly anywhere. Most cities and towns have parks or rivers where places can be found for it. While an intensive Eachtra should be done about once or twice a year, Peaceful Abiding should be done about once a week. The best times are the early morning immediately after waking, and late at night just before going to sleep. It is a simple form of meditation, for it requires no particular training in theology, metaphysics, psychology, or philosophy. However, it may interest the reader to know that the exercise of seeing "just the light" from an object is the method used by Impressionist painters, and also the foundation of a school of contemporary philosophical thought called phenomenology. The senses are to be transformed and made sacred, not disparaged as a distraction from "true" spirituality, nor rejected as a source of temptation to vice. And indeed it is the element of light which activates the visual sense and brings us into contact with the spiritual world. In most Western traditions including the Celtic, thought and consciousness is described with the metaphor of brightness and

light. Wisdom is always said to be "illuminating." For just as the rising sun in the morning reveals the world and gives it color and warmth, so does the light of consciousness illuminate the dark places of the mind. Knowledge and wisdom has therefore always been likened to the element of light. Thus the Old Celtic Gods are sometimes referred to as "The Shining Ones." Likewise, we say of someone who has obtained the benefits of spiritual consciousness that she is "enlightened." Thus we may say in a preliminary way that the instruments of the spiritual attitude are the physical, mental, and emotional organs of perception; the organs through which light may enter.

Although this activity sounds simple, it is not. Within moments, one becomes distracted by thoughts and feelings that draw one's attention away from the meditation. One might review things that were said and done recently, or anticipate things to come. Itches and twitching muscles might arise. Peace, it would seem, does not come easily to us. But with practice, it becomes easier to settle into the receptive, relaxed condition of peacefully inhabiting the world. Because it goes against our usual habits, it takes work to do nothing. The technique to overcome inner distractions is to acknowledge them, name them, and then refocus your attention back on the meditation. It may help if you try to relax the muscles in your face, especially in the brow and around the mouth, because these muscles tend to tighten themselves slightly while we are engaged in concentrated thought.

3. Speaking to the Sacred

On departure from your place of Peaceful Abiding, if it is outside your home, clean up any rubbish that doesn't belong, both your own and anything that may have been lying about when you arrived, and put out any fires. You have likely heard the phrase, "take nothing but photographs, leave nothing but footsteps." This is usually very good advice. But for this exercise, I recommend that you do not take even photographs, for you should etch the experiences into your own memory. Additionally, I recommend that you do leave something. For example:

Offerings and Memorials. Leave a token object of thanks and gratitude to the place. Be sure that it is biodegradable, and will not be mistaken for rubbish by another traveler, and will not harm the local environment. (Fruit, bread, water, juice, wine, and beer.) If you light incense sticks, be sure that you place them in a way that they will not accidentally start a fire.

In the ground, trace out the shape of a symbol or a diagram that best represents the spiritual path to which you are committed, or the thoughts and feelings you experienced during your stay.

Circles, spirals, labyrinths, triskeles, Celtic crosses, words and inscriptions, and mandalas are all appropriate.

Construct a cairn from stones. Start by gathering large stones into a base. Then balance a pile of stones on top of this base, forming an upright column. Consider the number of stones to balance in this pile, for numbers are also symbols and will carry a message. Consider what should go on the very top: a shell, a feather, a different-colored stone, a clump of moss or seaweed. This, too, will become a message. Construct a crescent-shaped enclosure of smaller stones around the base of the cairn.

The idea of leaving an anonymous marker of one's presence at a site of peaceful abiding is already widespread. Some years ago, I was walking along the shore of Lake Huron in the middle of the night, relaxing after a day at the Celtic Roots Festival in the harbor town of Goderich, Ontario, Canada. A brilliant full moon hovered over the lake, and a few meteors streaked across the sky from time to time as well. It was a sublime and peaceful night. Along the beach, I came across no less than four tall stone cairns, presumably built by an anonymous Celt who was also attending the festival. It was a beautiful evening, and a beautiful discovery. Several years later, while country walking on the fields of Inis Mor, the largest of the three Arran Islands off the coast of Galway, Ireland, I was happy to find that others who had already passed that way built similar cairns of their own. And so I constructed a small cairn of my own as well. It felt like the most natural thing to do. And on another occasion, while walking with a friend on the ancient Druidic center, the hill of Uisneach, I came across a small circle of pillar-sized boulders set into the ground, with a large rectangular standing stone in its exact center. This miniature circle had an extraordinary resemblance to the small rings and cairns I had been making all along the stone beaches of Galway City that previous Lughnasad. Also on Uisneach I found a natural spring-fed pool around which the ground had been cleared, to make it easier to sit by it and drink. I began to wonder if there is a natural impulse within our psychology to make a contribution to places of outstanding natural beauty.

Whatever memento of your presence you choose to leave, it should be representative of your spiritual path, personally meaningful for you, and assembled while one is holding the spiritual attitude. For example, the stone cairn described in the previous exercise has important symbolic connections with the principle of the Great Marriage. The upright column of stones is the phallic monument to the God of the sky, and the circular or crescent shaped enclosure surrounding it is the yonic monument for the Goddess of the land. It is not important that others recognize the symbolic associations of your memorial. It is important that *you* do. It matters only that you have left your fingerprint and signature. The memorial at the site of peaceful abiding is a trace of your presence communicating that you were here. It might be the gods, the spirits, or the ancestors who read the message. Or it might be a group of passing children, tourists, or animals. The purpose of such markers is to undertake a somewhat more interactive form of Peaceful Abiding and so reinforce the spiritual attitude. Additionally, the more anonymous the message is, the more likely that those who come by it will believe whatever they want to believe, and come away with a good feeling for having found it.

The kind of memorial described here is not a permanent structure. By contrast, the cairns, stone circles, and passage mounds built by the Celtic and pre-Celtic people of Europe were built to endure. Temporary structures speak of our frailty and fragility, the transience of things, and ultimately of death. Permanent structures speak of the will to overcome transience and bequeath our values, and indeed the story of our lives, to future generations, and so attain a kind of immortality. Cairns and mounds mark out centers, where correspondences between "above" and "below," cardinal directions, social relations, and so on, come together. The rings and circles of such monuments reproduce the architecture of the world. Thus they are natural symbols for unity, belonging, and continuity with others both past and present. "Gateways," like the entrances to passage mounds, the portal dolman, or the famous trilithons of Stonehenge, act as entrances to the Otherworld.

Clearly, different kinds of monuments represent different ideas. And one monument can have several of these features. The point, however, is that constructing monuments, big or small, permanent or transient, aid one's practice of Peaceful Abiding. The act helps to establish, or recognize, a place as distinctly related to the sacred powers of the world. And so it promotes the Spiritual Attitude.

The last level of Peaceful Abiding involves *speaking* to the sacred powers of the world, and using various things as carriers of our messages. Most of the time, when people send messages to God, they make *requests*—we seek out the gods because we want something. Our wants range from the most basic needs such as food and comfort, to "worldly" desires for love, money, and the fulfilment of dreams, to the most cerebral like the need for meaning and purpose in life. But in general, the giver of an offering wants to influence or control the powers to whom the offering is given, to court their good favor and win some kind of benefit from them. Here we have a pagan kind of prayer.

There are several kinds of offerings, based on the reasons an offering is made. The first is decidedly un-spiritual: the giver is in effect showing off to others. The giver of an expensive offering shows himself to be someone who is important, powerful, or wealthy. Another kind of offering is a material gift given to a deity in order to receive something else in return. It may also be given as a kind of payment for something already received from the deity. The sacrifices of harvest fruit and vegetables, of weapons and laborer's tools, etc. can fall in this category. In the case of offerings to malevolent or cthonic deities, the offering is intended to pacify the deity and prevent it from causing misfortunes and disasters. Either way, the offering becomes a vehicle for carrying messages to the powers or beings for whom it is intended. Religious sacrifices of all kinds, from the Wicker Man to the Catholic Eucharist, evolved from ancient customs for preparing and distributing food. As the anthropologist Marvin Harris wrote, "early ecclesiastical religions saw humans and gods as if they were enmeshed in a food cycle. Without help from gods, humans would never be able to feed themselves. But humans must feed the gods to obtain that help."[3] From a spiritual perspective, which need not be contrary to the anthropological perspective, to give an offering is to speak to the world, to be present to the world as it is present to you, and thus to open up a kind of dialogue.

We know from literary sources and archaeological discoveries that the

Celts sought to communicate with their gods and with the powers of the world by giving offerings and sacrifices to them through fires and waters. For instance, many small wooden human effigies were discovered at the source of the river Seine, in France, which portrayed people afflicted with injuries or diseases. These have been interpreted as offerings to the river god by people suffering the same afflictions, in the hope that the river god would heal them.

The type of offering you give can often communicate a special message just because of what it is, aside from whatever intention the gift may have. Food offerings are natural symbols for the organic fertility of crops, animals, and children, and so it is an excellent gift for issues relating to physical and sexual health, friendship and social relations, and so on. In the Celtic tradition, drink offerings, especially alcoholic beverages, are associated with ancestors and predecessors. Jewelery and decorative objects are associated with success in worldly affairs such as business, justice, politics, and the like. Feathers, bones, shells, flowers, and other natural objects can reflect the specifically religious or ceremonial associations of the animals or plants themselves (if any), or can signify that the spirit of the animal or plant which the offering came from is acting as one's messenger. Nearly anything can be used to send wishes, love, and prayers to the sacred powers of the world. It would be perfectly appropriate, for instance, to hold up a soap bubble ring and let the wind blow bubbles through it.

Both the offering itself, and the place where it is put (a fire, a river, etc.) can be treated as the medium of communication between this world and the next. On seeing one's bouquet of flowers carried off by the current of a stream, or one's written message on a piece of paper consumed by a candle, it is easy to imagine that one's message and intention is being transported to the Otherworld by the flowing water or the rising smoke. By contrast with the sacrifice of social prestige, this kind of offering is necessarily private (even if there are witnesses); it takes place between you and the gods. What matters here is the way in which speaking to the sacred powers of the world, be they gods, ancestors, or immaterial and impersonal forces, effectively treats those sacred powers as real. Whatever is requested, and whether the request is granted or not, the offering itself *affirms the reality of the sacred*. It tends to cultivate in the seeker the sense that the divine is accessible, reachable, intimate, and personal. This is especially true of performing music and poetry. As sound is projected across space and time, eventually dissipating in the distance or returning as distorted echoes, it seems to reach the immaterial, invisible realms of the Otherworld. The sound of one's instrument or one's voice, with or without the use of words, is a carrier of the performer's presence as well as of her messages.

This affirmation has an effect on the seeker herself—it tends to enhance the spiritual attitude. This effect on the seeker is not a consequence of the action but is an inherent part of the action itself. Thus, performing the act can, by itself, be intrinsically beneficial.

These preliminary activities are important simple exercises which will help the seeker retain her sense of place and being, and keep her aware of her connectivity with the world. They will also prepare her for more challenging things ahead.

Four:

Space, Time, and Magic

Having discussed some of the informal ways in which a person can promote the spiritual attitude, I shall now turn to more structured, deliberate ways. One's commitment to spirituality can be reinforced and sustained by constant reminders such as ceremony and ritual, the decoration of one's dwelling and any clothing or jewelry one might wear. These and other aids all serve to *create sacred space and time*, which is a time and a place deliberately set aside for the experience of the presence of the sacred.

1. The Meditation-Place

Sacred Space is an area reserved apart from most other practical matters of daily life, for it has been designated for religious purposes. One will eventually need to seek out powerful places in one's area, as well as research other places one could travel to for an extended adventure. But within one's own home, it is important to have a space set aside purely as a religious space. This will be the space where your ceremonial objects are kept, and where representations of your gods or symbols of your path are located and displayed. Such a space is usually called an altar. But because of the way in which I normally use my own, I prefer to call it the meditation-place.

A good meditation-place has two qualities. One, the most practical, is that it is accessible. You need to be able to see it and reach it in order to use it. In a flat where I once lived, I had symbolic objects on top of bookshelves, on mantles and windowsills, and even hanging from a long tree branch that was suspended from the ceiling. A Green Man across from the door blessed everyone who entered the house with his smiling gaze. But my main meditation space was in a private room and located at floor-level, on a board supported by a few bricks, so that when using it I could sit comfortably close to the Earth. An image of a deity or a symbol placed on top of a refrigerator, for instance, might serve as a niche reserved "for the gods," giving them a place in the ordinary tasks of our lives. But the place where we address ourselves to the world's sacred powers most directly should be an easily accessible place not used for any other purpose.

The other quality of a good meditation-place is that it is, in some respect, a model for the cosmological structure of the sacred world. It, therefore, has an object representing the Axis-Mundi, the World-Center, and the layout and geometry of the rest of the meditation-place are all designed to artistically or geometrically balance themselves around the center and draw attention to it. Ancient sacred sites in the Celtic lands were frequently built with the same principle in mind. One of the best examples is the royal site of Ulster, posted on the road maps as "The Navan Fort" and known as *Emhain Macha* in the Irish tradition. It is located in what is now called county Armagh, just to the west of

Emain Macha, the royal center of Ulster.

Armagh town, in Northern Ireland. There is evidence that the site was inhabited in the Neolithic period, but permanent settlement that is visible today dates back to the 7th century B.C. The most prominent feature is the artificial mound, surrounded by trees. It had, at one time, several concentric rings of huge oak posts inside it, and an entrance to the west. The largest post was in the center, which was carved like a totem pole. For reasons unknown, the structure was filled with limestone rocks, burned, and then covered over with sods. The building almost certainly was not burned accidentally. It may have been burned by attackers, or deliberately burned by the builders as a sacrifice. As Irish folklorist Dáithí Ó h-Ógáin says:

> ...the striking circular plans, the use of great oak posts, and the sealing off of the whole building, leave little doubt but that those responsible for both construction and destruction were in awe of the site and regarded it as sacred. The largest

timber post might have been intended as a sort of "world tree," at the sacred centre of the community's territory with a ceremonial function of linking the earth with the skies. As such it would have been a symbol of the prosperity of the tribe or sept, and important ceremonies would have centred on it.[1]

When you construct your own sacred place, then, what you choose to put in the center-place will be very important, for it will represent qualities or forces that become, for your path, your means of accessing the divine center of the spiritual world. They will link your "earth," your embodied life, with your "sky," your spiritual principles. Statues of saints or deities, candles, small cauldrons, mandala-images or works of art, symbols, tokens from sacred places, and the like, are all appropriate. The centering-object will represent the axis-mundi of your interior world, so think carefully about what centering-object you want.

Your meditation place should also have something to it which represents the gateway to the Otherworld. For it is by using the meditation-place, more than almost any other way, that the Otherworld and its forces and deities will become present to you. The meditation-place also functions as a gateway. A decorated curtain behind the altar, flanked on either side by long upright branches resembling a door frame, will serve admirably as a gateway that looks as if the seeker could enter it. You should be facing west when sitting before the gate, for west is the direction of the setting sun and of access to the Otherworld in the Celtic tradition. Alternately, you may want to face the direction of the nearest significant body of water where you live, or the direction in which the nearest river flows. In some respect, any symbol or deity image prominently displayed is a gateway, for it will function as a conduit for the presence of the deity or the forces and principles represented by the symbol. Such is the power of the law of correspondence. But for a certain kind of meditation called *Imramma*, it is useful to have something that more obviously resembles a portal, as we shall soon see.

2. The Apple Branch

Aside from these observations, the very activity of creating one and using it regularly is often enough to make the meditation-place sacred. One may then start to think about other ritual tools and ceremonial objects. One of the first instruments that someone on the Druid's path should obtain is the Apple Branch, also known as the Bell Branch. In most Irish stories of journeys to magical lands, an Otherworld being usually offers an apple, or a branch from the apple tree, to someone whom they wish to invite into their magical realm. The romantic hero Connla is given an apple by his otherworldy paramour, and it sustains him by itself and always remains whole. The glimmering girl who Wandering Angus meets and searches for has an apple blossom in her hair. Cormac is given a musical apple branch by the woman who invites him to the Otherworld to meet Manannan. The apple, therefore, is the tree for calling the attention of the Otherworldly powers and beings, for requesting entry into their world, or for inviting them to join us here.

Creating the Bell Branch. *At sunset, fill a chalice with wine (because alcohol is a magical substance, when it is respected), and share it with your Gods by pouring out some of it on the Earth. Think of it as the faerie food that takes you to the Otherworld. As you do, and in your meditations, ask the gods to show you a tree that will donate wood for you.*

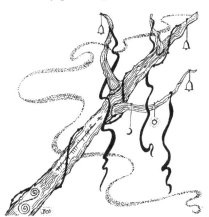

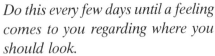

The Bell Branch.

Do this every few days until a feeling comes to you regarding where you should look.

Walk about that area for the space of about an afternoon, with one's mind in the condition of peaceful abiding, and get to know the landscape. Stop whenever a particular feature of the area attracts your attention. In that area, find a

tree. Walk around it, touch it, look it over on all sides. If you feel as if this tree will allow you to take a branch, then take one. If not, continue walking.

Once you have found a branch that you like, be sure that the tree from which it came "permits" you to take it. Spend some time abiding with it. Leave an offering or a token memorial near the tree, to serve as a kind of repayment and thanks for the tree's loss of one of its fingers. Explore the tree and the area where it is planted, to understand it and be familiar with it.

When you return home, clean the branch and set it on your meditation-place. Affix three bells to it at first. You may also wish to carve your name into its length using the Ogham alphabet. When you are finished, wrap it in a cloth or towel that will muffle the sound and keep it hidden from sunlight.

The best place and moment to ring your branch for the first time is a "between-place," such as a doorway or the edge of water, at dawn or twilight. Alternately, it is good to take it to the site from which it came from. When you have decided on the best place for its first ringing, take it there and carefully unwrap it, allowing the sunlight to touch it for the first time since it was made. Hold it aloft and ring it aloud. Announce, as you do, that this is a Druid's Bell Branch, whose music is heard in this world and the Otherworld, and which shall call the attention of the spirits and gods whenever it is used.

The Bell Branch can be a life-long treasure. At important stages in one's life, such as rites of passage, or on the achievement of certain significant goals, one can attach another bell to the branch, or a colored ribbon, or carve a symbol. Your Bell Branch will be all the more powerful if you develop a relationship with the tree from which it came, by returning to the tree often and using it as a regular site for peaceful abiding. If the tree should die, or if the branch was taken from a dead tree, one might still be able to develop a relationship with the site where the branch was found.

Brighid's Cross.

3. Druidic Symbols

Symbols of the path should appear somewhere among one's ceremonial tools and the decorations of one's meditation-place, as reminders of the mysteries and meanings that they represent, as well as reminders of one's solidarity with other practitioners of the same path. Some Celtic deities have their own symbols. Brighid has her cross of woven rushes, and Taranis has a wheel with twelve spokes, for instance. The most common religious symbols used by practitioners of Celtic spirituality are the triskele, the Awen, the tree, and the 20 letters of the Ogham alphabet. The triskele is the best known of Celtic symbols which come to us from Irish tradition. It consists in three spiral arms linked together at a central point. The most famous example of a triskele is the large triple spiral carved into the wall of the passage at Newgrange. It can stand for any of the hundreds of triads in Celtic literature, although it is normally taken to represent the unity of the "Three Realms," the life-supporting environments of land, sea, and sky, and also the unity of the bodily, mental, and spiritual "parts" of an individual person's being. The triskele can easily be seen as the Celtic equivalent of the Hindu "OM"

The Newgrange triskele.

symbol. If one image was superimposed on the other, the graphic similarity would be striking; but more importantly both symbols represent the primordial unity of the world and of the person.

British Druids usually use a symbol called the Awen to identify themselves and represent their ideas. It consists of three parallel vertical lines, the outer two leaning diagonally towards the top of

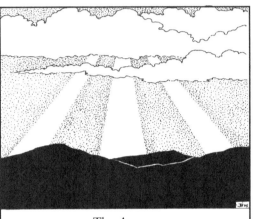

The Awen.

the middle one. Sometimes it is accompanied by three circles, either above the awen itself or concentrically surrounding it. It can be interpreted as three megalithic stones reaching up to the heavens, aspiring to the height of the sky. Likewise it can be seen as three pure rays of light shining down from above, like the sunbeams that can sometimes be seen in the sky on partly cloudy days. The Awen represents the "light" of enlightenment that shines from the primordial source of being, the spiritual realms that exist "above" us in the starry heavens. Something like the Awen appears as rock art inside the mound of Knowth. One of the carvings depicts a dot with numerous rays spreading out below it, and probably represents a standing stone casting shadows at different times of the year. Like the Hindu OM, the Awen is also

used as a phonetic sign: it is associated with three vowel sounds which British druids use much the same way Hindus intone the sound of the OM. The three sounds are an acoustic psychological inducement of semi-magical, spiritual attitudes of mind. One can only speculate whether the triskele also originally represented a phoneme, as the OM sign does to the Hindu today, although it is noted that Newgrange, like other passage mounds, has unique acoustic properties, as if custom-built for ritual singing and chanting. The ancient builders of Newgrange and other similar monuments certainly invented the technology of "magical sound," even if they did not invent a written alphabet to represent the phonemes of their language.

We do, as it happens, know what the ancient Celtic alphabet was, although we do not know if it was invented by the same culture that built Newgrange and other Neolithic monuments, or by a later people. It was called *Ogham*, and it was written mainly on stones to indicate burials, territorial boundaries, and other practical matters. The letters consist of horizontal or diagonal lines touching or crossing a central vertical line (usually the corner edge of the stone) that linked all the letters. It was read from the bottom to the top. It was also marked on wooden rings made from twisted tree branches called "withies." In these cases, an arrow-shaped line called a feathermark indicated where the message started and in which direction to read it. In the *Táin Bo Cuailnge* Cú Chullain creates an Ogham withy using only one hand, and on it marks a message to the armies of Connaught, warning them to continue no further.

There were originally 20 Ogham letters in total (although five more were added later to account for phoneme sounds in Latin and Greek), and they were named after 20 species of trees native to Ireland. The correspondence with months of the year is a 20th century innovation, created by Robert Graves in his work on the theory of poetry entitled *The White Goddess*. There is no literary or oral-tradition reference to any correspondence between the Ogham and calendar dates prior to the publication of his book in the year 1948. Other correspondences, such as with birds and trees, are well attested in the literary and traditional sources, as is the use of Ogham as a divination tool. More will be said of this later. Here, it is enough to say that one may wish to inscribe one's name, the name of a deity important to you, a poetic phrase or a special proverb, or the like, on to your Bell Branch or other tools using the Ogham.

This brings me to the trees themselves. The use of the tree as a symbol of spiritual identity is the most distinctive and instantly recognizable part of Celtic Mysticism. As seen, the word "Druid" comes from an ancient Celtic word for an oak tree. It is well known that trees are a part of the old Celtic religion and not only symbolized various spiritual ideas, but also were worshipped in their own right as well. Many Councils of the Church from the 5th century onward denounced the worship of trees, along with the worship of wells, indicating that the practice was probably widespread in Europe. As a symbol for spiritual identity and aspiration, I can think of nothing better. Trees embody the principle of "as above so below," connecting divine or celestial realms with cthonic underworld realms and our own mortal realm. For their trunks and branches reach for the sky, and their roots reach deep into the Earth. Their many angles of symmetry—radial from above, bilateral from the side—appeal to our aesthetic sense of balance and contrast. A tree's branches and leaves often repeat the shape, pattern, and symmetry of the whole tree. The annual regeneration cycle of deciduous (broad leaf) trees is a natural symbol for spiritual renewal. In ancient times, a forest would have been a mysterious and dangerous place. At a distance from the safety of towns and villages, forests were outside the realm of civilization, a home for things mysterious, dangerous, unknown: wild animals, outlaws, and the many fantastical and nightmarish creatures of imagination. People who made their livings in forests and wildernesses, such as shepherds and hunters, thus take on some of the magical associations of those places. This may be part of the reason ancient Druids set their sacred sanctuaries in a deep forest clearing called a *nemeton* (meaning "sanctuary," the common word used by Western European Celts for a sacred place). An Old Irish glossary indicates that in the *fiodhneimhidh*, (tree sanctuary) "the seers used to perform their rituals." And a 7th century Irish poem states a prohibition against cutting down those sacred trees.[2] Ireland's ancient law-code, the Brehon law, named seven species of "Chieftain" trees which could not be cut under most circumstances, no matter where they were found. (These were the Oak, Hazel, Apple, Yew, Holly, Ash, and Pine/Silver Fir.) Hawthorn trees were often planted next to holy wells, like a kind of spirit guardian. Yet trees are also plants of civilization: the wood gives us materials to build and heat our homes, as well as berries, nuts, and fruit to eat. So many of our most important architectural monuments are designed to resemble trees, or are decorated with lush foliage ornaments.

The modern Irish word for "tree" is the word *crann*, but there is another word, *Bíle Ratha*, which means the special tree at the center of a *nemeton*, or sacred place. The word can also mean "a champion protector." A *Bíle* is associated with the linking of Earth and Sky, the Great Marriage, and the "axis mundi." It is a "world tree" which links

the prosperity of the human community with the larger orders of the cosmos. In the story of the coming of Conn Céadchathach, Conn of the Hundred Battles, to the kingship at Tara, it was prophesized by a female seer named Rothnaimh that an ancient yew tree named Mughain would be discovered when Conn was born. This tree stood near Ballaghmoon in county Kildare until the last century. A modern example of the tree as the symbolic center of a human community is the official emblem of Canada, the red maple leaf. Historians will tell you the maple is Canada's symbol because of the importance of the tree to Canadian industry. But it may also have been chosen because mature maple trees possess such beauty, durability, and grandeur. We are naturally inclined to see tall and proud trees as the link between the earth and sky, between the human community and the order of the cosmos. This cosmic order includes all the great immensities of life within the cycle of birth, death, and the possibility or regeneration. Such is the intelligence of trees—such is 'what trees know.'" This knowledge is symbolized most directly in an architectural and artistic figure known as the Green Man—a mask of a human face emerging from leaves, or actually made of leaves. He appears on European cathedrals all the way from the Dark Ages to the Renaissance. Although there are not many examples of the Green Man on Irish buildings, the artistic representation of the intelligence in plant life appears in some of the illuminated manuscripts of Irish Christianity, including but the Book of Kells. There are, however, records of Celtic tribes in Gaul named after trees, and of a Celtic god, Sylvanus, who, like the Green Man, has leaves in his beard and hair. The most famous warrior band in Ireland is named for a tree: the Red Branch.

While it is clearly a part of Druidic tradition that trees are sacred, this does not mean that in ancient times, trees would never have been cut down. It is said that an entire forest was felled to build the palisade wall around the Hill of Tara. The ditch and bank of this palisade still exists, and is known as *rath na rí*, the Fort of the King. In modern Ireland, land planners and developers who build new housing estates or motorways sometimes find themselves faced with large and well organized protests, legal challenges, and even acts of civil disobedience to protect them. Certainly, environmental concerns are at work here, perhaps more than concerns about any remaining Druidic nature spirituality, for most protestors. The reason for respecting the land and the trees has changed, although in practice the material result is very similar, if not the same.

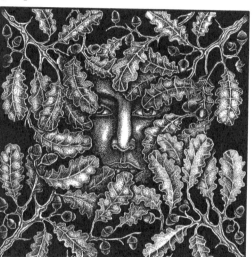

The Green Man.

4. Other Instruments

There are a number of other traditional instruments that Druids used in their ceremonies. For in many of the mythologies, the characters are able to perform extraordinary feats of magic with the possession of magical objects such as tools and weapons. I shall now turn to a description of some of them.

The Cauldron is important to the magic of material prosperity because it is a vessel for preparing and serving food, and the magical properties of mythological cauldrons reflects this. The Cauldron of Dagda, for instance, feeds whole multitudes. The cauldron can also dispense wisdom itself as a kind of food, a food for the mind. A mere three drops from Cerridwen's cauldron grants divine knowledge. The deities and figures which adorn the famous Gundestrup Cauldron illustrates this with graphic clarity that the cauldron represents plentifulness of not just material wealth but spiritual wealth. It represents abundance of that which we gain from the Otherworld. In ritual, any cauldron can become the Dagda's cauldron, dispensing both food and wisdom. Or it may function in ritual as a libation-bowl, in which case it receives the offerings made during a ceremony. Perhaps the witches of Shakespearean fantasy, mixing their magic potions in cauldrons, are a memory of the folk healers of the past. They knew how to use the parts of plants and animals to make medicines, aphrodisiacs, cosmetics, hallucinogens, fertility enhancements, abortion inducements, even poisons. With this knowledge they would appear to be wielding the power of life and death. To a people who lack the biological knowledge of today's science, this power would seem magical, and indeed dangerous.

The Chalice is a drinking vessel used not for preparing food but for serving it. As such it is a natural symbol for the knowledge and wisdom which nurtures the mind and the soul. King Cormac of Tara was said to possess a magical cup which would break into three pieces if lies were told in its presence, and mend itself again if rectifying truths were told. Any cup can be a Cup of Truth, dispensing joy and madness in equal measure, when it is ceremonially treated as if it contains water from the Well of Wisdom, or ale from the Feast of Age. With this attitude in mind, an ordinary cup can become the Holy Grail, the great treasure of the Hero's Quest. One of the names of Ireland's Goddess of Sovereignty, Meadhbh, has the meaning "she who intoxicates"—like the mead which the

sacred cup dispenses. The word "mead" itself originates in the same linguistic root as her name. What makes the cup a magical treasure, whether it contains milk, apple juice, water, or wine, is in large measure the attitude one takes to drinking it. The blessing of the Cup is what life feels like when love, poetry, music, beauty, and all things through which the divine reveals itself in the world intoxicates you like wine.

Musical instruments have an important place in Celtic Mysticism as well. The Irish father-god, Dagda, possessed a magical harp which had its own place of honor in the banqueting hall at Tara, and which would come to him when he summoned it by saying, "Come summer, come winter, Mouths of harps and bags of pipes!" On at least one occasion, the harp flew to his hands when he recited this summoning-spell and killed nine men who were standing in the way. A 9th century text called the *Instructions of Cormac* says, "All music is holy until it comes to the harp." The proficiency of a musician was measured by a triad called the Three Noble Strains: sleep music, joyful music, sorrowful music. Dagda was a master of all three, and used this mastery to put the Fomhoir occupiers of Tara to sleep so that he could rescue his harper, Úaithne, from their custody. The harp was also the favored instrument of the greatest of Ireland's high kings, Brian Boru. Brian united almost every tribe on the island and defeated the Vikings at the Battle of

Clontarf in the year 1014. His harp is on display at Trinity College Library, in Dublin. His military and political achievements gave the people confidence in their own power, pride in their identity, and a sense of membership in something bigger than themselves and their tribes alone. For this reason the harp has become a political symbol of the sovereignty of the Irish Republic.

For the purpose of a spiritual life in the Celtic tradition, musicianship is a very important skill. I shall be bold and claim that one does not qualify as a member of the human race unless one is learning or practising some form of artistic creativity. There are many kinds of art, but I think that music is best. Music is immaterial and yet real, like a spirit. Rhythm and the melodic interplay between harmony and dissonance are some of the oldest magical vehicles to reproduce the natural rhythms of life and nature, and so bring to bear the power therein. Although not mentioned in any Celtic story I know, drums are frequently used in other cultures where the developmental level was similar to that of the Iron Age Celts of Ireland about the same time. They are useful for keeping time during the performance of chant songs, and for meditative purposes. They get the blood pumping and the mind working. Through stimulating brain waves at particular frequencies the music of the drum can transport the drummer and her listeners to another perceptual world. The more art

there is in your life, and the more refined and uplifting the art becomes with practice, the more the whole of your life becomes a meditation-space; the more the whole of the world becomes sacred space.

We don't have precise details about the costume of the Druids, although we do know a few facts. We know they dressed flamboyantly, in bright colors, for "brightness" was considered a quality of wisdom. In the story of the "Colloquy of the Two Sages," a junior and a senior Druid compete for the right to wear a special ceremonial cloak, which was purple and decorated with shells, feathers, and colored stones. The clothes of a Druidess named Fedelm, who was asked by Queen Maeve to predict the end of the Táin Bo Cuailnge, are described in detail: she had "a speckled cloak fastened around her with a gold pin, a red, embroidered hooded tunic and sandals with gold clasps."[3] Celtic masks made from bronze have been unearthed. Although it is likely they were merely decorative, it is also possible that they had ceremonial uses. A priest or priestess might have worn one to impersonate a deity for certain rituals. Community folk in the early Christian era sometimes costumed themselves for special occasions. A 7th century Archbishop of Canterbury named Theodore denounced a New Year's practice in which men would go around their village in costumes and masks, dressed like animals or like women, and would sing and dance for anyone who offered them a bit of money, food, or drink. Guilty parties were required to do penance for three years. This may have been a folkloric remnant of a pagan practice, in which people enacted the roles of various mythological characters in order to take on some of the magical qualities of those characters. To have them dance for you would thus bring a blessing for the new year. Similar New Year practices existed elsewhere in Britain. And the same basic idea lies behind costuming customs of later origin, like the Mummers, the Wren Boys, and Morris Dancing. These costumes include all sorts of strange things: wicker baskets and straw "haycocks" covering the head and face; rags, tatters, leaves, branches, feathers, clappers and bells covering the body; and bright clashing colors and patterns. The best magical costumes are those which give physical representation to the person's spiritual fields of energy. As such they are magical instruments that facilitate the radiation of one's aura. They can make one appear larger than life—almost as large as her true self.

5. Parting the Mist

All of these tools, symbols, and other trappings may look nice sitting on the altar, but they benefit us only when we use them. It is when we have established a time and space for the experience of the sacred that we see the ideas embodied in our tools and symbols come alive. Most of the time, it takes only a slight shift in perception,

a change of intention, to open ourselves to the experience of the sacred. But it is also sometimes helpful to have a ceremony, with concrete actions and spoken words, to formalize the change of attitude in our consciousness. When a group is involved, ceremony can be an enormously useful way to coordinate everyone's attention and attitude, which tends to heighten the experience for all.

A poem from the Carmina Gadelica, the collection of Scottish folk prayers assembled in the late 19th century, has a short prayer I sometimes use as a way of beginning my meditations. It is called "The Three," and is described in the collection as a prayer of protection. It runs like this:

> *The Three who are over me,*
> *The Three who are below me,*
> *The Three who are above me here,*
> *The Three who are in the earth.*
> *The Three who are in the air,*
> *The Three who are in the heaven,*
> *The Three who are in the great pouring sea.*[4]

This is of course a Christian prayer, and the "Three" referred to here is the Holy Trinity of Father, Son, and Holy Ghost. But it is also a Celtic prayer: the figure of Three has been important to Celtic spiritual thought for thousands of years, even before Christianity. Here is another example. It is simply called "Fragment," and it reads as follows:

> *As it was,*
> *As it is,*

As it shall be

Evermore,

O thou Triune

Of grace!

With the ebb,

With the flow,

O thou Triune

Of grace!

With the ebb,

With the flow.[5]

Just reciting these prayers as mantras during meditation can have a calming, peace-making effect, relaxing the mind and making the spiritual attitude easier to adopt. I have picked these two in particular because they are instances of the ancient Celtic threefold arrangement of divinity. The oldest appearance of The Three is the beautiful triskele in the passage of Newgrange. It appears in the triad of "Land, Sea, and Sky" which together seem to make up the division of the world, on the vertical axis. It is in the hundreds of "Triads," short proverbs from the Celtic tradition describing "Three things which…" And finally and importantly, The Three appear in the many gods and goddesses who are paired with two siblings, and so are *triple* gods. Morrigan is a triple goddess when paired with her sisters Nemhain and Babd. The Tuatha de Dannan is the "tribe of the (goddess) Dana" and they are also referred to as *fir Trí nDéa* ("men of the three gods" or "men of the three goddesses"). It is not hard to guess who these three gods

are. When the Milesians, the tribe from whom the Irish people are mythologically descended, arrive in Ireland, they encounter three goddesses named Ériu, Banba, and Fódla. These are all names for the land of Ireland itself and so these goddesses may be taken as a three-fold image of the Goddess of Sovereignty. They are married to three divine kings whose names are Mac Cuill, Mac Cécht, and Mac Gréine (respectively meaning: "son of hazel," "son of the plough," and "son of the Sun"). These kings are identified as the grandchildren of the god Daghda. The royal deities of the Gauls described by the Roman poet Lucan are triple deities as well. Their names were Teutates, Esus, and Taranis. The first name here is also known from inscriptions in France and Britain, and may mean nothing more than "tribal god" as the word is cognate with the Celtic word for tribe (teutá). Taranis means "terrible." He seems to be identified with thunderstorms, and his symbols include a thunderbolt and a wheel with 12 spokes. Esus seems to be associated with trees. Further analogies may be made with other triple-goddesses of time and destiny known from other European mythologies, especially the three Norns from Scandinavia (Wyrd, Urverly, and Skuld), or the three Fates from Greek tradition who weave the tapestry of fate (Clotho, Laechesis, and Atropos). These goddesses may have been the inspiration for the three prophetic witches in Shakespeare's *Macbeth*.

When I recite these prayers, it is this ancient Celtic triplicity of the deity which comes to my mind, and which creates sacred space in the realm of my perceptions. The creation of sacred space, one could say, is the creation of a space that is fit for the dwelling place of a deity. For of all the ceremonial equipment here described, the most potent magical instrument a Druid possesses is her language. Through the power of the voice and the spoken word, certain realities can be called into being in the realm of our thought and perception. A contemporary Druid or Bard can make use of the many patterns of poetry available today, within which there is wide space for free creativity. There are hundreds of circle chant-songs which have become part of the oral folklore of the contemporary pagan community, for most of them were composed for the very purpose of producing group unity, focused intent, and a mild trance state in the singers and listeners. In my clann, we never used recorded music in our celebrations. We believed that only live voices and musical instruments could produce psychologically and magically effective sounds. Recorded music does not do justice to the immediacy and the presence of live performance. We were fortunate to have some very talented singers and musicians among us, and over the years our own original music became part of our shared repertoire, and our shared identity. Very little is quite as powerful and emotionally evocative as a well-trained choir.

Through the power of the voice combined with a compelling melody and rhythm, the speaker calls a certain intentionality, thought, idea, or image into reality as the sonic force of a Word of Sacred Truth.

Experiment with this for a while, for instance by singing a Carmina Gadelica prayer at the beginning of your meditations. We have seen how, in the Celtic cosmology, the world is divided horizontally into four realms which correspond to the four points on the compass. The experience of one's meditations can be intensified again when these four quarters are acknowledged while circumnabulating the center. Here is one way to do it:

Parting the Mist of Manannan. Stand in the center of the circle, and take up the staff. Breathe deeply to clear the mind. Thump the staff on the ground three times, or ring the Bell Branch, to make the magical sound that announces the beginning of a ceremony. Or walk sunwise around the center three times, perhaps while reciting a prayer which acknowledges the center, such as "The three who are over me.""

Face the North, and acknowledge it with a flourish from the Bell Branch or three thumps on the ground with the staff, and with words like these: "Powers of the North, the Winter and the Darkened Earth, the nights by which we measure time, and the direction from which came the Gods of my people, I (name) call upon you. As I face the North, the Land upholds me, the Sea surrounds me, and the Sky covers me. The spirits of the Land, Sea, and Sky to the East of this place are welcome to this circle."

Facing East: "Powers of the East, the Springtime, and the Rising Sun, the direction from which came the ancestors, I (name), call upon you. As I face the South."

Facing South: "Powers of the Wouth, the Summer and the Mid Day Sun, the direction fromwhich camethe Fromoire and towhich they were banished again,, I (name), call upon you."

Facing West: "Powers of the West, the Autumn and the Setting Sun, the direction where our departed ancestors go, I (name), call upon you..."

Finally, return to the middle of the circle. Using the Bell Branch, acknowledge an object which represents the Axis Mundi: a cauldron for the Well of Wisdom; a staff in the ground for the World Tree; a cairn of stones; or similar token. Say something such as: "As it was, as it is, as it shall be, evermore, O thou Triune of grace!"

A four-quarter invocation such as this one can be useful for small groups or for particular purposes, some of which will be described in the chapters to follow. You may find that just by speaking the words, your mind is forced to acknowledge as reality the things the words describe. The exercise here essentially reconstructs the world in the shape of the mandala of cosmology, three "realms" or "worlds" on a vertical axis, and four provinces, one for each cardinal direction, on the horizontal axis. The whole effect is to "ground" and "center" one in the world, having made it into a sacred space through the dramatization of its archetypal structure. It is a small scale repetition of the original moment of creation. The purpose of ritual, as Mircea Eliade put it, is to close the distance between the ritual performers and the original event of creation.

Through the paradox of rite, profane time and duration are suspended. And the same holds true for all repetitions, i.e. all imitations of archetypes; through such imitation, man is projected into the mythical epoch in which the archetypes were first revealed.[6]

This takes the mind and the imagination back to the place where the creation of the world began, which is also the dwelling-place of the archetypal powers of the world. Having arrived at that place, we may become participants in their existence.

Ancient people sometimes made entire landscapes into sacred places. For instance, on the Scottish island of Lewis, there is a large stone circle called Callanish. It is a wide ring of 13 stones surrounding a large central stone, with four avenues of stones extending in a cross shape outside the circle. The main axis is aligned to the midsummer solstice, and there are alignments with the rising places of bright stars like Altair and Capella. As seen from the center of the circle, every 19 1/2 years, the full moon skirts the top of a mountain range in the east which resembles a woman lying on her back, and is known locally as "sleeping beauty." It disappears behind her head, and re-emerges in a valley to the south. In former times, it was believed that at that moment the Earth Goddess would appear in the circle. By constructing their monument at just the right spot, and connecting it to a story of a divine manifestation, the builders of Callanish transformed the whole landscape into a temple.

6. The Sovereignty of Fire

Within the "magic circle," it is important to stand up from the passive and receptive position that characterizes "Peaceful Abiding," and begin to seek out the immensity more actively. To obtain the full benefits of the spiritual life, one must do more than simply listen and learn. One must enter into a dialogue with the world.

The most important way Celts did this in ancient times was through the use of *fire*. Historians have established with confidence that fire had a prominent place in the ceremonies of ancient Druids. The mythologies make this clear as well. When the Nemedians arrived in Ireland, for instance, their leader Midhe lit a fire on the hill of Uisneach to inaugurate the event. To light a fire on one of the royal hills of

Ireland was thus to proclaim the presence and the authority of one's tribe over the land. Saint Patrick's "illegal" bonfire, with which he inaugurated the arrival of Christianity in Ireland, can thus be seen as a continuation of that same ancient Celtic tradition. It is well known that a remnant of this practice still exists in certain Celtic countries where it is the custom to light bonfires on certain special nights of the year. On the night of 31st October, *Féile na Samhna*, most towns and urban neighborhoods all over Ireland light fires or launch pyrotechnics in parks, fields, and hill tops in celebration of Samhain, the Celtic New Year. People used to walk the boundaries of their properties carrying a burning branch, partly to assert their possession of the land, partly to ward off harmful influences. Less well known outside of Ireland is that Protestant neighborhoods in Northern Ireland burn large bonfires on the night before Orange Day (12 July), when they commemorate the Battle of the Boyne and the final end of the old Gaelic order in Ireland. With some irony, but without disrespect intended, it can be claimed that Patrick's Christian bonfire, as well as the present-day Protestant bonfire custom, are both continuations of the ancient Gaelic tradition of lighting fires in order to assert the sovereignty of a tribe.

What is it about fire that makes it so important, not only for Celtic tradition, but for humanity in general? Why are things like pyrotechnics, candles, torches, laser light shows, and so on, a part of our most important cultural events and celebrations, all over the world? Why do we still commemorate New Year's Eve, the Olympic Games, certain national holidays, and similar celebrations with pyrotechnics of all kinds? Why do we light candles for birthdays, funerals, and dinner parties? It seems that the presence of fire stirs up special feelings in us. Perhaps this is because there is something primal and archetypal about fire. In the words of Virtuvius, the ancient Roman historian of the sciences: "…it was the discovery of fire that originally gave rise to the coming together of men, to the deliberative assembly, and to social intercourse."[7]

When fire was first domesticated, hundreds of thousands of years ago, ancient people were able to create circles of heat and light which would become areas of safety in an otherwise dangerous world. Fire illuminated the space around it when the rest of the world was covered in the dark of night-time. Wild animals would not normally enter the

Re-enactors lighting a ceremonial fire on the Hill of Tara.

illuminated area. Thus it created a circle of safety. Fire after dark provided light and warmth for ancient people, enabling them to remain awake and active for longer. It must have given them an extraordinary sense of power: the ability to exercise control over a natural energy and push back the boundaries of night time darkness, to keep warm, to cook food, and to enable productive work to continue a little longer. They could have spent their evenings doing things involved in the development of language, family and community solidarity, friendship, art and music, and the beginning of culture. Philosophy itself could begin: people could now confront the unknown and the mysterious with curiosity and wonder instead of with fear. Gazing at the moving and changing light from the flames and glowing embers may have stimulated the minds of ancient people, instilling curiosity, and thereby preparing them for abstract thought. Perhaps fire has that feeling of familiarity because it has been with us for so long, and our use of it has made us what we are.

From the perspective of magic, a fire after dark could have been the first "scrying device." A scrying device is an object used as a visual aid in meditation, that helps to induce a mild hypnotic trance state. Smoky glass mirrors, crystal balls, bowls of water, shiny metal disks or dishes, candles and flames, and so on, are typical examples. The movement of light and shadow in generally repetitive patterns is what seems to make them work. This is what fire does—its light is always in motion, even as mere glowing embers. And as it is in motion, it appears to be alive. Also, its smoke rises up to the sky and disappears, giving the impression that the essence or the spirit of the fire is always reaching up to the celestial world above. So the smoke could carry messages up to the world of the gods. Diodorus Siculus wrote that the Celts did exactly that: at funerals

Statue of Brighid near her sacred well in Kildare.

where the deceased was cremated, people wrote messages on sticks and burned them in the fire, believing that the deceased friend or relative would be able to receive the message. The appearance of the smoke vanishing into the air as it flies upwards makes it a natural symbol for communication to the Otherworld. For as the smoke disappears, it seems to have gone everywhere and nowhere—it must then have gone to the Otherworld. It is not an accident, then, that fire came to be represented as a gift from a god (for instance from Prometheus, in the Greek world), used as a deposit for offerings and sacrifices, and even worshipped as the presence of a god in its own right.

The Celtic tradition has a fire deity as well: Brighid, pagan goddess and Christian saint. In a church in the Irish town of Kildare there is a "perpetual" fire kept in honor of Saint Brighid, the abbess of an early Christian convent who died on or close to the year A.D. 524 The site of this convent was a Druidic sanctuary before the coming of Christianity, as indicated by the very name "Kildare" itself, from the Irish *Cill Dara* meaning "oak-church." The goddess was also a patron of poets and musicians, and an early text on poetry claims that the goddess appears to poets while they are composing. The saint was also patron to midwives (she was the midwife of Christ himself, as the legend goes), and also a patron of milk cows, herbs, blacksmithing, and the morning dew. The use of fire is common to the religion of both Brighids. One meaning of the name "Brighid" is "fiery arrow." The perpetual fire, which had been burning since pagan times, was ordered extinguished by the bishop of Kildare around the year 1220. It was relit in 1996 by the Brigandine nuns, in a public ceremony in which nine women carried torches from Brighid's Well, just south of the town, to the grotto where the ancient fire was kept.

It is partly in relation to Her that the experience of being inspired by poetry or music came to be called "the fire in the head." The earliest use of this phrase in the Celtic tradition is in the Song of Amergin, and it also appears in the poetry of an ancient Welsh seer named Talieson. Yeats wrote that a fire in the head caused Wandering Aengus to enter a hazel wood to try to catch the Salmon of Knowledge. In acknowledgment of all these associations, a perpetual fire is something that every Celtic household should have. A safe and easy to maintain perpetual fire can be kept in a modern home using, for example, a fat candle. Here is part of a prayer from the Carmina Gadelica called "Kindling the Fire," which can be used when lighting the candle or when transferring the flame from an old candle to a new one.

I will raise the hearth-fire
As Mary would.
The encirclement of Bride and of
*   Mary*
On the fire, and on the floor,
And on the household all.[8]

Mary and Bride, the saints called upon in this prayer, correspond to Danu, the progenitor of the gods, and Brighid, the goddess beloved by Christians and pagans alike.

7. The Flash from the Sun

Another device that Celts and pre-Celtic people used to approach the mysteries of the world was the *sundial,* the first time-keeping device. The world's first sun dial could have been a single standing stone in the middle of a cleared field. A simple upright column called a *gnomon,* placed in a field

Celtic cross slab with sundial, in Inis Mor.

large enough for its shadow to be measured all year long, will enable a community to measure time for various purposes connected to seasonal food production: planting time, harvest time, hunting time. Celtic Christian communities made sundials with sticks set into upright stone slabs. The word "gnomon" comes from the word "gnosis," an ancient word for knowledge—thus the "gnomon" is a stone that "knows." It is the scientific instrument by which the ancient Druids obtained the knowledge of cosmology and metaphysics for which they were famous. For the sundial enables us to measure time and understand the world mathematically, as the movement of the gnomon's shadow by the hour and by the day is measured. In that measurement is the beginning of astrology and prophesy, as well as the hard sciences. For the simple idea that the world can be measured is also the deep idea that *the world is intelligible*, and perhaps predictable and controllable as well.

The fact that so many Neolithic monuments in Western Europe have solar and stellar alignments is now well known. When Gerald Hawkins published *Stonehenge Decoded,* this fact was a new discovery. Ancient people had constructed stone circles and passage mounds as elaborate and complicated sundials. These buildings were gateways to the mathematical purity of the celestial realms. Martin Brennan has demonstrated convincingly that some of the rock art designs on these

monuments are best understood in the context of the play of light and shadow cast on them by the movement of the sun through the course of the year. [9] Solar and lunar calendars are represented in the rock art shapes, including the most complex astronomical figures like the solar analemma (the figure-8 shape made over the course of a year by the sun's changing daily high-noon position).

The gnomon portends the future. But this is not a psychic or supernatural portent. The sundial grants the ability to measure time, and so places us into a relationship with the past and the future. It reveals time to be structured cyclically. We now know that this cyclical effect is produced by the rotation of the Earth on an axis tilted from the plane of the Earth's orbit around the sun. But from the point of view of an observer standing on the Earth, measuring how the sun changes its rising and setting places on the horizon each day, the sun keeps a predictable annual cycle. In these cycles, there is hope: winter-dormant plants will grow again and winter-darkened skies will brighten. The future is always a great unknown, but the gnomon presents us with a future to be hopeful for.

8. Passage Mounds and Interior Worlds

It is now entering wide acceptance, although not without controversy, that these buildings were gateways not only to celestial realms for scientific and social purposes such as timekeeping, but also to interior realms. For most of the stone circles and passage tombs in Celtic countries have properties which are useful for practices designed to induce altered states of consciousness. Several archaeologists have argued that art carved into the stones of Irish megalithic monuments were inspired by imagery spontaneously produced by the brain of a person in a hypnotic trance, and that the interior construction was designed to facilitate trance-inducing stimuli.

Interior of passage mound on Sliabh na Calleach.

First of all, the interior chambers of passage mounds are dark. No light enters them unless it is refracted from the entrance or brought into the chamber with candles and torches. Sounds do not normally enter from outside either, as the clay and earth of the mound absorbs sounds from outside, and the narrow chamber passage normally permits sounds only from sources directly in its line. Passage mounds are environments of sensory deprivation. Although there are many variations in the basic layout of the interior, the overwhelming majority have a long narrow passageway leading to a larger chamber with a high ceiling and two or three side chambers, forming a T shape or a cross. The effect of sunlight, which enters the chamber only on the special day of the mound's alignment, is already well known. Less well known is that these chambers have properties that make them conducive to producing extraordinary hypnotic effects with sound. The walls of dry stone reflect sound. A group of people chanting or intoning musical sounds with their voices, or playing drums in different ways, perhaps also using the drums to modulate the sound of the voice, can make people in the room think that the sound is coming from everywhere and nowhere in the chamber. Passage mounds can even *amplify* sounds produced in their interiors. The interaction of propagating sound waves and the shape of the stone walls produces high volume sounds (up to 120 decibels) at frequencies that are well *below* the threshold of human hearing (two beats per minute). This phenomenon is called Helmholtz Resonance, and its physiological effects on the human body can be profound. Volunteers exposed to low frequency sound generated by drumming in Camster Round, a passage mound in northeast Scotland, described dizziness, changes to their breathing and pulse, and a feeling of "ascent," as if about to levitate.[10] This may have added to the trance effect produced in people's minds during ceremonies inside passage mounds and chambered cairns.

Long passages and tunnels are also a common element in altered states of consciousness, such as in near-death experiences, or people induced to hallucinate due to severe illnesses, extreme sensory deprivation, drug-taking, or rhythmic sounds. This appears to be a near-universal, cross cultural experience. Here is one possible reason why. The area in the temporal lobe of the brain which is responsible for processing motion through space responds to four basic types of motion: expansion/contraction, rotation, spiralling, and linear movement through space. Thus when the temporal lobe has been confused by sensory deprivation, drug use, hypnotic sound, and the like, it tends to produce images of spirals, caves, tunnels, and passages. The English archaeologist Jeremy Dronfield has argued that this neurological effect explains the spiral shaped carvings in the stones of Ireland's megalithic passage mounds. Someone experiencing a trance state during a ritual in a passage mound would see these spiral images in his mind. It would then be natural for him to illustrate the structure with signs representative of the activities and experiences which takes place in it. The building's physical passage itself becomes part of the journey. The seeker distances herself from the outside world, following a passage that takes her into the darkness of the mound's interior, which is designed to recall caves and the dark interior spaces of the Earth. Then she follows another passage, this time a subjective, perceptual "passage" in her mind, to a destination in the Otherworld. The places described on the other side of the tunnel are numerous in kind, and less easy to explain as the effects of confusion in the neural network of the brain's visual cortex. All sorts of different landscapes, cities, and celestial realms are reported, although the most common experience seems to be meetings with dead friends and relatives. Perhaps this is because people experiencing these visions believed themselves to be dying, or travelling in spirit to the places where the dead "live," and so their visions confirmed their expectations. This would also have made it seem appropriate to use the passage mounds as places to bury their dead, or deposit the cremated ashes. Rock art in passage mounds may also therefore represent the relation of the living to the dead.[11]

What interests me more than the search for an explanation from neurology, astronomy, or occultism, is the effect it would have on the seeker's view of who she is, and the meaning and purpose of her life. Someone undergoing this experience would have had to possess great integrity of character. She would need it to control fear and to make sense of the spiralling, tunnel-travelling, disorienting visions produced by the journey to the

Otherworld. The things that appear in the vision would surely have an sort of timeless, overwhelming, and authoritative presence, the kind of presence we normally say is the experience of God, or of a deep spiritual mystery. Here it is not important whether these things are just the products of a confused brain, an actual vision granted by spirits, or an actual flight of the seeker's soul to celestial or cthonic spiritual realms. In response to the things encountered in the vision, a person would have to develop special qualities such as bravery, open-mindedness, calmness, and willpower. She would need intelligence to distinguish the "signal" from the "noise." These qualities would also be valuable in other parts of her life.

9. The Magical Game

Games, especially those which have an element of chance in them, have been a part of the practice of magic for millennia. Magical games probably began as prayers or offerings to a deity, in return for which a sign from the deity was expected: an unusual shape of a cloud, a passing bird or animal, a lightning flash, a gust of wind from an auspicious direction. This may have depended on knowing complex correspondences of cardinal directions, colors, animals, and the like, with esoteric meanings of various kinds. The folk practice known as "fith-fath," described earlier, probably functioned this way. Eventually this evolved into a more controlled activity with simplified rules, reduced or eliminated ritual and ceremony, and standard correspondences: in other words, games. Instead of waiting for random events in nature, we created random events on demand: a fall of notched sticks, bones, coins, colored rocks, and so on. Such actions were believed to provide messages about the future, one's fortune, one's fate and destiny. Each sign, picture, letter or number, or other symbol, refers to a particular force, influence, experience, or idea. Randomly turning up one or more of these signs in a reading transmits messages from the gods or from the hidden powers which influence the selection. They reveal themselves through the random selection—and so the fall of Rune stones, the shuffling of a Tarot deck, and so on, appear to be not really random at all, but the working of higher or deeper esoteric powers. The idea is that divine forces and powers which affect the world and your life also affect the random fall of the stones, enabling us to learn more about the nature of such forces and their present intentions. In a poem called "Time and the Witch Vivianne," Yeats refers to dice throwing as "food for antiquarian meditation." The magic game uses randomness to reveal the hidden order of the world.

A good evening's gambling with a divination game may have helped ancient people entertain themselves when it was winter and there was little or no work to do. It played a part in special holy days when the mysterious powers of the world seem closer, and important events such as marriages, births, battles, plantings and harvests, large construction projects, and so on. "Winners" could enjoy the thought that they have good luck coming to them, and could boast about what they will do with it. Those who "lost," those who find that bad luck will befall them, could enjoy being the recipient of special help and attention, or could boast about how they were strong enough to overcome it. Playing for luck could be as much fun as playing for money. Party games for special times of the year such as Halloween, New Year's Eve, or special occasions such as weddings, may have evolved from ancient divination games.

Yet we also consult such games when we are puzzled by a choice or decision. It is generally assumed that these kinds of games are magically effective forms of problem-solving: they enable us to gain knowledge which we would not gain through ordinary means, and thus they help clarify an issue or inspire a different perspective. They tell us about forces and powers at work in the world which are affecting one's life, and thus one may know whether some choice is favored or not favored.

Basic Ogham Divination. Draw a circle on the ground, the floor, a sheet of paper or of cloth. The circle should be about as wide as two lengths of your hand. Think of this circle as a sacred place, and as a model of the cosmos. You may wish to make marks on the four cardinal directions to indicate this. In accord with the division of Ireland into four provinces: the right (east) side of the circle is for materialistic matters; the bottom (south) side for artistic and creative matters; the left (west) side for matters to do with knowledge, information, and the intellect; the top (north) side to do with conflict and challenges. The circle may also represent the Wheel of the Year: spring in the east, summer in the south, autumn in the west, winter in the north.

Place 20 small finger-length sticks, each carved with the Ogham letter for a tree, into a bag. Select five sticks at random from the bag, without looking, and drop them into the circle. Assume that the sticks which land inside the circle are more important than those which land outside. Also consider the possible relations with the place in the circle, where each stick lands. Look also for any of the chieftain trees, which are the oak, hazel, apple, yew, holly, ash, and pine/silver fir, and consider what meaning might be communicated whether they fall inside or outside the circle.

Here is a description of the 20 trees of the Ogham. I have included a short description of the species, and some possible ways their appearance in an Ogham casting may be interpreted which I admit are entirely my own creation.

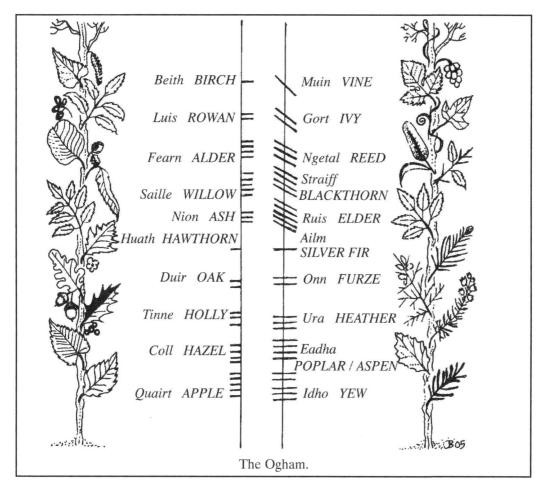

Beith BIRCH

Luis ROWAN

Fearn ALDER

Saille WILLOW

Nion ASH

Huath HAWTHORN

Duir OAK

Tinne HOLLY

Coll HAZEL

Quairt APPLE

Muin VINE

Gort IVY

Ngetal REED

Straiff
BLACKTHORN

Ruis ELDER

Ailm
SILVER FIR

Onn FURZE

Ura HEATHER

Eadha
POPLAR / ASPEN

Idho YEW

The Ogham.

- *Beith* (BEH) the Birch.

    A hardwood tree that can grow as much as 100 feet high. It reproduces quickly and can tolerate acidic soils, and so is often one of the first trees to colonize an area that has been logged. The birch's white paper-like bark makes it stand out brightly in a forest. Its thin, flexible branches were often used to make brooms, and at traditional "handfasting" weddings young couples would leap over a Birch broom to symbolize the clean new start they were making together.

    Interpreted: Beginnings, initiations, new things, quickness, brightness, cleansing, marriages.

- *Luis* (LOO-ish) the Rowan or Mountain Ash.

    A hardwood tree with red berries and small leaves that grow in groups. It can grow up to 50 feet tall. Birds enjoy the berries and the tree depends on the birds for the distribution of its seeds. A rowan branch hung somewhere in one's house was reputed to protect the house from thieves, lightning, and from curses. In Ireland the Rowan, and not the Oak, was the sacred Druidic tree.

Interpreted: Protection, sustenance, prosperity, security, survival.

⊕ *Fearn* (FERN) the Alder.

A broad leaf hardwood that thrives in dry soils of mountainous regions, but is also found near streams with Willows. The Alder fixes nitrogen into the soil and can be used to reclaim land from bogs and shallow ponds.

Interpreted: Alliances, shelters, rescuing, defending, things associated with masculinity and with the warrior.

⊕ *Saille* (SHALL-yuh) the Willow.

A tall tree that prefers to grow near streams and lakes. The willow's branches are very flexible, excellent for basket weaving and used in the wattle walls of Celtic roundhouses.

Interpreted: Flexibility, change, rapid growth, softness, beauty, receptiveness, things associated with the feminine, especially motherhood.

⊕ *Nion* (NEE-on) the Ash. A Chieftain Tree.

A tall hardwood tree which prefers lowland forests. It is the preferred wood for house posts, in part because of its sturdiness, but also because

the Norse "world tree," Yggdrasil, was an Ash tree, and so an Ash house-post makes one's house like a temple. Sick children would be passed through hollows in the trunk, as a form of healing magic. The Ash was the preferred wood for the sticks used in the game of hurling.

Interpreted: Unity, prosperity, sacredness, healing, completion.

⊕ *Huath* (HOO-ah) the Hawthorn.

A shrub tree with sharp thorns, and yellow or white flowers that bloom in early spring. This tree "guards" the soil in which it is planted. In the hollows of its roots it is easy to imagine windows and doors to faerie houses. It was considered bad luck to cut a hawthorn tree, and one could burn its wood only on certain days of the year.

Interpreted: Magic, guardianship, gateways, shelter, protection, springtime, fertility, boundaries.

⊕ *Duir* (DOO-ir) the Oak. A Royal Tree.

A broad-leaf hardwood tree which prefers forests and can grow as much as 150 feet and live as long as 900 years. It loses leaves roughly around Samhain, and grows its spring leaves usually in time for Bealtaine, hence why the Oak King "rules" for that half of the year (the Holly rules the other half). The oak was, for Druids of the continent, the most kingly of trees, perhaps due to its height, its sturdiness (it is an excellent wood for building houses) and because the mistletoe, a plant sacred to them for its alleged healing properties, grows on oak trees struck by lightning.

Interpreted: Wisdom, knowledge, strength, endurance, sturdiness, robustness, durability, authority, majesty, rulership.

- *Tinne* (CHIN-yuh) the Holly. A Royal Tree.

An shrub tree which thrives in hedges and the outskirts of forests. Its red berries are usually ready around Samhain. As it is an evergreen, it remains clothed in its sharply pointed green leaves while most other hardwoods are bare. Thus the Holly king "rules" the forest from Samhain to Bealtaine (the Oak rules the other half of the year). Cú Chullain uses holly as a weapon in several parts of his story.

Interpreted: Challenges, tests, ordeals, perseverance, festivals, celebrations, trickery, gift-giving.

- *Coll* (KOLL) the Hazel. A Chieftain Tree.

A shrub tree, but a tall one—often reaching 20 feet high—which prefers scrub forests.

Its hazelnuts are sweet and sought after by humans and animals alike. According to legend, nine hazel trees grow around the Well of Wisdom, and nuts from these trees were eaten by the Salmon of Knowledge who brings the knowledge back to humanity.

Interpreted: Wisdom, time, prophesy, knowledge, dreams, visions, inspiration, messages, enlightenment.

- *Quairt* (KWAIR-t) the Apple. A Chieftain Tree.

A broad-leafed hardwood with beautiful five-petal flowers. Of all the different kinds of apples, the apple of the Ogham was most probably the common crabapple, whose fruit is smaller and more sour than the apples in today's supermarkets.

Interpreted: Magic, wonder, beauty, mystery, food, material prosperity, gifts, beauty, the Otherworld, love, things associated with the feminine especially childhood and young womanhood. Separately from the Celtic tradition, it is also associated with "forbidden knowledge," temptation, sensuality, sin, and rebellion, because of the apple which Eve picked and gave to Adam.

- *Muin* (MUHN) the Vine.

A long lanky plant which clings to walls and other trees for support. Its stems can reach 30 feet long or more. The Ogham vine may have been the grape, although this is a rare plant in Britain and Ireland.

Interpreted: Desire, striving, sweetness, seduction, reaching for goals.

- *Gort* (GORT) the Ivy.

  The ivy is a creeping plant with wide leaves and short branches, that grows quickly to cover whatever surface it clings to (trees, buildings, etc.).

  Interpreted: Ambition, attainment, adornment and decoration, clinging on to others for support, stealing the strength of others.

- *Ngetal* (NYETT-l) the Reed.

  The reed of the Ogham is probably the giant grassy weed of the bogs and peatlands which can grow as high as 12 feet. In low winds reeds make a whispering sound that can be very ghostly and unnerving.

  Interpreted: Danger, unsettled times and situations, shifting focus, transience, quickness, surprise, fear.

- *Straiff* (STRAY-if) the Blackthorn.

  A thorny shrub with bitter tasting dark blue fruit. One would use a blackthorn walking stick to ward off malevolent spirits while travelling. But one must not bring blackthorn into the house.

The English word "strife," meaning hardship, and "to strive" meaning to work for a goal, are related to the name of this tree.

Interpreted: Danger, the destructive side of nature, darkness, loss, ghosts, barriers, obstacles, challenges, difficulties.

- *Ruis* (ROO-is) the Elder.

  A shrub tree with purple-black berries which prefers clearings and often grows near human settlements. A branch which breaks off from it can be pushed into the ground to take root as a new tree.

  Interpreted: Home, safety, security, the moon, things associated with the feminine during the later stages in life.

- *Ailm* (ALE-im) the Silver Fir. A Chieftain Tree.

  A member of the Pine family, and one of the only native evergreen coniferous trees in the British isles. It can grow in the poorest soils, and as its needles are acidic it often crowds out other species. It is the preferred tree for Christmas decorating.

  Interpreted: High places, mountains, perseverance, fire, the winter.

- *Onn* (UHN) the Furze or Gorse

  A small thorny shrub which grows in hedges, open

woodlands and pastures, and tends to clump together with others of its kind. Its distinctive yellow flowers bloom a few weeks before Beltaine and smell like coconut.

Interpreted: Springtime, growth, change, transformation, companionship, friendship.

⊛ *Ura* (OO-ra) the Heather.

There are several plants called Heather, including a mossy ground-hugging plant that grows on Scottish hills. The Heather of the Ogham is probably the 6-foot tall shrub which produces pink flowers near the end of the summer. From the name of this plant we get the word "Heathen," originally meaning someone who lives among the heather.

Interpreted: Hidden things, revealed things, surprises, the unexpected.

⊛ *Eadha* (EH-ha) the Poplar or Aspen.

A broadleaf hardwood that grows tall and thin, and is often the first to colonize an area that has been destroyed by fire.

Interpreted: Pride, stature, honor, status, reputation.

⊛ *Idho* (EE-uh) the Yew. A Chieftain Tree.

A very tall coniferous tree with broad evergreen needles. Because of its flexibility, the yew was the favored wood for making longbows. It exudes a mild poison which can make one ill if one fell asleep under its boughs. Yews are among the most long-lived of European trees—they can survive for more than 1,000 years—and their branches can bend down, touch the earth, and grow roots of their own to become new trees. They are traditionally planted in churchyards and graveyards.

Interpreted: Death, poison, longevity, mortality, old age, funerals, graveyards, rebirth, time.

There is, however, a deeper meaning to magic games like these. An effective divination device associates meaningful truths, ideas, and messages with *all of its signs*, and defines them broadly enough that *any of them may be true at any time*. We cast them at random, then we interpret the spread while meditating carefully on the ideas symbolized by what turns up. Then the reader finds herself believing that the idea was especially selected for her at that moment. And whatever her conclusions may be, the reader reconfirms the belief that the world is infused with magic, wonder, beauty, and, especially, purpose, and meaning. As previously described, the hidden purpose of magic is not so much to understand or control the world, but to satisfy our senses of wonder.

The hidden secret behind divination games such as Tarot cards, Runes, and other similar things is that, by using them, we trick ourselves into paying special attention to the philosophical message or meaning signified in the randomly-selected stone, coin, or card. To get caught up in the game is to trick ourselves into thinking the message is specifically for the reader, when it is, in fact, for all of us. Whether or not the magic of such games is real, whether or not they really do predict the future or reveal occult forces at work in one's situation, the games are tools for inducing thought and changing perspective. Interpreting the results of the spread of rune stones or Tarot cards, we are sometimes carried into a spiritual attitude, and we think about our lives more broadly than we normally do.

10. The Spirit of the Green Man

The technology of brewing and fermentation was another evolutionary leap in spiritual consciousness. The production of wine and the fermentation of fruit into alcohol are among the oldest and most potent natural symbols of psychological transformation and religious enlightenment. The fermentation process is a process by which the properties and qualities of various ordinary substances are changed. This symbolically corresponds to the process of becoming a transformed person, able to attain variously defined spiritual achievements. Today, fermentation is a well understood chemical and biological process.

But when the process was discovered and harnessed, at some unknown time in humanity's ancient history, it would have been seen as magic. For the properties of water, plant matter, and the other material ingredients, when treated with fire (another magical technology!) and allowed time, they are transformed into a substance possessing *very* different properties. To a people who did not have the scientific knowledge which we have today, the process would have seemed magical, the work of mysterious powers or spiritual beings. The word that modern occultists use for chemical reactions that symbolize spiritual transformations is "alchemy." Fermentation becomes a natural alchemy if one perceives that the same mysterious forces are apparently involved in the transformation of a person from a child to an adult to an elder. Metallurgy, blacksmithing, and even cooking are related natural symbols for spiritual transformation. The blacksmith transforms base "dead" materials such as copper and iron, into new "living" substances with different properties like bronze and steel, again using the semi-magical agency of fire. And the animals and plants we cook and eat, and the harvest seasons when they become available, symbolically links the community to life-and-death cycles in the environment such as seasonal changes, the passage of the sun, and the phases of the moon.

As everyone knows, fermentation produces alcohol. The very aim of the practice of brewing is to produce this chemical, which is a semi-magical substance because a semi-magical process created it and because it has properties which ordinary liquids do not have. It can catch fire, for example. And when consumed it produces the light-headed, uninhibited state we all know as drunkenness, which can bring pleasure or sickness to the body, and great clarity or great disorientation to the mind. Drunkenness is an age-old metaphor of spiritual bliss. The drunkenness effect can be seen as the spirit of the fruit or grain temporarily inhabiting the body and mind of the alcohol-drinker. The particular power which the process of fermentation appears to invoke is the spirit of the fruit or grains from which the wine or ale is made. Thus, among the gifts which the many gods of agriculture gave to humanity, which includes the seeds for our crops and the knowledge of how to make them grow, there is also the gift of the knowledge to create beer and wine as well. This is part of the poetry of harvest-time folk songs which personify the spirit of the plant as "John Barleycorn" or "Jack in the Green." Alcohol is also used in some rituals associated with ancestors and with hunting, where it apparently serves as a substitute for blood. It can substitute for the blood of ancestors which flows in our veins, the blood of animals killed in the hunt, and the hunter's own blood offered to the animals in return.

Drunkenness also produces stupidity, clumsiness, and aggression. Alcohol is an addictive, poisonous substance. If alcohol is thought of as a sacred substance we would regard intoxication and addiction as not just physically and socially destructive, but spiritually degrading as well. The experience of alcohol is the "spirit" of the plant because it enables the drinker to know what the plant-spirit knows, and to see the world as the plant-spirit sees it. "Jack in the Green" knows the world to be a realm of pleasure, inspiration, camaraderie, and play. He sees the world as a realm of beauty, growth, transformation, and love. Yet he has a dark side: violence, wickedness, rage, and death. These too are brought to the foreground by his gift on some occasions. For nature is, on one level, also harsh, brutal, and deeply impersonal. To deify the mind-altering qualities of alcohol is also to deify some of our vices and not just our virtues. It is thus a double-edged sword.

I recommend to any reader interested in brewing to obtain a good book of brewing recipes which also includes comments on proper use of equipment, proper cleanliness precautions, and so on. One may wish to add "magical" ingredients to the brew: a small (clean!) pebble carved with a magical symbol, for instance, could be dropped into the demijohn in order to impart to the final product the quality of being well suited for a particular meditative or ceremonial purpose. I like to put together a new wine on or close to one of the eight annual festivals in the old Celtic calendar. This makes it easier for me to remember when they will be ready, and magically associates the wine with the season in which it is made. As much as possible, obtain your ingredients locally, from a farmer's market for instance, in order to produce a brew which is in season for your area, and which is connected with the environment where you live. The man who taught me to brew wine, who for his excellent brewing skill was known in my clann as "The Lubricator," used to collect wild mulberries along the banks of a local river every year around Lughnasad. He produced a wine that was part of the season, quite literally a taste of the season itself. Thus he helped to keep all of us tuned to our environment.

11. Returning Home

When the ceremony or magic-working is complete, it can be psychologically helpful and dramatically elegant to do something which disbands the circle and resumes ordinary space and time. Here is a simple way to do so.

Resuming Normal Time and Space. Starting in the North, and in a counter-clockwise direction, disband the circle with words of thanks and blessings to each quarter, as follows: "Spirits of the North (West/South/East), I thank you for your presence in this circle. The ceremony is finished. Go if you must, but stay if you will. Come again at the time of your calling, the time of our need, and in your proper season. Slan leat, agus go rath maith agut (Goodnight and thank you)."

Returning to the center. Extinguish the fire, turn the cup upside-down, and

say, "I declare the circle is complete. Thanks and a safe journey to all who partook of the work accomplished here. Slan leat, agus go rath maith agut. Farewell, and Blessed be."

The use of magical techniques like these can give one the feeling of coming into more knowledge of the gods and mystical powers of the world—whose qualities are, at the end of the day, exaltations of our own, whether positive or negative, whether real or desired. It is thus a set of practices which, indirectly, subversively, bring us into knowledge of ourselves. They do this by stimulating our sense of wonder. The gods of plant life, like the Green Man, have big bushy beards, long thick hair, heavy builds like tree trunks, and warm cheeky faces from centuries of youthful exuberance and big-hearted laughter, representing the energy and virility of life. However, to those who do not give him his due, which means to give him the space to be himself, he plays vicious tricks which reflect the hard-hearted person's own resentment. The maiden-goddesses of spring planting and agriculture have well-endowed hips and breasts, big eyes, long thick hair, and a disposition to be generous and playful, also representing material prosperity and abundance, and enjoyment of life. Of course she also deals harshly with those who treat her poorly or spurn her gifts. When Cú Chullain refused the Morrigan's love, she attacked him by becoming an eel and causing him to trip and fall during his fight with

Ferdiad. These are our deities. These are our virtues and our vices. We find this idea in a poem by Yeats called "The Indian Upon God," in which an Indian hears a duck, a lotus flower, a roebuck, and a peacock all describe God as one of their own kind. Blake observed it in his poem *The Divine Image*, one of his "Songs of Innocence," where he said:

> *For Mercy has a human heart*
> *Pity a human face.*
> *and Love, the human form divine,*
> *and Peace, the human dress.*

This is an ancient idea, recognized by philosophers throughout history, from Lucretius and Xenophan in the ancient world, Spinoza in the Renaissance, and in the modern world by Feuerbach and Nietzsche. The direction to "know yourself," the initiating principle of Mysticism, leads directly to this extraordinary realization. Furthermore, Blake astutely observed in one of his "Songs of Experience," *A Divine Image*, that the same principle is at work in some of our vices: "Cruelty has a human heart/and Jealousy a human face."[12] This is, as I see it, one of the unacknowledged secrets of pagan spiritual life.

This concludes my short tour of some of the simple things that have traditionally been a part of the practice of magic. They are fairly simple: one can try them out and benefit from them even with only a "suspension of disbelief," so to speak. There are other practices in the Celtic tradition which require more than just a superficial shift in attitude and perspective. They entail transformations of consciousness itself. These activities serve as preparation tasks. Let us turn to these deeper activities now.

Five:

The Fire in the Head
and The Sea Journey

Beloved, gaze in thine own heart.
The holy tree is growing there...
—William Butler Yeats,
The Two Trees

By this time you should have been practicing the simple meditation of Peaceful Abiding for at least a season or two, and are able to enter the Spiritual Attitude, the state of relaxed receptiveness to the world. For it is my experience, and the experience of most spiritual people whom I have known, that by first establishing a dialogue with the world through the spiritual attitude, the world begins to respond.

1. Divine Inspiration

The spiritual attitude, which the meditation of Peaceful Abiding cultivates, is the attitude of mind that looks at the world and finds within it things which symbolize, or manifest, a spiritual presence. At some point in the practice these presences might seem to thrust themselves upon one's perceptions apparently of their own initiative. You may be engaged in the most mundane and ordinary tasks, when suddenly a glimpse of the sky through a window catches your attention. Perhaps when introduced to someone by a friend, you find a certain light around the edges of his or her face, and a sudden fleeting thought of another time and place enters your mind, as if you knew this person before. You may be walking through a forest, a garden, or even a city neighborhood, and feel an unignorable feeling of familiarity for the place. This is what happens when, by means of the spiritual attitude, the soul-energies within us are stirred, aroused, and then through action circulated into the world and back into our perceptions again. This was called "the eye of piety" by a visionary living in the west of Ireland who described to William Butler Yeats the manner in which one can see the gods, faeries, ghosts, otherworldly castles and islands. It is sometimes also called "the world of faerie," momentarily revealing itself from behind the veil of the ordinary world. One's perceptual range of awareness constitutes a world in itself, and when that world starts to include subtle magical notes and accents such as these, then one is entering a new perceptual world. Things remain what they are, and yet they become more than what normally meets the eye.

Some people have a greater sense of the spiritual presence behind and within the normal world than others. While most people feel little more than emotional pulls of familiarity or repugnance towards particular sights, sounds, people, and places, or perhaps fleeting glimpses of unidentified movement in the peripheral vision, some rare few are able to enter whole new perceptual worlds. The Irish mystic George Russell, also known as "A.E.," was such a person, and he described what it is like in his work on spiritual perception from a Celtic perspective, *The Candle of Vision*:

I could not escape from it even in that busy office where I sat during week-days with little heaps of paper mounting up before me moment by frenzied moment. An interval of inactivity and I would be aware of that sweet eternal presence overshadowing me. I was an exile from living nature but she yet visited me. Her ambassadors were visions that made me part of themselves. Through the hot fetid air of the gas-lit room I could see the feverish faces, the quick people flitting about, and hear the voices; and

then room, faces, and voices would be gone, and I would be living in the Mother's being in some pure, remote, elemental region of hers. Instead of the dingy office there would be a sky of rare amethyst; a snow-cold bloom of cloud; high up in the divine wilderness, solitary, a star; all rapt, breathless and still; rapt in the seraph princes of wind and wave and fire, for it was the hour when the King, an invisible presence, moved through His dominions and Nature knew and was hushed at the presence of her Lord.[1]

Russell's capacity for vision was so strong that he would be perceptually transported to another world completely, even while in the most mundane environments like the printer's office where he worked at the time. In this otherworldly realm, as we read in his text, the world is much the same as our world except that the presence of even the smallest element was heightened to the level of the immensity. Everything has a presence that can hold one in a state of aesthetic arrest, captured and even overwhelmed with beauty, peace, love, and even sorrow. The other thing to notice about this passage is Russell's claim that the experience of the sacred can happen in very nearly any situation, so long as the seeker has the right attitude.

Let us explore a technique for inducing that state of mind. The generation of energy by means of *Imbas* is a powerful magical technique and at the same time an opportunity for the seeker to psychologically unbalance himself. For these activities require the seeker to put her mind into a mild trance state. Before attempting to gain Imbas for the first time, try these preliminary exercises for a season or so first.

Controlled Breathing. Sit down by your meditation-place and take a moment to obtain the spiritual attitude through Peaceful Abiding. Breathe out, and as you do think the phrase, "I am breathing out." Breathe in, and think as you do, "I am breathing in." Take as much time with each breath as is needed to think the phrase fully.

Lengthen the rate of breath each time. You can do this by using a longer meditative phrase to think while you breath. Breathe in, thinking, "As I breathe in, I breathe in the world." Breathe out, thinking, "As I breathe out, I breathe myself into the world."

Lengthen your breaths again. Breathe in, thinking, "As I breathe in, I breathe into myself the energy of the world." Breathe out, thinking, "As I breathe out, I breathe the energy of myself into the world."

The words of the mantra ("I am breathing in"), and the power attributed to them, may be different from one tradition to another. But the breath exercise is common to almost all magical practices around the world. It has been especially refined in Eastern traditions such as Yoga, Tantra, and Zen.

As you practice controlled breathing, you may become aware of the cycling of energy within your body. This feeling is, in part, brought on by the way in which the exercise forces your lungs to process oxygen differently. It is possible to accidentally hyperventilate or to become light-headed and pass out. The breath exercise also has a stimulating effect on the channels of psychic energy within your body. These energy channels, by no coincidence, tend to be represented with the very same symbolism of the Axis Mundi of the spiritual world. They are in the Celtic tradition the streams that flow into and out of the Well of Wisdom. These are metaphorically represented as streams of water from a well, but as a metaphor it represents the streams of energy that flow through the body of the spiritual seeker.

This energy is in part a physical energy—the "life force" of oxygen that flows through our lungs with every breath. All the words for "spirit" in the Indo-European family of languages are rooted in ancient words for movement and breath. In Irish the word for spirit is *anam*, which has its root in the Latin word for spirit, which was *"animus,"* from which we also get English words like "animal" and "animation." Something able to move of its own accord, then, is something inhabited by spirit. Animals, plants, and people are obviously included here, along with water, fire, and the wind. The English word "spirit" comes from the Latin verb *spirare*, meaning "to breathe." Spirit is thus the movement of breath. In mystical traditions, Spirit is also the breath-movement of the psychic energy of thought and feeling that cycles through the mind on a wheel of external perception, internal consciousness and imagination, and outgoing speech and action which returns to perception again. This is the great secret to understanding spirit. It is not just a "thing" that we carry around inside us alongside our bones, muscles, and internal organs. It is an activity, a movement, a force. Spirit is not something we "have." It is something we *do*. We reveal our spirit most of all through the voice, which is, of course, carried on the vehicle of the breath. And to hear this knowledge, to receive this spirit, is pleasurable to us. We can be intoxicated by it. Spirit is energy in motion. We say of someone who is lively and energetic, spontaneous and courageous, that she is "spirited." We say the same of animals such as horses or dogs that are rambunctious and hard to tame. The experience of receiving, exercising, and producing this spirit is called in the Celtic tradition "the fire in the head."

One way to "see" these streams of energy is a meditative technique for controlling and releasing the internal sense, the imagination. This technique is known as creative visualisation. It is used by Buddhist monks, Hindu sadhus, Gnostics, Shamans, Masons, and nearly every kind of magical practitioner almost universally. It was recommended by Ignatius Loyola as "The Spiritual Exercises," his training curricula for Jesuit Catholic priests. It was recommended by the Russian drama theorist Stanislavsky for training stage actors to see their characters and thus portray them more effectively and believably. His method continues to be used in drama schools around the world. There is good circumstantial evidence that the ancient Druids knew this technique. In the darkness of the passage mound, the cave, or the souterrain (artificial cave), with nothing to stimulate the senses, the mind and the imagination "kicks into overdrive," to fill the void. A technique of creative visualisation would have enabled the seeker to make sense of the images and sensations that flood up from the imagination and subconscious. It would help her keep from being consumed by confusion or subconscious fear. The thoughts and visions which come to her would have been interpreted as the wisdom of the spirits and deities of the Otherworld. At least one archaeologist has interpreted the rock art in various passage mounds and stone circles as representative of the images that appeared in the minds of ancient Druids during dreams and shamanic trances. Newgrange is only the most famous of these structures. There are many more, such as the cairns of Sliabh na Calleach (Hill of the Witch). There are also several natural caves modified for the purpose, such as the Cave of the Cats, at Cruachan, now known as Rathcrogan, in county Roscommon.

One can further refine the controlled breathing exercise by not only thinking the words through, but also visualizing the movement of water in the streams. As one inhales, the life-refreshing water flows into your Well of Wisdom, and as one exhales, the purifying and cleansing waters flow out, taking with them all blockages and impurities. In the ancient world, those who studied meditation as a vehicle for the pursuit of enlightenment often described energy as flowing in streams through the body. One of the ways in which this flowing energy is described in the Celtic tradition is as the growing and blossoming of a magical tree. An Irish king at

The passage mound on Sliabh na Calleach.

Tara named Cathaoir Mór once had a dream of a grand and magnificent singing tree with sweet smelling flowers and abundant fruit. He asked his Druids to interpret the dream, and he was told that the tree was himself. Its fruit was his generosity, and its music was his eloquent speeches at public assemblies.

The contemporary revival of Druidry uses an exercise called the *Tree Meditation* to train the seeker in the technique of visualisation. It also enables her to balance the flow of energy within her, grounding herself so that she holds neither too much nor too little. You may want to have a helper read this text to you as you attempt the technique, until you are familiar enough with it to do it on your own.

Spring Tree Meditation. Sit down near by your meditation-place and close your eyes. Take a moment to obtain the spiritual attitude through peaceful abiding and controlled breathing.

With the eye of piety, observe the sapling of a tree emerging from the ground underneath the place you are sitting, and unfolding its first precious leaves within your body. Feel the first roots shooting down into the Earth below at the same time.

Breathe in, breathe out. See the tree strengthen and grow taller, now reaching the height of your waist, and delving equally as far under the surface of the Earth. See how its stem has become a sturdy wooden trunk.

Breathe in, breathe out. See the tree send forth its first branches as it grows up to the height of your heart. Observe the leaves unfold and grow into a healthy green canopy. Feel the roots reaching further down to towards the center of the Earth.

Breathe in, breathe out. See the tree reach into your head now, and see the branches multiply and fill out your legs, arms, and all around you. Feel the roots spreading through the ground equally as distant as the trunk and branches above.

Breathe in, breathe out. See the tree obtain its full, mature height, with its crown above your head. Feel the roots reaching down and touching the centre of the Earth. See the top-most branch reaching up and touching the sun in the sky.

The Tree meditation has a counterpart which I would like to call the Autumn Meditation. It is, in some respects, the reverse of the Tree Meditation, to come at the end of any session that began with the first meditation so that the consciousness of the seeker is returned to the ordinary world easily and gently. As can be attested by anyone who has ever passed out, unconscious from drunkenness or from a blow to the head, sudden interruptions of reality are highly disorienting. One needs a clear sense of transition from the ordinary world to the Otherworld and back again. The Autumn Meditation serves that purpose for the Tree Meditation. An experienced helper, again, can be invaluable for this purpose. Like the stone cairn, the autumn tree meditation forces a recognition of the transience of things, but leaves the seeker with the promise of future renewal.

Autumn Tree Meditation.

Breathe in, breathe out. Visualize the tree as you saw it growing within you at the beginning. Feel the depths of the roots and see the height of its branches.

Breathe in, breathe out. Observe the color of the tree changing from its deep summer green, towards the orange, yellow, and red of autumn. Feel the roots become less malleable and soft, and become more hard and sturdy.

Breathe in, breathe out. Feel a breeze from over the sea blowing across the branches. One by one, and then branch by branch, feel the leaves flowing in the breeze and then detaching, carried away in the wind. See the branches recede as they loose their leaves. Feel the roots dissolving into the soil, first at the tips and then up towards the tree.

Breathe in, breathe out. See the height of the tree come down, as the branches weaken and fall off, or wither and retract. See them become covered with grass and soil where they fall.

Breathe in, breathe out. Now all that is left is the remains of a trunk surrounded by the branches and leaves on the ground where they fell. But look between the roots of the tree: a single acorn fell there. Know that, with this acorn, the great tree within you can be replanted and reborn.

Breathe in, breathe out, and open your eyes.

Experiment with these techniques. When the tree is fully grown, hold it there for a length of time and explore it in your mind. What species of tree is it? How many branches does it have? Are any birds or animals living in it? What does it feel like to have this tree growing inside you? While holding the meditative image in your mind, you may begin to find details and features which appear to you and which do not feel as if produced with your own effort of imagination. These are the first inklings of *Imbas* entering you, and the first flickerings of a clear and sustainable eye of piety.

The tree meditation can create in your mind's eye an internalized "axis mundi," the great vertical column at the center of the four-fold world of sacred space which unites the sky with the earth. In the tree meditation, the seeker represents her own spinal column as the axis mundi of her internal world of perception, imagination, and consciousness. For the spinal column unites the body and its bones, muscles, and internal organs (the "earth") with the brain and the mind (the "sky"). It is a part of the tradition of many ancient cultures that the axis mundi within the body is a channel for the movement of psychic energy, both upward and downward, and that this energy can be projected into one's life for various purposes.

2. Imramma

Imramma means "sea journey." In the modern revival of Celtic spirituality the word has come to denote the Celtic version of the Shamanic practice of "spirit flight." The pattern of the spirit flight has been studied by anthro-pologists, theorists of religion, and by contemporary seekers for a long time. It is reflected in the mythological pattern of the Hero's Journey, and its destination is the Otherworld. In this pattern of mythic storytelling, a hero leaves the everyday world and enters a magical world where he encounters strange forces and beings. He or she is either given or must win a treasure, with which the hero returns to the mortal world. Imramma, as a form of meditation, uses this pattern of mythological storytelling to create in the mind of the seeker the impression of travelling in spirit to the Otherworld.

The Imramma is the spirit-flight to the Otherworld, and thus a more elaborate and advanced visualization than the tree meditation. Prepare a space where you will not be disturbed. Bring your Bell Branch, your cup, and drink to fill it. Wine is best because it is formed by human work and the life within it, but any natural drink, such as water or milk, will do. Apple juice is another good choice because it comes from the most magical of fruit. This is not only an offering to the guardian of the gateway, but when you ring the Bell Branch and speak the Imramma Prayer over it, it becomes the faerie food that enables the seeker to travel to the Otherworld.

Almost all seekers, as well as most anthropologists who study shamanism, magic, and indigenous religion, generally agree that spirit-flight has the following main features in some variation, either as part of the preparation ceremony, or else internalized into the vision itself. (1) A gate-way, boundary, chasm, or threshold which separates the ordinary world from the spiritual world. This boundary is usually a river, a lake, or other body of water which the seeker must cross, or it is a doorway, passage, or tunnel that the seeker must enter and pass through. There also may be more than one. (2) A guardian, gatekeeper, or a sentry on the other side of the threshold who controls access to the Otherworld. This guardian may demand a gift or a payment, or require a certain question or puzzle be solved, before the seeker is allowed to continue. Again, there may be more than one. (3) A guide, mount, boat, vehicle, or pathway which enables the traveller to navigate safely. (4) Finally, and most importantly, a particular purpose or goal which the journey seeks to achieve.

Boundaries and thresholds almost always feature in the architecture of temples. For example, the kerb-stone before the entrance to Newgrange is carved with beautiful spirals and circles that appear like the waves of the sea, although there is a vertical line in its middle which is aligned with the rays of the sun that enter the inner chamber on Midwinter morning. All the spirals on the left side of the divide are inward-spirals (that is, following the spiral-lines clockwise takes you to its center) and on the right side are outward-spirals (in which following the lines clockwise takes you to the edge). This roughly corresponds to the apparent movement of the sun in the northern

hemisphere between the two halves of the year. Newgrange was also traditionally approached from the south side of the Boyne valley, requiring travellers to cross the river Boyne to make their way towards the mound.

With these thoughts in mind, we can reproduce the Imramma as a form of meditation. It can be preceded with a short ceremonial invitation or invocation of the Mist of Manannan which includes techniques for inducing a mild trance state. For some people, the sound of someone speaking an invocation poem is hypnotic and convincing enough by itself to induce the trance. The ceremony may also include music and sound, especially from the Bell Branch, as well as candle lights, masks or veils to cover the seeker's face, and so on. Anthropologists have found that shamans around the world often use a substance of some kind: hallucinogenic plants, for instance. My own preference is for a small amount of alcohol, usually red wine. This is, in part, because it tends to relax the muscles and the mental inhibitions, and also because it can be poured out as an offering. Food and drink calls to mind the "faerie food" which captures anyone who eats it in the Otherworld. Here is an example of the trance-induction ceremony, using poetry that I wrote many years ago which I and some of my associates have found quite effective.

Summoning the Mist: *If you would seek a vision, take up your Bell Branch and go on a sea journey,* across the waves to the Otherworld, where the Well of Wisdom and its five streams and nine hazels hold all knowledge.

Face the gateway of your meditation-place. Announce to the spirits your presence and your intention to enter into their realm by ringing the Bell Branch at each of the four quarters of the circle. Ring the Bell Branch over the offering, and then cast the offering into the offering bowl to the north, the direction where the Four Cities of the Dannans were, to invite their presence and attention. Ring the bell branch over the offering and then cast the offering into the bowl to the south, where the Fomorians were, to placate them lest they disturb you.

Prayer to Summon and Part the Mist:

A cloak of mist about my home
I raise today with Manannan
That none shall see who dwells within
But I shall know all who dwell here.

Shake your cloak, O Manannan, between me and all hurtful things, As you did for fair-haired Fand And for bright Cú Chullain.

A Druid Mist about my self
I raise today with Manannan
That none shall see me as I pass
But I shall see all who pass me.

Shake your cloak, O Manannan, between me and all hurtful things, As you did for fair-haired Fand And for bright Cú Chullain.

Ring the bell branch a final time now over your cup and drink, and it will become the faerie food that takes you to the Otherworld.

Imramma Prayer:

Let the Sacred Fire be lighted
And the Old Ones be invited
Water of Life, my gift to thee
and acorn seeds, and poetry
Speak of things, forgotten far
The apple tree, the shining star
The Wonder House, the burning head
The Spiral Path that old ones tread.
And though a thousand secrets see
They all withhold one Mystery
That you were not from nature torn
You were not made, but you were born.

Drink of the faerie wine three times and share the rest with the Gods. If you have a spirit who is special kin to you, sing an invitation song to him or her, and share the drink with him or her, and he or she will accompany you as you travel.

Close your eyes, and enter the realm of faerie. If your will is strong, your intentionality relaxed, your mind without disturbance, and your sight clear, the Mist of Manannan will part for you. Then you may follow the path from your place of meditation to the shore, where waits a boat to take you to the magical Land-Under-Wave, and the grove of the Well. There you *will find good and wise friends to give an answer to your wondering.*

The journey begins when you close your eyes and visualize. Imagine the rising Druid mist that obfuscates the gates to the Otherworld surrounding you where you sit at your meditation-place. Then visualize yourself departing from your meditation place and reaching the threshold to the Otherworld in the form of a body of water with a bridge or a boat to cross it.

The guide through the Otherworld may appear here. It cannot be understated how important the guide is. In the story of the Sons of Tuireann, the three heroes take a special boat called the Ocean Skipper, with sails woven from the hair of the god Daghda, on their journey. Oisin rides to Tir na n-Og on a magical horse given to him by the goddess Niamh who rides with him. Just as in any journey across the surface of the physical Earth we consult maps, signposts, satellite GPS locators, and so on, in the geography of the Otherworld it is also useful to have the direction of a guide. Normally, in a visualized-meditation like this one, a guide will appear spontaneously, in the form of an ancestor, an animal, or even the footpath on the ground. One may eventually find the same guide appearing most times, if not every time, you attempt this meditation. It is also helpful, especially to the inexperienced, to have a human guide, who takes you through the visualization by describing the landscape in which you are travelling.

Imagine the Druids from thousands of years ago in their deep forest groves at night, or in their underground ritual chambers, the souterrains and the passage mounds. They are chanting and singing, beating drums, all focused on the one Druid who sits in the center, who is wearing a veil or a mask, and has been denied food and sleep for a day or more, and perhaps has had a bit of wine or mead. They have been there all night. After the ceremony, the singing and dancing, and so on, has gone on for some time, one of the Druids in the circle steps forward, and begins to speak to the one in the center:

The Gateway to the Grove

See yourself at the entry way of the passage mound.

It is night time, and the world is silent.

A dome of bright stars hangs over the Earth,

A grove of green trees surrounds where you stand,

A river flows past the grove of the mound.

Turn and face the mound, see the passage gate,

And see into the black interior.

You are walking into the passage now,

Leaving behind the stars, trees, and the stream

Entering the dark, entering the dark,

Entering the womb of the sacred world.

See the shadows drape the carved passage walls

As you walk deeper into the blackness.

And now you reach the great inner chamber

With its high ceiling of great vaulted stones

Deep within blackness, deep within blackness,

Deep within the womb of the sacred world.

Now turn towards the way in which you came

Facing the passage towards the outside.

See the dim light from the star-filled night sky

See how it glows with increasing brightness

Morning is coming, and with it the dawn.

Suddenly light beams stream into the chamber

The sun has awakened, and brought forth the day.

See the strong light rays push back the darkness

Feel the convergence of Earth and of Sky

Rising within you, married within you,

Bringing you love from the birth of the world.

Just as the chief Druid finishes describing the passage to the Otherworld, the sun rises and its first rays strike the seeker in the center of the circle. All drums and chanting stops. The seeker's mind is shocked into a state of "between darkness and light," between silence and sound, the state of quiet that is also the state of vision. And then he begins to speak.

That is what it may have been like in ancient times. I leave it to those who wish to reproduce this ceremony to discover the Otherworld on their own. Again, I emphasize that one should take appropriate safety precautions, such as having a helper nearby, in case the seeker hyperventilates, or falls over, or is frightened by an unexpectedly lucid vision.

Just as the Tree Meditation requires the Autumn Meditation to return the seeker to the ordinary world safely and easily, so the seeker on the Imramma requires a means of transition back to the ordinary world. One can arrange beforehand a signal with a helper. For instance, the helper could talk the seeker through the meditation, describing the encounter with the threshold, the guardian, the journey to the center, the revelation there, and the journey home again. The seeker could also arrange for a helper to produce a certain sound, or light a certain incense, after a previously-agreed period of time, or when the seeker make a certain signal, or when the helper observes that the seeker is finished. The "grounding" at the end of the meditation could go like this:

Returning to Earth. If there is a helper, he should assist the seeker to return her consciousness to the ordinary world by changing the rhythm of the music to the rate of a heartbeat, calling the seeker's name, and saying "return to us, return to the world." He should describe the seeker's journey back the way she came: through the passage, through the gate, over the stream, and back home.

When the seeker has returned to this world, be sure that the powers and beings who were encountered on the journey are properly thanked. The seeker should pour out the offering-bowl onto the Earth, saying a thank-you prayer to the beings encountered in the vision.

In the mythologies, the purpose of the journey tends to be the acquisition of a particular treasure, with which to heal or restore some disordered state of the mortal world. *Imramma*-journeys are, after all, instances of the universal pattern of mythological storytelling called the "Hero's Quest." In terms of personal spirit flight, the treasure could be the answer to a question or a chance to meet the Gods, learn from them, or request a service from them. I have found that the Imramma is a very helpful meditation for dealing with personal problems, clarifying one's goals, stabilizing heath or coping with chronic disease, and curbing negative emotions such as anger and depression.

3. The Feast of the Bull

Imramma is also frequently used as a technique of prophesy, for gaining knowledge of the future, learning about psychic connections with other people and places, and one's destiny. The myths describe another form of magical prophesy which appears similar to the spirit-flight meditation described here. It was called the *Tarbhfheis*, which means "feast of the bull." In the story of Cormac Mac Art, the ceremony went like this.

This is how they did the bull-feast—a white bull was killed and one man consumed his fill of its meat and of its soup, and he slept after that meal, and a charm of truth was sung by four Druids over him, and it would be revealed to him then in a vision the identity of the man to be made king, as to his form and his appearance and the nature of the actions he would do.[2]

When Cormac arrived at Tara, it was seen that he fit the description of the man in the dream. After a short confrontation with the king who was there at the time, Cormac was installed as the ruler at Tara.

Here is a variation of the Tarbhfheis which a contemporary Celtic group may wish to attempt instead. I present it here as a variation of the Imramma for groups rather than for individuals or intimate couples. For the Imramma is, it may be claimed, the Celtic technique for obtaining wisdom and prophesy through magical means. It is similar to the practice of *Seidr* found in Northern European Asatru or Heathen traditions. It may also be compared to the Wiccan practice of "Drawing Down the Moon," but the Imramma technique does not involve the assumption of a deity's consciousness into one's own. Imramma employs a technique no more dangerous than sensory deprivation and repetitive sound in the form of mantra chant-singing (although that can be hypnotic enough, and hence dangerous enough, by itself). A guided meditation assists the seeker to visualize being inside a passage mound at the morning when the sunlight enters its inner chamber.

The Tarbhfheis: If you would seek a vision, and it is your tribe that requires a vision from you, assemble the tribe and lay out a feast before them. Though gone are the days when we can sacrifice a bull and feast upon it the very same day, still it is well to prepare a meal, however small.

Prepare the meal and feast together, for those who share a meal at a common table are united as a tribe, but let the one who is to journey to the Otherworld feast lightly. Give praise to the souls of the creatures whose bodies are laid out as food before you, for they will accompany you to the Otherworld. Cast some of the food to an offering place for the Gods. Then, proceed to the prepared place.

Let the one who is to receive the Imbas from the Gods be stripped of clothing and jewels, and covered with warm blankets and wraps. Lay leaves, feathers, stones, shells, and branches over the covered Druid. Let all the other Druids stand in a circle about the Druid under the coverings, and over the covered

Druid they shake their Bell Branches and sing their magic songs.

While the Druids in the circle sing their magical songs, at least one Druid should assist the meditation of the covered Druid by guiding her through the worlds, saying something like this: "See yourself at the entry way of the passage mound…"

The magic song should continue until the Imbas flows through the covered Druid and she begins to speak. Then let everyone fall silent and listen to the wisdom that she pronounces.

When the seeker indicates that she has said all that there is to say, she should be brought back to Earth.

Interestingly, the Tarbhfheis may be one of the pan-Celtic ceremonies, for there are records of Gaulish Druids and even early Romans performing bull-sacrifices at the inauguration of kings. The parts of the bull sacrificed for the feast would be distributed among the attending guests. The part of the animal's body which each guest would receive would correspond with the part of the world-body he came from, and thus everyone is united as members of a common social body. Similarly, at the end of the story of the War of the Bull, the Black Bull of Sanglain carries the slain body of the Brown Bull of Cuailnge back to Cruachan on the ends of its horns. Parts of the slain bull's carcass drop off on the way, and new names are given to the places where they fall. This is familiar from other stories around the world. There is, for instance, the fight between the Babylonian god Marduk and a dragon-goddess named Tiamat. Another example is the battle between Odin and his two brothers against a giant named Ymir. In each case the world is fashioned from the dismembered body of a deity. This may be just the mythological representation of the historical event of one tribe conquering another. But it is also the idea that the world is the body of a deity, and is not the material handiwork of a distant, separated deity. In ancient Celtic tradition, the land is the body of a goddess, whose name is the Great Queen.

4. Dangers and Rewards

As controversial or as unwelcome as it may be for me to say it, one must be careful to avoid trap of wishful thinking and self-fulfilling prophesy here. Sometimes we want so much for something to believe in, sometimes we want so much to believe that we are living in a magical universe, that we will unconsciously create that universe in the realm of our imaginative perceptions. Suddenly every random rustle of leaves is a message from beyond, communicating secret messages about "what is meant to be." Ideas and beliefs have the hypnotic power to do that to us. The paranoid who believes in conspiracies soon enough finds them where there are none, and the insecure, emotionally depressed person finds slights and insults in the smallest of other people's comments and accidents. Similarly, someone who wants to believe in deities, faeries, spirits, ghosts, even monsters and demonic creatures, soon enough sees them everywhere. Even when performed properly, these psychological techniques can have an effect on the seeker's ability to tell the difference between what is real and what is not. When performed poorly, the technique may well grant the seeker no results at all, or totally disconnect the practitioner from reality. For example, I was having a conversation with a someone who said he was a Druid, concerning the four tornadoes which devastated the Caribbean and the east coast of the United States in the fall of 2004. This man told me that the storms were caused by Arabian shamans magically attacking the United States in retaliation for the invasions of Iraq and Afghanistan. This silly explanation was preferable to him because it presupposes that the world contains magic, and so gives him a chance to become magically powerful himself. The alternative and more likely explanation, that 200 years of industrial pollution has disturbed the chemical balance of the atmosphere, causing global warming and climate change, presupposes a mechanistic view of the world. We might find this world view ungratifying, but we should not trade one empty and soulless-world view for another. Therefore, if you think you can benefit from these techniques without putting your sanity at risk, then think again.

There are further questions to ask here. Are the experiences of the Otherworld which these trance inducing meditations produce "real"? Are the gods and spirits real? And are they really speaking to us? Or is it all in the mind? Are we simply short-circuiting the perceptual apparatus of the body and the brain? Are we hypnotizing ourselves? Are the spirits, gods, and landscapes we encounter nothing but projections of our own inner hopes and fears? Are we making it all up just to gratify our egos? The answer to all of these questions, as I see it, is "yes."

Meditation is all of these things. The really important questions, however, have to do with the effect that the cultivation of the spiritual attitude has in the practitioner's life. The effect on the life of the aforementioned gentleman is that it made him barking mad. (On another occasion, the same fellow told me that the "evil spirits," which once inhabited Irish household fireplaces, have now invaded microwave ovens!) The effect the spiritual attitude has on other people's lives is that it makes them more peaceful, happier, healthier, stronger-willed, more capable of persevering through personal hardship, and often, surprisingly, more willing to demand social justice. The people who benefit most from spiritual practice are usually those who remain "grounded." They bear in mind their limitations, especially their mortality.

Another question arises. How shall we tell the difference between the real presence of something supernatural, such as a spirit or a deity, and the illusion of one unconsciously created by our desires, hopes, wishes, and even fears? How can we know that we are seeing something only because we want to see it? This is a problem we really ought to take seriously. In ancient times, the answer would have been to appeal to the authority of professional religious specialists. People relied on the word of public religious experts to know when some event was a real manifestation, and when they were fooling themselves. These public figures did not simply claim authority for themselves and then impress or intimidate people into obedience, as happens so often today. They underwent long and difficult training and education programs to earn their authority. We have already seen how they were taught in large colleges for as long as 20 years. We might not like to do things that way today. We like to believe that people without formal education can sometimes be very wise. In fact there *is* a certain injustice to introducing authority structures into religion. But it seems to me that we must avoid being drawn towards unconsciously-created fantasy worlds.

By way of explaining another answer to this problem, here is a story of an experience which happened to me, in Killarney National Park, Ireland, which I visited with my sister and some of her friends in the spring of 2002. This park is mainly a landscape of grand old trees and lakes, with occasional limbs of rock emerging from the thick undergrowth of plants and mosses. I felt very comfortable and at home there, and perhaps as a consequence of this, I felt the forest as a personal presence. The path we were following led past the demesne of a mansion house, along a straight open stretch with pastures on either side, directly toward three mountains, clad in the blue-green mantle of evergreens and crowned by the clouds. This mountain was old, the kind of old that one imagines possessed by a strong, able bodied man with a youthful face but with eyes that see into time itself and thus are older than can be reckoned. At the end of the path, in a cleft between two of the mountains, was Torc Waterfall, pouring over many crevices and crags and tree trunks, where I sat and meditated for a while. When it began to get dark, we decided to return to the car. I went back a few steps to look at a bridge built over the stream, which my sister had pointed out to me to see, and then went to find her to walk back, but she had gone. So I cut down the hill to the bottom, and regained the path back to the mansion, saying goodbye to the mountain and promising to return again. I got to the mansion house, but I did not see a sign indicating which road to take. As I had taken a hiking trail along the lake instead of the roads from the car park to the mansion, I knew that if I kept the shore of the lake to my left, then whichever road I took, I would be going back the way I came. This I did, and as I walked along the road, passing joggers and bicyclists, I was resisting the urge to jump into the forest again and walk closer to the water. But it soon became apparent to me that I was walking a longer distance than I expected. Moreover, the sky was darkening in preparation for night. At one place along the road, there was a fence

separating park land from a field, and just on the other side a herd of deer was grazing. They perked their heads up, one at a time, watching me as I passed, as if wondering if I knew where I was going.

I found an indicator for a hiking path marked with an arrow, so I followed it, hoping that the entrance I was looking for would be at its end. The trail markers appeared every few hundred yards, and were numbered, so I thought I knew how long I had to walk. But the trail veered off the paved road and into the woods again, adjacent to a sign indicating a place called "Meeting of the Waters." At this place, I noticed shorelines and water on both sides of the road, and so I knew with certainty the suspicion that had been growing steadily in my mind, that I was on the wrong road, and that I had indeed become lost. I had been walking along a peninsula between two lakes. I began to jog along the path, so that, if I did become hopelessly lost, at least I could end up at a place where I could be found by others. The path came to a fence so I followed it instead, into a field, hoping to find a gate to a road. I was in the field with the herd of deer I had seen before, who saw me coming, looked me up and down, decided that I was an idiot, and scampered away. Eventually I found a gate, but it was the gate of the numbered hiking trail, and because it was all I had, I got on it again. I followed the numbers, still jogging, and hoping I would not break my ankle on a root or a stone that I could not see. If the god of the mountain wanted to keep me here, that would be one way to do it. I was beginning to become irrationally afraid. In my head ran stories of people abducted by UFO's, and of faerie-led people returning to civilization after dozens or hundreds of years which to them seemed only an evening. I passed a numbered marker, and excitedly hurried along to what I hoped would be the end of the trail and a meaningful sign for what direction to go. But I eventually found the very same sign on the very same road that I had followed in the first place. I had come full-circle. From here, I reasoned that I had to double-back to the last intersection. There I found a sign pointing me in the right direction. My travelling companions were sitting around the car waiting for me. In good humor, they made me believe that I had been missing for three hours. There was a spiritual lesson in the evening's events, especially in the irony of getting lost in the landscape which I wanted to worship only a few hours before.

I raise this experience to illustrate that a genuine spiritual experience always has some element, great or small, that is *not what you expect*. It is always different, surprising, and strange, one way or another. The genuine spiritual experience throws you out of the ordinary attitude, and shakes you up. It has no tolerance for passiveness and complacency. The "mystery" of Mysticism is precisely the "otherness" of the experience: the experience is other than my expectations, other than my beliefs, other than *me*. Even while holding the spiritual attitude, it goes beyond one's expectations. Quite often, therefore, it is frightening, and this is true more often than we may like to admit. It is also *the response to the mysterious* that marks a genuine spiritual experience. A full spiritual experience inspires the person to change her life, in great or small ways. The person might be sadder or happier, more centered and grounded or more listless and lost. The change might last for a few days, or for the rest of her life. But in general, it is the effect on a person's life, that is the true test of the genuine spiritual experience. Her sense of herself, her character and ego, and the purpose and meaning she finds in her life, is uplifted, transformed, or even destroyed.

These simple observations about the spiritual experience can, of course, be elaborated. There is one last quality I should mention, which needs no explanation. In the moment or in retrospect, in whole or in part, and whether it is wonderful or fearful, the genuine spiritual experience is essentially *beautiful*.

Six:

Gathering the Clanns

Even kings would not be so bold as to make a decision or take action without the Druid's council...

—Dion Chrysostom (40-112 C.E.), *Orations.*

Celtic spirituality is socially expressed. The notion of a completely personal, inner belief as we understand it today would have been unthinkable to most ancient European people. Someone who wishes to pursue her spiritual needs and aspirations through Celtic Mysticism should therefore think seriously about bringing together her closest friends and relations into a group of some kind. For nothing reinforces and advances a spiritual life more than the companionship and encouragement of family and good friends.

1. What brings people together?

In the ancient Celtic world the *tuath* ("tribe"), and not the individual, was the basic political and economic unit of society. A *tuath* was a multi-faceted community of 2,000 or 3,000 people, resembling a corporation, a political party, a labor union, a family, and a commune, all rolled into one. It was this *tuath*, and not the individual, which owned land, paid or received the dowry of its married women, paid the debts of its members incurred by committing criminal offenses, and received the compensation for criminal offences inflicted on its members. A *tuath* also exercised territorial sovereignty. It could raise an army from all of its able-bodied men, and many of its women, to drive other tribes out of its territory or even to capture more land. A professional class of warriors within the tribe, who had better armor and weapons, would be almost constantly engaged in warfare, from cattle raids and border skirmishes to full scale campaigns of conquest. And finally, it was as a member of a particular *tuath*, having the various social relations that membership in a *tuath* affords, that individuals addressed themselves to the Gods, the spirits of the world around them, the ancestors, and all the supernatural powers which were important to them. In modern Irish, *tuath* is the word for the nation-state.

There are many names for the kinds of groups that modern pagans form. Wiccans normally refer to their groups as Covens. A Celtic group composed entirely of Druids or apprentice Druids is usually called a Grove. A mixed Celtic group of Druids, Bards, warriors, artisans, and so on, is often called a *tuath*, or sometimes a *clann* (a family). A common word for a gathering of pagans of any kind is a "circle," after the circle in which participants of ceremony sit or stand together. Whatever it is called, it is a smaller, more intimate kind of community than a Christian congregation, as it is not normally more than 15 to 20 people. This size tends to foster the deepest, most intimate kinds of friendship among the members. Our innate emotional resources can form intimate family bonds with only a limited number of people at any given time. As in an ancient Iron Age Celtic community, a modern community of Celtic spiritual seekers should have variety: there should be Druids, Bards, poets, seers, warriors, artisans, and craftspeople. Each of these roles has its own body of skills, traditions, and standards of excellence which can be internalized to form the basis of a spiritual path. And most importantly, there should be a sense of togetherness, of safety and strength, and of belonging. To achieve this, we should ask, What brings people together? What are the bonds of community? How can a community resolve disagreements, suppress freeloading and cheating, overcome scandals, maintain cohesion if membership changes, and perpetuate itself into future generations?

The first thing that a newly constituted group is likely to want to do to affirm their unity and their identity is to invent symbols. People create complex systems of signs, emblems, and even codes and ciphers, to communicate messages of group identity, and shared purpose, as well as to motivate and inspire. Ever since the 1974 film *The Wicker Man*, a white flag with a shining and happily smiling yellow sun has been the almost universal emblem of Pagan community and culture. This should not be surprising, because the worship of the sun is one of the mainstays of Paganism around the world, certainly including Celtic Mysticism. A young boy carrying a sun-banner has been part of the Tara Midsummer Festival's fire-lighting ceremony re-enactment since the festival's inception. To fly a flag over the meeting place of one's clann, bearing the standards and symbols of one's tribe or one's religion, therefore, is to make a public announcement of one's allegiances, beliefs, commitments, and shared values. Your community may wish to design, for itself, an emblem, a symbol, or a flag to represent your tribe's spiritual path and your shared commitment to each other. One may also wish to designate someone to be the carrier and protector of that banner, either for particular occasions or for fixed terms of time.

Symbolism, however, is not all that there is to community life. There is also all the many ways in which people relate to one another and pursue common goals, which the symbols represent. Aristotle wrote that "man is by nature a social animal," and by that he meant that it is natural for people to want to live together, and to form social and also political relationships. He wrote that friendship is a necessary part of the well-lived life, something that no one would want to live without even while possessing all other good things. It is certainly undeniable that we are able to form communities quickly and easily. I observed this myself while waiting in Frankfurt Hahn airport, in Germany, for a flight that was delayed seven hours. During that long afternoon, the travelers got to know each other and some of the airport staff. People made the waiting more bearable for each other by sharing food, newspapers, mobile phones, and of course conversation. A common experience had made almost 200 total strangers become friends. It felt a little bit like being a member of a special club. Even language barriers were overcome. Having been through that common experience, I noted people continuing to help one another even after finally arriving at Stansted: arranging transport and accommodation together, for instance.

It is this sense of common experience, this sense of an event or an activity happening to a group of people together, which brings people together and forges the initial bonds of community. It is not enough that people live and work in the same town or city. It is necessary that there are shared experiences which belong to everyone. There are many things which can be a part of a community's common experiences. The various events of ordinary life form the bulk of them, as each generation that grows up together has a similar time with childhood, education, adolescent emotional discoveries, military service, and the like. At the end of a particularly special events such as sports victories, excellent music concerts, and theatrical productions, the boundaries between people tend to be lessened. It becomes easy, even natural, to talk to perfect strangers who were in the same audience. Common experiences bring people together because they tend to generate common purposes. With common purposes, people work together to achieve something that will benefit everyone. Little brings people together more dramatically than shared traumas and tragedies. Most of us have a sense of sympathy that cannot bear to see the suffering and deprivation of others, and compels us to help those in need. The work of healing and rebuilding after storms, accidents, wars, natural disasters, and death, is a common purpose which tends to pull people together in powerful and long-lasting ways.

The idea of a common heritage and origin also tends to pull people together. We have seen this already in the practice of making burial monuments the most important centers of social identity and territorial sovereignty. If a group of people believe they belong together because they have the same ancestors, this creates bonds of solidarity, enabling people to call upon each other for help and protection. It provides a special reason to treat certain others, if not all others, with respect. The lineage of a teacher or leader can often be equally as important as the lineage of family. The belief makes it possible for people to think of the accomplishments of their ancestors as their own accomplishments as well, and to think of the praiseworthy qualities of their ancestors, their beauty, strength, wisdom, and so on, as potentials dwelling within them. Continuity between living people and time, the past and the future, is thus made possible. A toast or a formal expression of praise for ancestors is also, in this way, an affirmation of solidarity between the speaker and others who have the same ancestors. It also calls upon the spirit of those ancestors to be present, so that their honor, glory, wisdom, skill in combat or musicianship, or other praiseworthy qualities can manifest in their living descendants. At the feasts and gatherings of one's own tribe, then, one should start with a toast to one's ancestors, perhaps also with a brief retelling of their story, and an invitation to them to join the feast.

2. Feasting

Economic relationships can pull people together as well. Hunting, gathering, planting and harvesting, cooking and preparation, all require group effort. They also require ways for people to trade with each other.

The anthropologist Marvin Harris wrote, "Giving and taking, or exchange, is the glue that holds human societies together."[1] Every human society has developed a system of trading services and material goods, and sophisticated systems of cooperation emerge as trading becomes bonding, friendship, and even political alliance. Harris claims that this began in the societies of our ancient proto-human ancestors, who probably traded sex, food, and grooming services the way modern chimpanzees and other primates do. This prepared them for group life, and forced the development of memory, attention, and intelligence. Then, once our ancestors' lives became governed more by language and culture than by genetic evolution, long-term relationships could be formalized. We could keep accounts of our transactions, and also exchange material goods and services in return for immaterial rewards like "status" and "prestige." Harris says:

> ...once cultural takeoff had been passed, exchange relationships could evolve rapidly into different kinds of economic transactions: gift exchange, barter, trade, redistribution, taxation, and eventually buying and selling, salaries, and wages. And to this day it is exchange that binds people into friendships and marriages, creates families, communities, and higher order political and corporate bodies.[2]

Harris is a cultural materialist, and so his ideas might be unsatisfying to those who prefer spiritual or esoteric explanations for things. Many people prefer to believe that the bonds of friendship and love are magical and spiritual. But we should not dismiss Harris' words lightly. For we also believe, for instance, that friendship is shallow and false if the friends are not willing to share their toys with each other. We can expect that our friends will help us in times of need, and we expect that we will have to help them in their need. In an ancient Celtic society, people were housed, clothed, and fed by an economic system of redistributive exchange and barter. Food and other valuable material goods would be collected by a wealthy tribe or clann leader to be distributed again to everyone in lavish feasts, resembling the *potlatch* ceremony of native tribes along Canada's west coast. These feasts would last for days or even weeks. They are the setting for some of Celtic mythology's most well known and funniest tales.

Feasting distributed not only food but also honor. In ancient Celtic society, someone could gain prestige for himself by throwing a feast. Indeed one could pursue a career in politics that way. Tribal leaders were expected to be efficient providers, as they were responsible for distributing the tribe's wealth and resources. They had to have big parties from time to time to keep their supporters happy (especially the ones with the big swords). These parties demonstrated that they had not lost the favor of the land goddess to whom they

were ritually married. If someone else could prove himself to be as good or better a provider, then he stood a better chance of becoming the next clann chief. A certain particularly tasty part of the animal's body would have been given to the man at the feast regarded by the host as the best man there. We don't know what part of the animal it was but we do know that it was called the "Hero's Portion." Several tales describe arguments and even fistfights over the right to claim it. The story of how Setanta earned the name of Cú Chullain takes place at a feast presented by a man named Cullain, a blacksmith who was wealthy enough to entertain the King of Ulster, Conchobar Mac Nessa, as his guest. Setanta was invited to join them as the King's foster-son, but arrived late, and had to kill the great wolf hound guarding the door. Cullain was, understandably, very angry about that, so Setanta volunteered to take the dog's place until a new pup could be reared and trained. Thus Setanta earned the name "Cú Chullain," or "Cullain's Hound."

Celtic tribes in Britain and the continent produced coins; but for the most part, the unit of exchange in Celtic marketplaces was a live animal: a cow. Everything had a price measured in cows, including a person's social worth. This was called the "honor price," the number of cows that person could be fined for committing certain criminal offences, or could expect to receive as compensation for suffering an injustice.

Using cattle as currency would have been an excellent way of ensuring that trade was always connected to the clann's material productivity. Cattle are useful in themselves as a source of food and clothing. It is probably correct to say that the ancient Celtic economic system combined bartering with redistributive exchange. One could not have "currency speculation" as we do in modern banking, which is disconnected from productivity, although perhaps the herd's birth rate is similar to what we today call interest!

At present, the social system which houses, clothes, and feeds us is international market capitalism. It follows that the members of a modern Celtic clann are likely to be working class or middle class people meeting their survival and prosperity needs in separate jobs, instead of with and for their extended families and clanns. Indeed the other members of the Clann may not be blood relatives. This simple fact is more important in the revival of Celtic spirituality than may be obvious at first glance. It means that if someone is unhappy with a group, she does not risk starvation, ostracism, and homelessness by leaving it. It also means that modern Paganism and earth-spirituality will almost certainly remain a small subculture. Unless by some historical surprise the Pagan community became a nation, able to exercise political and territorial sovereignty, this is unlikely to change. Those who do not wish to step outside "the system" should nevertheless do some of the economic activities that a

Celtic clan used to do. Some of them can be revived easily enough—feasting, for instance. Anyone can pool their money to buy food, commit time to preparing it, and enjoy eating it together. Those who have space for vegetable gardens could grow their own contributions to the feast as well. The more people share their labor and spread its rewards around, the more they will be bound together as a genuine community, and better able to realize the benefits to her spirituality which community offers.

3. Ceremony

The economic ties between people should be taken in their proper context. A society in which all human relations are based on market transactions would be a horrible place to live. It would exclude so many things which have little or nothing to do with property and money. The bonds of love and friendship, nationality and citizenship, family life, and shared spiritual identity, are *not* economic relationships, even if economic ties sometimes strengthen them. A society in which everything can be owned, bought, and sold, would become a plutocracy—a totalitarian state ruled by the rich. The *Testament of Morann* advises the would-be king about the dangers of the pursuit of material wealth: "Tell him, let not rich gifts or great treasures or profits blind him to the weak in their sufferings".[3] It is difficult to imagine a present-day economist offering such advice to the leader of a modern developed nation.

In an economic and political system where the "pursuit of happiness" has come to mean the same as the pursuit of money and prestige, this is a subversive statement.

What other ways exist to bring a community together? Joseph Campbell, the scholar whose life work it was to present the psychological foundations of mythology, made this observation in a 1966 essay called "The Emergence of Mankind":

> ...the most evident distinguishing sign is man's organization of his life according primarily to mythic and only secondarily economic, aims and laws. Food and drink, reproduction and nest-building, it is true, play formidable roles in the lives no less of men than of chimpanzees. But what of the economics of the Pyramids, the cathedrals of the Middle Ages, Hindus starving to death with edible cattle strolling all around them, or the history of Israel, from the time of Saul to right now? If a *differentiating* feature is to be named, separating human from animal psychology, it is surely this, of the subordination in the human sphere of even economics to mythology.[4]

Campbell's opinion here is a natural counterpart to the cultural materialism of Marvin Harris. Mythology unites people because of the way it encodes into narrative symbolism certain beliefs about who we are and the structure of the world we live in, and the way it honestly relates these symbols to experiences in our lives. When events in our lives are corresponded with moments in a shared mythology, people are able to relate to each other as equals and as friends. They are thus better able to form strong friendships and to help each other respond to change and tragedy in their lives. Shared mythology is in art and architecture, like the great temples and cathedrals Campbell mentioned. It is in music and literature. It is also in rituals and ceremonies. Indeed, I have found that for modern pagans, the presentation of ceremonies has replaced feast-giving as the most important way to get social prestige and status. In rituals, mythology is publicly expressed. We redramatize mythology for each other using ritual, and in so doing, express and reinforce our commitment to our values. Thus it gives life a sense of order and meaning. As Campbell says:

> The structure of ritual, as I understand it, is to give form to human life, not in the way of a mere surface arrangement, but in depth. In ancient times, every social occasion was ritually structured and the sense of depth was rendered through the maintenance of a religious tone. Today, on the other hand, the religious tone is reserved for exceptional, very special, "sacred" occasions. And yet even in the patterns of our secular life, ritual survives. It can be recognized, for example, not only in the

decorum of courts and the regulations of military life, but also in the manners of people sitting down to table together.[5]

We have seen how a tribe can be gathered for a ceremony by raising a flag or lighting a fire. Another way to gather the tribe is to make music and sound. Horns, bells, gongs, drums, and the like, cannot be missed the way a flag can if someone is looking the other way. For sound invades our consciousness with an unignorable quality unlike any other kind of stimulus. In fact the Celts used horns and trumpets for many purposes, having particular sounds and flourishes for marching, war, and calling together a council. Another popular way which I have experienced is a procession. While one or more celebrants prepare the space where the ceremony will take place, others involved prepare themselves at a hidden location. When messengers have communicated to both groups that everyone is ready, the hidden group emerges and makes its way to the site of the ceremony. The parade follows a path that makes them visible to everyone at one place or another, and which also traces a symbolically appropriate direction: approaching the circle from the east, for example, or spiralling clockwise into it.

Celtic tradition informs us that the Druids had the social power to open and to close public assemblies. The Druid would speak first at any important gathering, even before the chief or the king. Perhaps it was the Druid's social privilege, as the figure responsible for social unity as the holder of society's religious knowledge, to simply open and close official gatherings where the people would act and decide together as a tribe. That way every public decision, even practical ones, had the air of a ritual, and magic was brought to bear to ensure that justice would prevail. Here is an example opening declaration with which to begin any ceremony or community-unifying celebration such as seasonal festivals. I wrote this text for the inaugural ceremony of An Conradh Draoithe na h-Éireann, the Convocation of Irish Druids, which occurred at the winter solstice of 2002, on the Hill of Tara. Its structure is loosely adopted from the opening preamble of the Constitution of the Irish Republic.

Announcement of the Gathering. *When the Druid rings the branch, the community quiets itself to hear the ceremonial declaration:*

"Listen to the word of the Sacred Truth which is spoken at every beginning and at the moment of every creation.

"We, who are the people of the land, the sea, and the sky, from all quarters of the Holy Ground of Ireland, having assembled at this sacred place,

"Mindful of our duties to the enduring Earth and Sun who lovingly sustained and nurtured us all through our centuries of trial,

"Gratefully remembering our long-suffering forbears who kept

our traditions close to their hearts, who nurtured them in secrecy, and who painstakingly assembled again what had been lost, so that in some future time perhaps the need for secrecy may die and we may worship our Gods openly and joyfully again,

"And seeking to promote the common good, with due observance of dancing, singing, feasting, making music and love, so that the dignity and freedom of the individual may be assured, true community solidarity and unity attained, the wisdom of our traditions restored, and concord established with other traditions,

"Do hereby declare, invoke, and pronounce this festival open."

In accord with the principle of correspondence, a well-performed ceremony re-enacts the original cosmogonic event of creation. It performs this re-enactment both in the visualized imagination of the participants, and also theatrically. For ritual is the origin of theatre. The world's first theatrical productions were raised in ancient Greece, having emerged from public religious ceremonies in which important mythological narratives were dramatized. Thus there is a kind of continuum, or spectrum, between theatre and ritual, and not a hard and fast division. All ritual is, in part, a theatrical performance, whether performed by a coven of Witches performing the rite of Drawing Down the Moon, or by trained actors performing a Shakespearean comedy. Moreover,

all theatrical performance is capable of raising energy, in subtle or overt ways, much as a well-enacted ritual can. That is, in part, what we find appealing about theatre and why it continues to be a powerful form of art and communication. At one end of the spectrum is "pure" theatre, where everyone involved knows the event to be role-play and does not assume anything more is going on. At the other end is "pure" energy-raising, without any script or characterisation of any kind. But no play in a theatre is ever perfectly "pure" in this respect, as our human feelings and intelligence are always engaged by the story, and in that small respect energy is raised. Likewise, no ritual is ever perfectly "pure" in the sense of being entirely without rhythm or narrative. For the participant is always a character (herself, if no one else!) encountering or engaging with another character (a deity, a spirit, an ancestor, another human being, or even an impersonal force or an immaterial principle). And there is a sequence of events which follows a narrative order, even if the ritual enactors do not speak the same words every time for the blessings and invocations. It is that theatrical element in ritual that gives the sense of *story*. Storytelling is a powerful instrument for raising energy, focusing the consciousness of each participant, maintaining continuity with previous ceremonies, other practitioners, and with the many parts of one's own life over time. Community is brought together when the people are all living their lives according to the same story—they are all seeing themselves and each other as characters enacting their own part of a grand unified narrative of human life in relation to the great immensities of the spiritual world.

4. Leadership

Is shared ceremony and mythology enough to bring people together? Is it all that we need to affirm and strengthen the bonds of community? It seems to me that the answer is "no." I must therefore discuss, however controversially, the issue of leadership. In leadership, all the other elements of social unity find expression.

Many Pagans today cultivate a healthy disrespect for authority. They tend to insist that their groups should function as a democracy, from simple-majority to unanimous consensus. Likewise there is great resistance to investing the symbols of power and authority on one person to the exclusion of others. On the face of it there is nothing wrong with this. But we know that ancient Celtic culture was not a liberal democracy. The ancient Druidic practice was institutional, aristocratic, exclusive, and elite. Its criteria for authority was advanced education. In order to be counted as a Druid, one would have had to complete a tough education program. On this criteria, the only people among us today who qualify are those who have at least a Bachelor's degree, if not a Master's as well, from a recognized university.

Many people hold the attitude that wisdom has little or nothing to do with formal education, and therefore it is possible for an uneducated person to be very wise. Some even claim that "book knowledge" is an obstacle to wisdom. But the question, of course, is not just what the ancient Druids actually did. That is not an unimportant question. But our primary question is what we, today, ought to do. It is up to us, today, to decide what Druidry is, and what it ought to be. There may be parts of ancient Celtic culture that we should *not* revive—head hunting, for instance. We may find ourselves severing ties with the past with such decisions, and thus lessening our right to call our path "Celtic." However, if we make such decisions judicially, and keep in mind that the important aspects of a spiritual tradition are its mysteries, we will not loose sight of what really matters.

There are large differences between then and now regarding how social power was justified, distributed, and exercised. Here I take social power to be the ability to make and to follow through with decisions concerning group identity and action. Where earlier I defined power as the ability to do whatever one may want to do, social power is the ability to engage others to do, or assist in the doing of, whatever one may want to do. Any group of people who bring themselves together to form a community will almost inevitably face the problems and the realities of social power. Today's cultural environment prefers justifications of power based on more firmly democratic, egalitarian, or consensus-based principles, rejecting ideas such as "hereditary right," or even rejecting any justification for social power at all. This is totally unlike how it would have been done in the time of the Celts who these groups claim to be like. But this may not necessarily be a bad thing. For instance, the idea of hereditary right can be used to justify extraordinary injustice, violence, and oppression. The solution to this cluster of problems is fairly simple. Let us face up to the fact that we are a modern people, living in this place and time. Let us not pretend to be other than who we are. Let us acknowledge how much of our inheritances are recent as well as ancient. Let us learn how our forebears lived, decades or centuries ago, in order to help us decide how we ought to live now.

For today's Druidic grove, I believe that the most important decisions, such as inviting new members, should be made democratically. But in other respects, the coherence and the stability of the group in large measure rests upon the decision-making of the leaders. It is up to each group to decide for themselves how the leaders will be chosen, what their responsibilities and powers are, and how long they will serve in that capacity. Here are some possibilities.

- *Regular elections.* The leader(s) are elected by all of the adult members of the group. (Note that "adult" here might include some teenagers, especially if the group provides rites of passage for its adolescent members.) The election might take place once every year, every three years, or nearly any other regular period which everyone can agree is a reasonable amount of time and which has some appropriate magical significance, for instance every Beltaine, etc.

- *Rotating leaders.* All the adult aged members of the group take turns. Leadership changes every year, or at the end of an agreed-upon period. The rotation is alphabetic, or perhaps on the basis of "seniority" (that is, the order in which people joined the group).

- *Irregular elections.* The leader(s) are elected by the adult members and remain in position permanently, unless a significant amount of dissatisfaction with their leadership arises. In that case, someone else may challenge them and force a new election. Alternatively, a leader may choose to retire and call a new election.

- *Permanent leaders.* The leader(s) install themselves and remain in their position until they retire. Normally, the permanent leader is also the founder, who has announced the group's existence and invited other like-minded people to join.

If anyone should eventually become dissatisfied with the leader, they simply leave.

If you wish to commit your group to having no leaders, think carefully first. Even in groups that claim to be completely egalitarian and non-hierarchical, there will still be one or more people held in higher esteem than others for various reasons. In actual practice there really is no such thing as a leaderless community. There will always be one or two individuals who take more initiative than others, who have more experience than others, who are consulted for advice more often than others. If not, then there will be one or two people who are just more loud and outspoken, able to bully others to do what they want. I have seen more "egalitarian" groups than I can count which imploded when people with knowledge and initiative were accused of "trying to take over." The subsequent infighting brought about the collapse of the group and created long-lasting and needless grudges among everyone

involved. Much of this can be avoided by respecting each other's strengths and talents, including the talent for leadership.

We have ample evidence that the model of "irregular election" was used in ancient Celtic times. The adults would vote for a leader from among themselves, usually choosing someone who was not too young and inexperienced, nor too old to wield a weapon effectively. Celtic society was a militaristic society after all. But there were also "royal" or "noble" families, in which the leader was "chosen" by hereditary right. Such a leader claims his right to lead on the basis of being descended from an ancient priesthood, a mythological hero, or even a god. For instance, the Connachta sept, which came from the West of Ireland and conquered the Boyne Valley in the 3rd to 4th century A.D., claimed that Meadhbh, the goddess of sovereignty of Tara, was one of their ancestors. They claimed she was buried in the West, on top of the hill of Knock Na Rae in Sligo, and not on Tara

Burial mound of Queen Maeve, Knock na Rae

(which still has a rath named after her). Thus the name of Meadhbh came to be the name of the great queen of Connaught in the story of the Táin Bo Cuailnge. As another example, a Germanic prince from Saxony named Cerdic landed in Britain in the year 495, and established the kingdom of West Saxony, or Wessex, in 519. He claimed to be the eighth-generation grandson of Wotan, a god-king of the northern European world. When Christianity arrived, the geneology was "extended" so that it would fit into the Christian world view. Cerdic and Wotan became descendants of Sceaf, the son of Noah, and hence descendants of Adam who was created by God himself.

The leader's presence in the tribe as a descendent of a divine ancestor was effectively the presence of that ancestor's power. Of course, a connection to a special predecessor does not by itself make someone fit to be a leader. He or she still had to earn the right to be a leader, through the usual process of diplomacy and warfare. If he was unpopular, he could still be voted out. But the idea of hereditary power received from a special predecessor is a *very* powerful idea, both spiritually and also politically. In non-religious contexts it still exists, for instance in sports teams, political parties, crime syndicates, banks and corporations, or any organization that sees itself as carrying forward the vision of its founder, or the spirit of some past member who achieved excellence.

There are other models of leadership which a modern tribe may use. My clann is a multi-generational group, with members ranging from middle-aged adults to their teenage and pre-teenage children. It was, in this sense, an actual family. Although no one in particular is "in charge" in any formal sense, the older adults are the natural teachers due to their greater knowledge and experience, and it usually falls to them to organize our gatherings and ceremonies. Even with this core of experienced adults, nothing stops the younger or less experienced members from taking initiative to do something of interest to them. It is the job of the adult members to encourage them. And, of course, the adult members can continue their own learning process as well. To an outsider, our model of leadership might look like this:

- ☉ *"Council" of Elders.* The important decisions are made at open meetings. All members, young and old, are entitled to speak. Decisions are made when the adults or the most senior members of the group have achieved a consensus among themselves.

This may be described as a kind of aristocratic democracy, and in combination with the model of irregular election, it is probably the closest to that which was actually used by our Pagan forebears. No matter what style of leadership selection you choose, the leaders themselves should in some measure be the people that the group regards as most deserving of the position. The man or woman selected should be the one who possesses the most knowledge, experience, and other qualities which everyone can generally agree are necessary for leadership. Celtic tradition held that the tribal kings had to be free from physical blemishes as well as blemishes of character. On one level, this is because it was believed that if the king possessed any such blemishes then the Goddess of Sovereignty to whom he was married would be displeased. This displeasure would be transmitted to the land and people in the form of bad weather, poor harvests, and so on. But on an ethical level, the king is required to represent the best of the tribe. Thus someone convicted of theft, murder, oath-breaking, and the like, was automatically disqualified. The leader is supposed to be the person who best embodies what the people believe to be an ideal human being.

We have a few written sources describing what ancient Celtic people expected from their leaders. For instance, the 7th century *Testament of Morann*, an example of a "wisdom speech" recited at the inauguration of Irish kings, says that a leader should be "merciful, just, impartial, conscientious, firm, generous, hospitable, honorable, stable, beneficent, capable, honest, well-spoken, steady, true-judging."[6] Note the emphasis on intellectual qualities. The ideal ruler is not just a good fighter. He or she is also a good thinker. The chief of a Celtic clann is chosen for his ability to emulate and embody these qualities. For it seems that these are the qualities which arouse the goddess, and her pleasure in him is reflected in the condition of the land and people. The *Testament of Morann* refers to corrupt leaders as "bull rulers," and describes them as follows: "The bull ruler strikes [and] is struck, wards off [and] is warded off, roots out [and] is rooted out, pursues [and] is pursued. Against him there is always bellowing with horns."[7] In other words, the bull ruler is always under attack, apparently from his own people.

As noted, physical blemishes would disqualify someone for the kingship. To us, this seems arbitrary and irrational—what does someone's physical constitution have to do with her ability to lead? In the mythologies, physical blemishes function as outward signs of character defects. Usually they are deliberately brought out of the unjust ruler by the cutting satire of a maltreated poet. It is a mytho-poetic way of saying that if the leader has any flaws, particularly *moral* flaws which physical flaws represent, then it will reflect badly on the tribe. It is these moral qualities which matter. So a physical disability shouldn't disqualify someone from leading a modern Druidic clann.

The kind of power granted to these leaders should be relevant for the responsibilities they will bear. A Celtic clann chief combined the functions of legislator, court justice, and high priest, as we would know these roles today. A good leader continues her own learning process while guiding others with theirs. She isn't so authoritative that the other members of the group rely upon her for everything, or cannot act without her blessing. This gives them no space for their own learning and growth, and indeed would wear them out. It would also give the others no opportunity to acquire experience of their own. Everyone should feel that they are able to take initiative of their own and will be respected if they do, and be able to give and receive both praise and critical commentary. The leaders may also wish to assign tasks from time to time to those who they think would benefit from them. Such tasks might be to design and lead a ceremony, to research something, to find or to create a ritual object. I remind the reader that such assigned tasks should be relevant to the person's spiritual path. If your tribe's leader has been granted the responsibility to write and to lead your ceremonies, then he cannot use that power to tell you how to handle your personal finances!

A newly-formed tribe may want to spend a season or two simply getting to know each other, finding everyone's strengths and interests, and organically discovering who takes initiative and who tends to be the one that others turn to for information and advice. At some stage, then, you may want to formally name your leaders and prepare a ceremony of recognition for them. In my clann, we had an annual selection of the "May King and Queen," every year at Beltaine, in addition to more

traditional activities like leaping over a bonfire. The kind of "leadership" they provided was ceremonial rather than authoritative and not really fitting into any of the aforementioned categories. They would fit better in a category like this one:

⌾ *Ceremonial figureheads.* These leaders possess no actual authority or power, but are called upon at most, if not all, of the group's events to perform special ceremonial functions. They may be called upon to say a blessing before meals, to carry and protect the clann's flag, or take certain important parts in ritual re-enactments of mythological events.

These leaders are purely symbolic figures. Ours were responsible for magically promoting general fertility for of the clann in whatever way they felt best. This, in combination with the "council of elders" model, is the style of leadership which I recommend for modern Celtic groups. Ceremonial figureheads need not possess any real power. However, in my group we found that the selected people had to undertake serious work nevertheless. They found they had tasks to complete, obstacles to overcome, potentials to develop, and often discovered new talents for leadership and responsibility in the process. Some found they had personal ordeals associated with their karma or their destiny to resolve. Everyone, including myself in my turn, found that the position, originally intended mainly to be fun, demanded real self-exploration and resulted in greater spiritual awareness.

The method of selecting the king and queen can vary, according to what everyone agrees is symbolically or magically significant and appropriate. The Tarbhfheis, described earlier, could be re-enacted for this purpose. Some groups I have encountered use Ogham divination, which can make it appear as if the leaders were chosen directly by the gods, communicating through the fall of the sticks. One year the selection for my clann was performed as follows.

Selecting the King and Queen.
Assemble the tribe at the gathering place and create the sacred space. The queen of the previous year summons her king and requests from him the crown. This given, it is placed in the center of the circle.

The men are then sent out of the circle to forage for a long stick. They are told that whoever brings back the longest stick will have won the first round of the selection process.

When the men return, each bearing his stick, they are lined up together. Each is then required to recite to the women the great, glorious, and heroic deeds which they accomplished in the time since the previous year's selection of the king. The length of the stick determines the speaking order: he who brought back the longest stick speaks first.

The women listen, and whenever the speaker says something that impresses them, they tie a ribbon on to his stick.

When all the men have spoken, the ribbons are counted. He whose stick has the most ribbons becomes the new king for the forthcoming year.

But his last task is to choose his queen. He must choose one of the women who, in his sight, best embodies the Goddess of Sovereignty. He must express his love and dedication to her, and if she finds his expression acceptable, she offers him a drink from the chalice and places upon his head the crown.

You can guess what a fun and ribald event this was. One fellow pulled a massive fallen log into the circle. Another, suspecting that the length of the stick may be a ruse, had a finger-length twig hidden in his shirt pocket, just in case. We had to make a rule: the stick can not be so large that its finder could not take it home. Once the ribbons were counted, the newly-selected King had to romance one of the women and try to make her fall in love with him. If he couldn't do this, he couldn't be king either. (And this is why the men usually chose women with whom they already had a relationship.) If he failed, it would fall to the man with the next highest number of ribbons on his stick to court the lady of his choice. Thus the king is chosen by the women, and the queen by the men, although the women have an edge on the balance of power. One reason for this is that in Celtic tradition, the deity of sovereignty is almost always female. The historian Alfred P. Smyth noted a custom for selecting the king which obtained in Leinster, the east province of Ireland, and speculated that it may also have existed in the Scottish kingdom of Dal Riada. In this custom, a man becomes king by marrying the daughter of the previous queen.[8] Sovereignty is thus passed along the female line. A man wields the political power but receives his right to do so from a woman. This custom may have been based upon the conception of sovereignty as a female principle. But this is not the same as saying that ancient Celtic society was matriarchal. For in all but certain famous exceptional examples, political power was in fact wielded by men.

Another element in the selection of the king and queen obtained from recorded Celtic customs is the offering of a drink. There is a Scottish marriage practice in which a woman would choose a husband from among various suitors by offering a drink to the man of her choice. Aristotle recorded something similar among the Gauls in what is now Marseilles, France, and elsewhere a similar custom is recorded among the Hindus. In a story of the Hidden House of Lugh, Conn of the Hundred Battles is on the Hill of Tara, consulting with his Druids, when a mist arises. A spear-throwing warrior emerges from it, and invites Conn to accompany him to his house. Conn follows him to a rath in a beautiful plain, with a golden tree at its door. In the house was a beautiful young woman who offers Conn a drink of red ale from a golden cup. The warrior explains that he is Lugh Lamh-Fada, and the woman is the Sovereignty of Ireland. Note that the offering of a drink to the king does not place her in a subservient position to him, as it may seem. The drink of acceptance is a special blessing which is only hers to give, and which not just anyone can receive. A man who receives this gift is honored by her, but also in some sense *subordinated by her power to give.* It is she who holds the power to give or not to give, and to decide to whom she will give. There are symbolic sexual associations in this ceremony and clear reflections of the Great Marriage and of mythological artifacts like the Well of Wisdom and the Holy Grail which should be obvious. As Mircea Eliade wrote, "Marriage rites too have a divine model, and human marriage reproduces the heirogamy, more especially the union of heaven and earth."[9]

In your circle, of course, there is no reason why women cannot compete as well. After all, Celtic mythology has an abundance of great queens.

5. Justice

There is also a need for what might be called "regular maintenance." For bitterness and resentment will emerge in your community quickly if there is no system for making decisions, enforcing them, airing grievances, resolving conflicts, and hearing debate. The first year may well be a magical time of intimacy, intensity of emotional bonding, and greatness of future plans. But unless some of this energy is carried forward with care then it is only a matter of time before the community breaks down in petty disagreements, and the members split into smaller groups or go their separate ways altogether.

The ancient Irish system of justice was called Brehon law. It had a long and complex system for gathering evidence, hearing grievances, and arbitrating among competing claims of wrongdoing. Someone with a complaint would obtain an advocate to speak on his or her behalf. The plaintiff would then choose one of five "paths" with which to plead the case. These were the paths of *fir* ("truth," regarding property, allegiance, or perjury), *dilged* ("entitlement," regarding unfulfilled contracts), *Cert* ("justice," to change an unfair contract), *Téchtai* ("propriety," apparently having to do with old issues), and finally *Coirn athcomairc* ("proper inquiry," to include anything not covered by the other categories). Then the plaintiff would pay a surety bond, like a "peace bond" today, to demonstrate his commitment to the case. There were five different kinds of sureties he could pay, most of them in the form of milk cows or property in land. He could pledge himself as a surety, such that if the other

kinds of payment defaulted he would become a bonded servant until the debt was paid. The defendant had to pay an equal surety. Then each side is given a chance to plead its case, and to rebut the case of the other side. The judges can also hear the testimony of "expert witnesses" (tribal chiefs, other lawyers, etc.) Then the judgement is announced in public. The losing side has three days to appeal, otherwise the decision is final. The judges all supervise each other, and if one makes a poor decision, he can be forced to pay a fine.[10]

This is interesting stuff, but the complexities of Brehon justice may well turn out to be an aspect of ancient Celtic culture we need not revive. Most modern day Celtic tribes are informal groups of friends, not large semicorporate entities with thousands of members. There are easier ways to air grievances which may be more preferable for smaller groups. Simple open dialogue may well be enough. You may wish to use some of the wisdom texts as guides on how to conduct a fair and inclusive debate. One of the old Irish wisdom texts, the *Instructions of Cormac*, has a short section describing the signs of bad debate to be avoided. They include: "contending against knowledge," "taking refuge in bad language," "hair-splitting," "despising books," "shifting one's pleading," "inciting the multitude," "blowing one's own trumpet."[11] These are points which philosophers today recognize as common logical errors. In Iron-Age

Celtic culture, where many of the decisions were made in big outdoor public assemblies, it was important for the community elders to follow guidelines such as these to keep the debate rational and productive, and prevent it from becoming a useless shouting match. My clann uses an idea borrowed from the native people of North America: the talking stick. At our meetings, no one but the person holding the stick is allowed to talk, aside from minor interjections. It is an effective way to ensure that everyone who wants to comment about some issue has a chance to speak. If a decision needed to be made, this method is effective for determining exactly what the decision is about, and enables everyone to vote quickly. If you use this method in your group, then the object you use as your talking stick should be something that everyone can generally agree is the right kind of object for your group. It might be a staff, a cup, a special ring, or even a chair or seat which speakers sit in. Everyone should have a hand in making or decorating it. Perhaps the task of taking care of it between meetings could be one of the functions of the group's ceremonial figureheads.

6. Passages

I wish to discuss at length a specific dimension of spiritual community life: the provision of "rites of passage." Passages are the ways that every spiritual tradition acknowledges a person's transition from one phase of life, now at an end, to another phase, now at its beginning. Passages give people a great sense of belonging, purpose, identity, and strength. At various points in everyone's life, we begin a new phase in which we becomes, in effect, a new person, having new responsibilities, new powers, and occupying a new social role. Most of these events are physiological and hence inevitable, such as the changes associated with sexual puberty and adolescence. Others are social in nature. They include being born, entering adolescence and puberty, entering adulthood, becoming eligible to drive a car or to vote, graduating from school or university, getting married, bearing children, retirement, old age, and death. These are all passages. In religion, some of them are acknowledged by ceremonies called "initiations." These ceremonies transform the natural symbolism of physiological development into a tradition-bound symbolism of psychological, moral, and spiritual development.

The origin of the word is the Latin *Initium*, meaning a beginning or commencement. All initiations imply a community: there is a group of people sharing a group of customs, practices, techniques, and teachings. The initiation allows the postulant to "join the club" and gives her access to the customs and teachings, enabling her to use them, contribute to them, and to think of them as her own. It also creates continuity between generations.

As described by the prominent American Druid Isaac Bonewits, there appear to be three different kinds of initiations, and all religious communities practice some form of at least one of them. They are:

- ☯ *Recognition of a status already gained.* These initiations tend to give people a fairly well defined group of goals to achieve. The ceremony itself is not the place where the work of achieving those goals is undertaken. It is presumed that the initiate has already succeeded, and so the ceremony is often little more than a publicly-expressed affirmation of the initiate's success. School graduations and the attainment of adulthood are examples of this type.

- ☯ *Ordeals of transformation.* These include practices designed to encourage, or even to force, the initiate to confront the great spiritual mysteries and immensities of the world and/or within himself. Tests of physical endurance and psychological willpower are usually involved. Other kinds of ordeals have historically included live (temporary!) burial, food and sleep deprivation, sensory deprivation, tattooing, infliction of bodily injury, and even sexual ordeals.

- ☯ *Transmission of the gnosis.* In this type, a special status, psychic benefit, etc., claimed to have originated in an ancient or mythological progenitor, is bestowed upon the initiate. He or she is then able to access those ancient figures as a source of power and knowledge, or act as their spokesperson.

The presence of community and of continuity between generations is clear with each type. If there is no continuity of contemporaries and predecessors, then there is no initiation. There is no one to recognize a status already gained, no one to judge whether the ordeals of transformation were passed successfully (indeed, no one to assign such ordeals), and no one to transmit the gnosis from one generation to the next. In every case, community is systematically presupposed. The community either recognizes that the postulant has attained the appropriate level of knowledge and character development, or else uses the initiation ceremony to get the process of striving for those attainments started. In either case, the community is involved.

For the first type, it may appear that community involvement is superfluous. Children grow into adults whether there is an initiation ceremony for them or not. That is a biological fact. Yet community involvement makes those biological facts *count* for something, and so contributes to their meaning. Part of the function of a community is the provision of a sense of place, welcome, belonging, and status to its members, and initiations are one of the ways in which a community provides this. To be initiated is to be recognized as a member of a particular group, having a particular place in it, and occupying a particular role. In the case of stage-of-life initiations such as the passage from youth to adulthood, there are obvious physiological changes which happen regardless of whether someone receives social recognition for it. But the essential point is that an initiation is a social event. Being an "adult" is a social category, defined by social factors such as emotional experience and maturity, readiness for responsibility, and the like. The two categories overlap each other, but they are distinct.

What about self-initiation? One of the unusual things about contemporary Paganism is the general attitude of acceptance towards it, although this acceptance is not without controversy. Most pagans agree that people initiate themselves in various ways, in part just by growing up and having various experiences in life, and by taking on the responsibilities of the new stage of life. A self-initiated person may claim that he or she knows within herself that she has attained the appropriate level of knowledge and maturity to be deserving of initiation, and thus does not feel she requires the recognition of a community. However, the plain fact is that self-initiation as a Druid would have been unthinkable to someone in an ancient, Iron-Age pagan culture. For such a person, his place in society constitutes his identity—his social role is what he *is*. Even his status as a human being is a matter of social recognition. No one could be a Druid just by announcing herself to be one. But we are not, of course, living in the Iron age. What should we, who live in the modern age, believe?

I am inclined to believe the following. The simple choice to take up a profession like law or medicine, the choice to start a hobby or learn a new sport, and so on, are all forms of self initiation. Everyone is "self initiated" who make a commitment to live her life according to a certain principles, such as to pursue a certain goal and to develop skills that will enable success in the pursuit. It is the same for the spiritual path. This may or may not be associated with any particular ceremony. Spiritual experiences, such as for instance encounters with death, or feelings of great cosmic unity, brought on by meditation or by the wonders of nature, can by themselves constitute initiations. How we respond to such experiences, and how we change as a result of them, is "the proof of the pudding," the sign that an initiation has taken place. If someone initiates herself with her choices, she answers the Morrigan's Call, which is the call to discover and to decide who you are. This is a dynamic, powerful moment in people's lives, and should be honoured. Self-initiation does not make you automatically a member of a certain community. But it can make you ready to join one. It does not make you a Druid, but it may be one of the things which you must do to deserve being called a Druid. Certainly, self-initiation can "put you on the path." It is appropriate for a community to be sceptical of the self-initiated, at least at first. After all, how many "enlightened teachers" have we heard of who later turned out to be frauds, seeking only to have their ego stroked or their pockets filled? But all other things being equal, it can be unjust for the members of a community to refuse to accept a self-initiated person. Such a person may later be offered a ceremony of social recognition, put on by some community that is willing to welcome the person as a new member.

At an initiation ceremony, there are many themes and symbols at work. One is the theme of movement. The ceremony's purpose is to ritually flag the moment when a person moves from one state of life into another. The ritual expresses what happens at the boundary. Therefore, in some initiations, there is a definite gate for postulants to walk through, like a special arch constructed of leafy branches. There may be a person serving as "guardian at the gate," who requires the traveller to pass some test or answer one or more questions before passage is granted. The

correspondence with the spirit-flight to the Otherworld is clear: for the theatrics of initiation ceremonies are often based on the psychological experiences of spirit-flying seekers.

Another theme is that of growth and maturity. An initiation recognizes that the postulant has changed or improved herself in some way. Alternatively, the initiation might be designed to cause certain changes to take place. Between childhood and adulthood there are natural changes in the body, which are taken as the analogy for the changes of mind and character in the process of maturity. Similarly, in passages that have to do with the transmission of gnosis, the natural relation of parent to child and teacher to student is here taken to be the natural relation between the ancient predecessors and the new initiate. Related to this, there is the theme of death, the ultimate "change." As an initiation is a beginning, so it implies an ending. Thus some kinds of initiation, usually the second or third kind, ceremonially enact the postulant's death and subsequent resurrection. She might be left alone in a silent and dark room, for instance. In some ancient cultures people were literally buried alive and mourned as if dead, and then released from the tomb after a few hours, or sometimes days. It is thought by some scholars that the Biblical character Lazarus, whom Christ "raised from the dead," was actually undergoing a mystery-tradition initiation that involved live burial.

The moment of change can be marked in various ways. An oath might be sworn. Special garments might be given. A new name granted. The announcement proclaimed to the four quarters. Gifts are exchanged. Events from the mythological past are dramatized. Objects, artworks, or people who incarnate the deity are revealed. An arch or gateway may be entered. The ceremony that precedes and follows this magic moment sets the dramatic action in time and space, anchoring the affirmation into the initiate's consciousness and in the energy of the world.

Did the ancient Druids have any initiatory secrets? I believe I can make a partial answer to this question. Consider the following famous statement about the Druids, recorded by one of history's only eyewitnesses, Julius Caesar:

> They [The Druids of Gaul] also have much knowledge of the stars and their motion, of the size of the world and of the earth, of natural philosophy, and of the powers and spheres of action of the immortal gods, which they discuss and hand down to their young students.[12]

This fragment indicates the possibility that the Druids taught an initiatory tradition. The poet Lucan seems to confirm this in another fragment which reads:

> To you alone it is given to know the truth about the gods and the deities of the sky, or else you alone are ignorant of this truth, the innermost groves of far-off forests are your abodes.[13]

Lucan seems to have meant something similar to what we mean when we say, "he's either a genius or a lunatic."

These two fragments indicate that the Druids may have had had an organized system of master and apprentice education, which taught a special body of knowledge not available to the rest of Celtic society. The system may be similar to the kind of education that today's doctors, lawyers, and skilled trades people like carpenters, receive. These too have initiations of a sort— the conferral of a certificate or diploma. So these fragments here may *not* indicate anything similar to the secretive initiations of Freemasons, Rosicrucians, or other modern-day secret societies. It was probably more like a professional apprenticeship followed by a graduation of some kind.

However, because the Druids were a religious order, I do think that there was a mystery tradition involved. A mystery tradition is one in which there is a certain body of information that is available only to those who have gone through a special ceremony, a special education program, or some other selection process. It is also distinguished by the kind of information it possesses: "mystical" information. This is normally information of a philosophical, ethical, or cosmogonic character but presented in the form of mythological or historical narratives with religious significance. Some physical artifact which has a relation to the narrative might also be a part of the "secret" that the members of such a tradition possess and protect. With that in mind, look again at the quote from Julius Caesar. Information about the size of the world, of physics, biology, and astronomy ("natural philosophy"), and of the gods, was in the ancient world considered philosophical and cosmological knowledge, rather than scientific knowledge, although it included information obtained through scientific observation and experiment. This came together with ideas about the greater structures and powers of the cosmos ("the immortal gods," the "size of the world," etc.). These are normally the province of mystical practices like meditation—about which it *is* possible to be "scientific," in a manner of speaking. It is possible to rationally and systematically study our own spiritual experiences, and to talk about them and share them with others. This is the sort of thing that was probably within the body of information the Druids protected.

Secrecy might be the instrument for controlling who accesses this information. But it is also an important part of the character of a mystery tradition that this special body of information is not secret, but actually freely available to anyone who knows how to look for it. The knowledge might have been available to anyone who seeks out the right kind of spiritual experience. And there might be special ceremonies designed to create those experiences. Alternatively, the special information may be encoded, or portrayed in non-obvious ways. In this case, the information is available to someone who possesses the right attitude of mind, or makes the right choices, or enlists the right kind of help. If someone is smart enough to figure it out, then she has the right to know. All of the world's most important philosophical and spiritual truths are "secret" in this open and public way. If someone can't figure it out, she effectively debars herself from the spiritual discovery. Opening up all the secret books, hidden crypts, and closed curtains to such a person would do her no good at all.

The ability to create the conditions for the revelation of mystery is the power and promise of Mysticism. It is openness to what is mysterious in this sense which is taught by a mystery tradition. A mature mystery tradition also offers help and encouragement to those willing to do their own work to find, experience, and understand the mystery. Tight-lipped protectionism of "secrets" from the "uninitiated" (or better still, the "unworthy") is not the mark of wisdom. It is the mark of paranoia.

People who are committed to that kind of "secrecy" are normally only trying to impress and intimidate others. Or they are protecting themselves from embarrassment should their secrets turn out to be stupid.

As with so much of the symbolism and pageantry of theater and ritual, the whole drama of an initiation ceremony is played out to instill in the mind of the postulant a concrete sense of connectivity, sacredness, and wonder. We have so few rites of passage in the larger society: school graduations, marriages, retirements, and funerals are about the only life transitions that have remained celebratory occasions in our secular society. Perhaps one reason why people sometimes feel displaced, or feel they are leading unfulfilling lives, is because we are not experiencing our stage of life transitions as sacred, community affirmed, mysterious events. Initiations establish place, identity, achievement, connectivity, and purpose. They reward certain virtues and discourage certain vices. They make people feel honored and respected. Most of all they instill a sense of *belonging*. And without them, we can find ourselves at a loss to know who we are.

7. From Childhood to Adulthood

Given this absence, a private or semiprivate Celtic spiritual community should arrange rites of passage for its young members. There are several stories in the mythologies which describe a Druid announcing that a child shall be known by a certain name, implying that there was some kind of Druidic baptism. Fionn MacCumhall and Cú Chullain all received their names after special events in their childhood: Fionn tasted the flesh of the Salmon of Knowledge, and Cú Chullain killed the guard dog at the fort of Cullain the Blacksmith.

More recently, an informant described to me a naming ceremony for a baby which took place in one of the ancient ring-forts of the western islands in the summer of 2005. It involved traditional music, speeches from the parents and grandparents, and lastly an announcement from an elder of the community: "I declare this child to be (name)." Then the child was raised up high for everyone to see. There was a cheer, followed by gift-giving, more music, and a reception at a local pub. "It's not Catholic, or religious, it's just Irish," my informant told me. Still, it was a rite of passage, in the Celtic style.

In ancient Celtic society, young boys were socially recognized as adult men when an elder of the community gave them their first weapons. We also know one of the traditions connected to the presentation of a sword. Before being given to the person who would eventually own it, it would be placed in or under the bed of an unmarried woman, who would sleep with it there. The future owner would come to collect it the following morning, accompanied by members of his family. The ceremonial associations that may be gleaned from this tradition are fairly clear. The unmarried woman represents the Goddess of Sovereignty. It may be important that the warrior should receive his weapons from such a woman. It would impress upon him that his right to wield a weapon comes from the Goddess, and that he is also taking up a psychological commitment to her and to the tribe she sponsors.

Here is a reconstructed ceremony that a clann can use as a passage for its younger members. Alternatively, it can be used as a welcoming ceremony for new members at the time they join the group.

Presentation of a sword. The warrior who shall eventually own the sword, having chosen it or having chosen the craftsperson who will forge it, should spend time in the evening in peacefully abiding upon the question, "What sort of man can wield the Sword of Nuada?"

When the sword is ready, it must be collected by one of the community's Druids and brought to the home of an unmarried woman. The Druids place it in or under her bed. As they do, one of them rings the Bell Branch over the sword, the bed, and the woman, while reciting a roscann (magical poem) over her, declaring her to be the representative and the embodiment of the

Goddess of Sovereignty for this time and place and this sacred purpose.

The following day, the warrior is brought to the entrance of the tribe's sacred place. The Druid knocks thrice on the gate and calls to the woman within:

"We are the people of (name of the tribe). We request the Woman who holds the Sovereignty of our Clann, to allow us to enter, for (name of warrior) is with us to receive his arms."

The woman either emerges from the house or invites the group to enter. She bears the sword, within its sheath. She asks the warrior, "Do you know the secret of the Sword of Nuada?" The warrior answers her according to his insight.

When this is done, the woman presents the sword to the warrior. She might press the sword heavily into his hands before releasing it, to represent the weight of responsibility that a sword-bearer takes on, saying, "(name of warrior), you have spoken wisely. Receive this sword from the hands of the Goddess, and know that you are welcome in our clann." The warrior then unsheathes the sword and holds it aloft. A general celebration should follow.

The biological changes which the young undergo are distinct from the social changes, and call for a different set of symbols in the initiation ceremony. The voice changes, hair grows in new places, the arms and legs grow longer, and the sexual organs develop—on one level these have to do with *appearance*. They make the person look different. They also make the person physically capable of taking on new social roles: a mother or father, a heavy laborer or soldier, a public speaker and leader. Here, initiation consists in ordeals which put these new found powers to the test. Recognition from others is required here: it is precisely that recognition which entitles the person to take on adult privileges and responsibilities. Other changes happen within the person's body, and have less to do with appearances. Especially for women, the capacity to reproduce makes someone into an adult without any need for social affirmation. The biological changes, the onset of the capability to reproduce, requires an initiation which recognizes a status already gained.

We do not know what ceremony the ancient Celts performed for young girls on becoming new women. This information simply wasn't important to the all-male Christian chroniclers who wrote the mythologies down. I would like to suggest that the presentation of a chalice could serve girls the way the presentation of a blade serves boys. This ceremony here is a representation of birth, signifying that the child is reborn as an adult, and takes on new powers and rights as well as new responsibilities. It is based on the rite-of-passage for young women which a number of my female friends have described to me (for as you may expect, I have never undergone it myself). It is also heavily dependent on the symbolism of the Chalice, described earlier, as a special object for women.

Presentation of a Chalice. The girl who is to be presented with a chalice should spend some time in the evening peacefully abiding upon the question, "What pours forth from the Holy Grail?"

At the beginning of the ceremony itself, the girl is placed under heavy coverings so that she is in darkness. The women of the tribe then enter the space and stand around the covered girl, and begin the ceremony. They call upon the powers of the four cardinal directions, the Earth, Moon, and Sun, and various goddesses, to descend upon the initiate, bless her life, protect her, and bring her good fortune.

Then the older women line up in front of the covered girl, facing away, and stand with their legs apart. The blanket is lifted, and the girl crawls out, through the legs of the older women, until she has been "birthed" again by all of the women present.

The new woman's mother (if she is present) or the oldest woman there (if the mother cannot attend) produces a chalice, covered under a veil. She says to the new woman: "Behold the Cup of Truth, which gives us knowledge and healing, and which is revealed only to she who knows the secret. And so I put to you the question: Do you know what pours forth from the Holy Grail?" The new woman answers according to her insight.

The woman then says, "You have spoken wisely, and so the Cup of Truth shall be given to you, that you shall know you are welcome in our clann." The chalice is then unveiled and given to her. A general celebration should follow.

After the ceremony a party in honor of the new woman is enjoyed by all, with music, food, gift-giving, storytelling, and any other fun thing the new woman wishes for a second birthday. I am told that one of the traditional gifts is an article of red clothing, for reasons that are surely obvious. In the years I have been involved in the community, I have personally seen, or had described to me, many variations on this basic theme. There are some groups who require the initiate to strip herself naked, crawl under the legs of those already initiated (to be "born again"!) and then be dressed in new ceremonial clothing. This symbolizes rebirth in a very dramatic way. One group which I once knew incorporated the shedding of blood into their coming-of-age

ceremony for both boys and girls, as a demonstration of commitment to the requirements of the new stage of life. Another group I once knew incorporated tattooing and ear-piercing. Those today who find such practices repugnant are not at a loss for alternatives.

Should it be possible to "fail" one of these initiations? Insofar as they acknowledge a status already gained, clearly the postulant has already passed all the relevant tests. It would be wrong to deny someone proper recognition of a standing they have already earned. Especially in the case of passages from youth to adulthood, to withhold social acknowledgement of a biological fact about a person's development would be irrational. An initiation that involves an ordeal of some kind is slightly different. It *should* be possible to fail it. However, there are ways of dealing with this which can save people from embarrassment and shame if they do fail. First of all, the leaders who perform the initiation should not allow the ordeal to go ahead in the first place if they think it likely that the postulant will not succeed. After all, it would be wrong to set someone up for failure. Secondly, the ordeal could take place in the days leading up to the ceremony, making the ceremony itself a rite of recognition which would not go ahead of the postulant fails the ordeal. The Eachtra, described earlier, can function as such an ordeal, which can be honored with a rite of recognition when the adventuring seeker returns home.

An example of an initiatory ordeal from mythology is the story of Gawain and the Green Knight. The story begins as King Arthur and his courtiers are enjoying New Year's Eve festivities. A knight in green armor arrives, carrying a mighty axe, and offers to allow anyone the chance to cut off his head, so long as the next year he may do the same in return. Only Sir Gawain agrees, and he strikes off the Green Knight's head. Then the knight picked it up and carried it home under his arm. The following year, true to his promise, Gawain travels to a castle where the Green Knight is appointed to meet him. The master of the castle says he is welcome to stay, so long as any gift he receives while staying there is passed along. Gawain agrees. Each night, the woman of the castle kisses him and attempts to seduce him. The following morning Gawain kisses the host. On the third night, the woman of the castle also gives Gawain a girdle, which she says will protect him from harm. Gawain keeps it secret: the following morning he passes on the kiss but not the girdle. When the Green Man finally arrives, he swings his axe three times only to give him a light tap on the neck. This is in recognition of his bravery in taking up the challenge. However, the knight also reveals himself to be the master of

the castle, and his wife's seduction attempts were deliberate tests of Gawain's virtue. So on the third stroke blood is drawn from Gawain's neck as punishment for keeping the girdle a secret. A similar story appears in the Irish tradition. In the story of Bricriu's Feast, the champions of Ulster were arguing over which of them should have the Champion's Portion. They ask a Druid named Uath mac Immoman to judge, and he offers a challenge: each of them can cut off his head, and the next day, Uath would cut off theirs. Only Cú Chullain accepts, and he hacks off Uath's head immediately. The next day, the Druid comes back, head on his shoulders where it belongs. So Cú Chullain bears his neck in fulfilment of his promise. The axe falls three times, and each time it reverses at the last instant, acknowledging Cú Chullain's bravery and integrity to his promise, and so confirming that he was the greatest champion there.

There are a variety of interesting symbols at play in these stories, which tell us about the way ancient Celts symbolized the sacred: the importance of heads, of New Year celebrations, of feasting, and the like. Both the Green Knight and the druid Uath mac Immoman are related to the god Cernunnos and the Green Man, for instance because of the color green on the Knight's armor, and because of the antlers which adorn the headdress of both figures. There is also something very Monty Python about the story as well. What could be more surreal and silly than a man who invites another man to chop off his head, and offers to do the same in return! But for the present purpose, it is important to notice that both stories feature a man who acts as an initiator, who puts someone's honesty and courage to the test.

8. From Follower to Leader

For a modern day Druidic initiation, something similar may well be in order. For instance, a postulant may be required to remain in darkness and silence, fasting and meditating, for a day and a night before the ceremony. At some time in the evening, some other members of the tribe visit him and coax him off to the pub. If he stays at home, he demonstrates commitment, and thus he succeeds. Another thing a modern Druidic initiation should put to the test is the postulant's knowledge. The Druids were renowned across the ancient world as possessors of great knowledge and wisdom. This should be maintained in the present movement. A Druidic initiation, then, should give the postulant a chance to demonstrate that he possesses the knowledge that a Druid can be expected to have. One way to do it might be to expect that the community's Druids should be university or college educated, as is expected of any Christian priest, Muslim cleric, or Jewish rabbi. Ancient Druids were learned, intellectual people and modern Druids

should be as well. I recognize that I am making a controversial statement here. Most people in the Pagan movement believe that someone without formal education can nevertheless be knowledgeable and wise. This view is impossible to deny at face value. But it sometimes hides intellectual laziness or even an anti-intellectual prejudice. It can hide a desire to obtain a certain kind of social prestige while doing as little of the work to earn it as possible. If modern Druids are unwilling to seek higher education when it is available to them, or are even ready to reject the value of education altogether, then they are *not* the modern-day equivalents of the ancient Druids. The authority of advanced education simply cannot be swept under the rug. Having said all that, however, I understand that education is always a collaborative activity, and does not happen only in schools. The important factual information connected to Druidry (history, archaeology, etc.) should be learned in universities with the experts and professionals. The spiritual knowledge can be learned from person to person, for instance in relations of individual student to teacher. Finally, the direct encounter with the presence of the sacred is always discovered, and perhaps only discovered, by yourself. The three kinds of knowledge are irreplaceable: they do not substitute for one another. Rather, they support one another. Indeed each may well be nearly worthless on its own.

Another way to give the postulant a chance to prove her knowledge is to show her certain objects or people which embody certain mysteries in the Celtic tradition, and ask her to identify them. This is how it happened in an Irish story called Manannan's Three Calls to Cormac. I have believed for many years that this story recounts an initiation, in particular Cormac's ceremonial inauguration as a king at Tara. The story begins when Cormac is offered a magical apple branch by a mysterious stranger. The branch rings with a magical sound that comes from the land "where there is nothing but truth, and where there is neither age nor withering away, nor heaviness, nor sadness, nor jealousy, nor envy, nor pride." This is, of course, Tir na n-Og. The giver of the gift demands in return his daughter, his son, and his wife. Cormac gives them, but to quell the anger of his tribe he immediately rings the Bell Branch. Then he sets out on a sea journey to bring them back. He arrives on an island where he is shown first a house on which a band of riders are thatching feathers into the roof. A blast of wind scatters the feathers each time the job is done. Then he is shown a man kindling a fire with an oak tree, and the fire burns through the tree faster than his ability to stoke up the fire with another one. Finally he is shown a fort with the Well of Wisdom at its center. The lord and lady of the fort invite him in, offer him a bath and a meal, and a place to stay for the night. A third man carrying a pig for the meal soon arrives, and Cormac is told that the pig will not cook unless four truths are told, one for every quarter of it. Each person there, then, must tell a story, and each story becomes a riddle for Cormac to solve. Cormac solves them by correctly identifying the lord and lady of the fort as Manannan and his wife. Cormac is then put to sleep, and when he wakes his family is returned to him, and the further gifts of an honor guard of 50 warriors and a magical truth-detecting cup is also given to him. The three wonders he encountered on the island are explained to him: the riders thatching the house are "the men of arts and the poets, and all that look for a fortune in Ireland, putting together cattle and riches." There is a moral lesson here, concerning obsession with wealth. The man kindling the fire is "a young lord that is more liberal than he can afford, and everyone else is served while he is getting the feast ready, and everyone else profiting by it." This teaches Cormac about the dangers of the pursuit of public honor and acclaim, and how it is possible to put others before oneself to one's own detriment. And the final wonder is of course the Well of Wisdom. These moral lessons here remain relevant to our own time. The pursuit of wisdom, above the pursuit of material wealth and public fame, belongs to the life of the Sacred King.

We have now seen three different things which an ordeal-style initiation could test: self-awareness, nobility of character, and finally knowledge. I would like to propose these three things as a kind of triad: they are the three things which together constitute the happy life. A Druidic initiation, then, is a ceremony in which the postulant is recognized for having attained them, or is put on track towards attaining them.

To fill in some more details, here are a few additional things we should expect from the Druids of today:

- First and foremost, a Druid should know where she came from, who she is, and where she is going. These are the things which show she has taken up the Morrigan's Challenge, and has taken seriously the mythological demand to "Know Yourself."

- A Druid should have had at least one transformative spiritual experience. It may have been deliberately created in a ritual, or spontaneously realized in a natural environment. Whichever way it comes, he or she must be able to show that it lead him or her to a greater sense of connectivity with the land, sea, and sky, to a Celtic god, or the landscape in which he or she lives.

- A Druid should understand her spiritual experiences in terms of the symbols and mysteries of the Celtic tradition. A Druid should know how to Part the Mist, drink from the Well of Wisdom, and speak the Sacred Truth.

- A Druid should know the important trees, plants, animals, and climate conditions of the bio-region where he lives. Ideally, he should travel to the Celtic homelands at least once in his life, to see the environment where the tradition began. But a Druid must develop his spiritual relationship with the land he actually inhabits.

- A Druid should have an excellent working knowledge of contemporary Celtic culture. She should be familiar with the food, music, sports, dances, arts, and so on, and should be an avid practitioner of some of them.

- A Druid should know who his tribe is, for the role of the Druid is a social one. Those who have no tribe should make some effort to find or create one. With the variety of festivals, pub moots, open circles, and Internet connections, this should not be difficult. You may find that by simply doing the Druid's work, and by doing it well, a community will eventually find you.

⊛ A Druid should know the history, mythology, and literature of the Celtic people. She should know at least the basic principles of psychology, philosophy, law, and related disciplines. This is the body of knowledge that is best learned from books or from higher education.

⊛ A Druid should have an ethical lifestyle. He is not an alcoholic or drug addict, does not abuse his partner or children, and does not exploit money or sexual favors from his associates. He is committed to environmentalism and social justice.

⊛ A Druid should be a capable teacher and leader. She should be able to resolve conflicts and tensions with compassion and justice. And she should be able to pass on what she has learned. Yet she does not impose her will on others, for instance by teaching and leading in a patronising, intrusive way.

⊛ A Druid should know how to create music, poetry, or some other kind of art. As described earlier, poetry and art are intimately connected with magic in the Celtic tradition.

⊛ A Druid should have had a full and unconditioned confrontation with death. This might be her own near-death experience, a situation in which she herself faced possible death, or the loss of a beloved friend or family member. There is no substitute for such experiences, however terrible they may be. The recognition of our mortality is the recognition of who we are.

⊛ And most importantly, a Druid should know how to love, and how to be loved.

9. Initiation of a Druid.

Given the nature of the historical sources available to us, an "authentic" reproduction of an ancient Druidic initiation is probably impossible. However, we know a great deal about the ideas and principles which guided spiritual thinking of ancient people, and it is on that basis that we can "reconstruct" Druidic ceremony. Here I shall attempt do so.

Initiation of a Druid. The postulant for initiation is brought to the site of the ceremony but made to wait outside. The ceremony begins with various commencement proclamations: the Announcement of the Gathering, a toast to ancestors, calls to the four quarters, and invocations and offerings to various deities. Then the postulant is called forward by the Druid who is leading the ceremony, to stand in front of a gate. The Druid says, "You have sought the Druids, learned much, and passed many tests. Is it your wish to continue?" The postulant answers yes. The Druid continues, "There is yet one last test you must pass before you can be counted among the wise. You must pass through this gateway. It is the holy gate to the Otherworld. It is the perilous bridge, the hidden cave, and the secret path. It is followed only by the wise, the heroic, and the seekers of Truth, who hear the calling of the Sidhe! The Mist of Manannan floods between its posts. Only she who knows herself can enter."

The Druids of the tribe, starting with the leader, ask the postulant several initiatory questions which should include, among any others: "What is your name? Do you come here of your own free will? From where have you come? What do you stand for? What trees do you know? What Gods have you seen? What is the secret of the Great Marriage?"

This series of questions should continue until the presiding Druid is satisfied. She then announces, "This seeker of wisdom has proved her quality. She shall be welcomed through the gate." The postulant is then allowed to enter the circle.

The senior female Druid, in her role as the embodiment of the Earth Goddess of Sovereignty, offers the postulant a drink from a cup. She says, "I give to you the wine of the Cup of Truth and the Holy Grail, from the womb of the Goddess of the Sovereignty of the Land, in the names of (the tribe's preferred deities). Know that they live within you, are embodied by you, and that you are a Druid in the tradition of your people."

Then the senior male Druid, as the embodiment of the Sky God of the Tribe, holds the bottom of a lit candle or torch to her forehead. He says, "I bestow upon you the fire of the sun, from the head of the God of the Sky, in the names of (the tribe's preferred deities). Know that they live within you, are embodied by you, and that you are a Druid in the tradition of your people."

Other assembled people present as gifts various ceremonial symbols, objects or clothing which identify the possessor as a Druid. The senior male Druid then says, "These are the teachings of the Druids, which you are now charged to carry within your heart and to embody in your words and actions." He reads from a wisdom-text describing the qualities of the Sacred King: the text can be the Triads of Ireland, the Testament *of Morann, the Instructions of Cormac, or another source of wisdom from the Celtic tradition preferred by the group.*

She is then taken to each of the four quarters in turn, and the presiding druid announces, "Behold, spirits of the East (South, West, North), this is (postulant's name), who has proven her quality. We declare that she is a Druid, and we are well blessed to have her among us."

The newly initiated Druid is then brought to the center of the circle, where Ogham sticks are cast to prophesy the forces and influences present at the time of the initiation, and with which she will be strong in her career as a Druid for the coming year.

Finally, the circle is closed down, and the tribe returns home for a "proper" celebration!

I make no claim about the historical accuracy of this reconstruction.[14] But it is safe to imagine that something very similar to this would have happened in ancient Celtic times. All the symbols, phrases, and gestures are all intended as dramatic repetitions of the spiritual principles which the Celtic tradition embodies. As a template, it has room for innovations and embellishments with which each tribe may make it "their own." It should be treated as a rite of passage for those looking to take up leadership responsibilities in their community. It presupposes that the postulant has gone through some kind of training program, yet does not assume that her learning process is finished after the ceremony is done.

The "question and answer" structure I have presented here is another way to test the postulant's knowledge, and it comes from a story called the *Colloquy of the Two Sages.* In this story, a younger poet is challenged by a senior poet with a series of esoteric questions. It opens as with the death Adne, the Chief Poet of Ireland at that time. His son Nede, away in Scotland, hears the news and returns to Tara. On the way, he is met by Bricriu who tells him that he should be Chief Poet, and gives him a decorated purple cloak appropriate to the rank. Bricriu then heads north to another poet, Ferchertne, and tells him that a younger low-ranking poet has usurped his place. Ferchertne rushes to Tara and challenges Nede to a series of questions, which Nede answers eloquently. Then, with the arrogant confidence of a rebellious youngster, he tosses the questions back in Ferchertne's face. The questions are, "Whence have you come? What is your name? What art do you practice? What are your tasks? By what path have you come? Whose son are you? Have you tidings?" and finally, "Who is greater than you?" Each of these questions, it would seem, are designed to determine whether Nede "knows himself." They are the kind of questions that someone who has attained intellectual and emotional maturity can be expected to answer. For there is a philosophical dimension to each them. Someone could answer them with the details of his or her birth certificate, school diplomas, family tree, career path, and so on, but that kind of answer would miss the point. "Initiatory" questions like these require the answerer to look at her life in the larger context of its direction, purpose, meaning, and values. They can be answered properly only by someone who is *responsible* for her own life: that is, someone *able to respond* when her life is called into question. A "correct" answer, if there is such a thing, is an answer which demonstrates that the person has become the author of her own biography. The questions give the postulant a chance to demonstrate that he or she can speak the language of wisdom along with the others, and so deserves to be counted as one of them.

The second-to-last question, "Have you tidings?" is particularly interesting. In the context of the story, Ferchertne was asking Nede if he was capable of magical prophesy. The younger poet, Nede, described a future of prosperity and happiness. The elder poet, Ferchertne, described a future of corruption, famine, and evil. The story makes it clear that this darker prophesy is the better one, for Nede immediately acknowledges Ferchertne as the superior poet, and kneels at his feet. Ferchertne now has a chance to punish the younger poet's boldness, but instead chooses to recognize and reward his self-awareness. Nede is invited to stand and take a place at Ferchertne's side as an equal. This was the right thing for Ferchertne to do: It would have been unjust to refuse to recognize the level of self-knowledge which Nede had demonstrated. There are many lessons we can take from this story. A readiness to stand up to authority, to think on one's feet, and to be bold in the pursuit of beneficial opportunities, is part of what it means to be mature. Yet maturity also includes respect for the wisdom and knowledge of others. Moreover, one need not always defeat one's opponents to "win." Sometimes opportunities arise in which everyone may win, and often such opportunities can be created, not just waited for.

Bricriu, the troublemaker who instigated the whole situation, is a lot like the trickster-gods of various cultures who stir up the status-quo in order to make possible some new revelation. The role of the troublemaker, like that of the satirist poet, is well-established in the Celtic mythological tradition. He does not make trouble for its own sake. He does it as a way of aiming for a beneficial social change. When, for instance, Cairbre spoke the first satire every spoken in Ireland, which humiliated King Bres for his lack of hospitality, his satire was effective because it was already true that King Bres was an unjust, inhospitable, corrupt ruler. The magic of the *glam*, the satire poem which causes blemishes, does not create the situation but draws attention to it in a special and unignorable way. The best protection against satire is to be a just, honorable, upright ruler of one's life. The hooks and barbs of satire cannot catch on such a person, and they fall away of their own accord. The trickster-figure in the context of the initiation ceremony is the person who gives the postulant a nudge out of the door of his comfortable status quo, and so starts him on an adventure of discovery and transformation.

The pursuit of self-knowledge is the vehicle that drives the journey from childhood to adulthood, from youth to maturity, and from "innocence" to "enlightenment." Every passage through the different stages of life is made possible by a transformation or discovery of self-awareness. Therefore the spiritual life is initiated, sustained, and brought the greatest extent of its flourishing by the simple instruction, "Know Yourself." It is the impulse which, when taken up as a life-long vacation, transforms you from an animal of the species *Homo Sapiens* into a full-fledged human being.

10. The Blessing of Belonging

What if you find yourself alone, with no family or friends who would be interested in forming a spiritual community? Although the Celtic community is alive and flourishing, the Druids and pagans among them are few and far-flung. Someone in that solitary position does have a few options available: regional gatherings, internet connections, teaching programs available by mail or by e-mail, and the like. And aside from these, there are still many things that can be done on one's own. Indeed there are some practices which can really be performed only on one's own. I have described some of them already. But there are other important things that require a community. Finding others to work with spiritually is a bit like finding a boyfriend or girlfriend: you must make yourself available, take risks meeting others, and as you meet them decide how intimate with them you really want to be. Appearances can be both revealing and deceiving. One must open one's heart to another and thus leave oneself vulnerable to being hurt. And yet when one connects with someone who matches you well, the benefits are enormously valuable, making the whole effort worthwhile.

The practice of Peaceful Abiding tends to develop in the spirit of the practitioner a certain sound, vibration, or resonance which can sometimes be sensed, just under the surface of consciousness, by other people whose spirits resonate at the same frequency. Just by living the spiritual life, and living it well, one will normally attract other like-minded people around you. This is how the phenomenon was described by George "A.E." Russell:

Around a pure atom of crystal all the atoms of the element in a solution gather, and in like manner one person after another emerged out of the mass, betraying their close affinity to my moods as they were engendered. I met these people seemingly by accident along country roads, or I entered into conversation with strangers and found they were intimates of the spirit. I could prophesy from the uprising of new moods in myself that I, without search, would soon meet people of a certain character, and so I met them… The concurrence of our personalities seemed mysterious and controlled by some law of spiritual gravitation, like that which in the chemistry of nature makes one molecule fly to another.[15]

Russell has surely said with elegance all that needs to be said about the spiritual affinities people sometimes recognize in others. Some people can sense that they have a future with someone after only a few moments of conversation, or even after a single moment of eye contact. This spiritual gravitation may well be the strongest force to bring people together: stronger than shared symbols, experiences and purposes, economic interests, and leaders.

"Belonging" is a blessing people give to each other. It makes people feel welcome, safe, and valued. It discourages freeloading. It attracts new members, and holds on to old ones. It reinforces commitment to one's ideals, and fosters confidence and courage in their pursuit. Above all it instills a sense of home, place, identity, and purpose. A clann that wants to foster the sense of belonging should have more in common with one another than their practice of the same religion. In addition to participating in ceremonies together, you should also share things such as meals and meal-preparations, vacations, child-raising responsibilities, labor projects such as cleaning or renovating houses or planting gardens of flowers or vegetables, organize movie-nights or pub-nights, and so on. If there are musically talented members, they should sing and play together, and learn Celtic music along with other styles they enjoy. If some of the members of your clann are athletic, perhaps they could learn the indigenous Celtic games such as hurling, and look for other tribes to play with. If there are enough warriors, perhaps they could stage re-enactments of historic battles for the public, or hold sword-fighting competitions with each other and with other tribes. A regular meeting should span an entire weekend instead of a single evening. On the Friday night, for example, everyone arrives after the workday is done and meets each other again, catching up with the news since the last meeting if they have not been in touch during that time. The Saturday afternoon can be spent preparing a meal together, to be eaten in a grand feast after the ceremony. On the Sunday, in the morning or early afternoon before it is time for everyone to go home, hold teaching-workshops for the younger or newer members, watch a movie together, make music, play games, or go for a walk in a local park, forest, cemetery, or public garden. The more you have in common with each other, and the more things you do together, the more you will solidify the sense of belonging.

Seven:
The Renewal of the World

It was in a mist the Tuatha de Dannan, the people of the gods of Dana, or as some called them, the Men of Dea,
came through the air and the high air to Ireland.

—Lady Gregory,
Gods and Fighting Men (1904)

Having begun at the level of the individual seeker and moved from there to the level of immediate family and community, it is well that the continuation of one's practice of Mysticism should reach the expanded level of the whole of the world.

1. The Celtic Creation Story

Most people think that we don't have complete and perfect knowledge of what the ancient Celts believed about the origin of the universe. We do, however, know a great deal about the basic mythological and philosophical ideas that animated the ceremonies they enacted. As a general rule, community ceremony would have re-dramatized the story of the creation of the world at the appropriate time(s)

of the year. This would have been the culture's most important community ritual. It served the purpose of reaffirming solidarity through the shared experience of being in the same geographical or regional landscape, holding the same mythology in common, or being descended from the same ancestors. On the level of religion and magic, the re-enactment of the creation of the world subdues the forces of transience, death, and primordial chaos. It prevents or postpones the destruction of the world, and reanimates the powers of animal and plant fertility that lie dormant in the winter. It was believed that the community's ability to procure justice, its economic prosperity, its military success, and its artistic greatness can all be perpetuated by ceremonially linking them to environmental, lunar, solar, and cosmic cycles, and indeed to the beginning of time when all was in proper harmony. We then find that the process of creation is perpetually ongoing. Like a living body, the world has biorhythms that can be symbolically associated with the breath or the heartbeat of a human being. It might even be claimed that it can have diseases. But there is an unseen, mystical implication as well. The ceremony of re-enacting the creation story makes us contemporaries with the creation event itself. *It enables members of the community participate in the creation of the world.* If you can participate in the creation of the world, then you have the potential to be a cocreator of the world.

That may be the proper way to understand the famous claim made by Irish Druids that they themselves "created heaven and earth, sea, sun, and moon".[1] On one level, this might be nothing more than propaganda designed to secure the Druid's hold on social power, rather like the Christian claim that unless you receive their baptism, you will go to hell. Or it may have been Roman-made, anti-Druidic propaganda, painting the Druids as full of decadence and vanity. But in terms of a personal spiritual practice, we can decide *what* world is created and renewed by spiritual practice. The reality is not so much that Druids create the world, but that through their magical practices, as well as their exercise of social power (educating the young, rendering court judgements, and so on) they participate in the creation of the world as an ongoing event. The world is sustained and enabled to continue through their magical power.

There have been a number of literary attempts to create or recreate a creation story for the Celts. Consider the story of "The Earth-Shapers" published by Ella Young.[2] Her version starts with the goddess Brighid, living in Tir Na n-Og, hearing the sound of the unborn Earth dreaming of beauty and crying out to be born. She convinces the other deities to travel down with her to the primordial waters, raise up the seafloor and shape it into the hills, valleys, fields and landscapes of the Earth as we know it today. Young was writing an original children's fable, not recounting an artifact of folk storytelling. But inside the simplistic writing style some philosophical ideas emerge clearly. For example, the gods co-operate as they shape the world. And they make it into a realm of peace and beauty. Young also presents a four-fold correspondence of the Four Treasures with the Four Cities from whence the gods came, and with the four cardinal directions. This I take to be an instance of the principle of the Four Green Fields, the "horizontal" four-fold division of territorial space, combined with a "vertical" three-fold division of celestial, mortal, and cthonic (underworld) realms. The whole forming a complete sacred cosmology. At the center Young places the Stone of Destiny.

George "A.E." Russell published a "Celtic Cosmogony" in *The Candle of Vision*. By contrast with Young's story, it is directed at the adult, for it is written in a more intellectual style. It begins with the God of the Sea, "the boundless Lir, an infinite depth, an invisible divinity, neither dark nor light, in whom were all things past and to be."

Aengus Og receives more dignity as the "all-pervading divinity who first connects being with non-being." Russell's purpose was not only to describe the origin of the world, but also to claim a particular metaphysical point about the nature of the world, which was that the world is not a mere artifact, but is a living being. It is one-half of the primordial being which split into two, a Great Father and a Great Mother. The deities involved do not craft the world like a potter or a carpenter, leaving the world at the end of the process essentially a mass of non-living matter, separate from its creator, as in the Biblical Genesis story. The idea here is that the world is the very body of the deity involved, and that because the world is the body of a deity its process of creation continues on. We can see that his purpose is metaphysical, and more than literary, because he also claims that the names of the deities involved are less important than the cosmogonic function they fulfill, and so are in some sense interchangeable with the local deity-names for other particular regions of Ireland, and of the world.

Russell also placed his Celtic Cosmology in relation to other philosophical systems of the world which he had been studying at the time. As pointed out by historian Ronald Hutton, it was Russell's purpose to place Druidic Ireland on an equal footing with the great ancient religious civilizations of Greece, Egypt, and India. For this purpose, he placed the Great

Marriage at the center of the Celtic creation story. This is a near-universal principle but with several uniquely Celtic manifestations. It is dramatized in Newgrange by the light of the sun every year at Midwinter. It appears in the story of the lovemaking of Dagda and Morrigan. Indeed it is re-enacted by every loving couple in the world. To Russell, the Irish deities are simply different masks for the same God: they are, to him, the regional names for the same deities described in the Upanisads. His cosmology, then, is Irish mainly in its detail; its underlying cosmogonic principle is much more universal.

Russell's vision of the world is the vision of a universal gnostic monotheism. In this vision, there is one and only one overseeing principle of order and meaning, influencing and informing everything that exists in the visible, material world. It is known primarily through the personal, partly intellectual and partly imaginative grasp of an individual seeker. Because this single divine being appears in a wide variety of forms and faces, its place on the traditional distinction between immanence and transcendence is hard to pin down. On the one hand, the overseeing principle of order and meaning exists "in" and "with" the world, animating it with life, and assigning to everything a purpose, place, function, and relation to the whole. The world is the personal body of a deity, the Great Goddess. It is not the impersonal product of a deity's handiwork. On the other hand, there is an Otherworld, called by Russell "the Many-Coloured Land," where lives the Great Father who created the physical world, and it is invisible to the physical senses. It is not subject to the ravages of time, transience, decay, and mortality as is everything else in the material world. Indeed Russell's and Young's accounts emphasize the distance and distinction between the physical world and the mysterious forces and powers of the sacred world. As we have seen, Russell described himself as "an exile from living nature." In his poem "Farewell of Pan," he represented earthly beauty and joy as limited, incomplete. The deity most well-known for celebrating bodily pleasures, the Greek god Pan, declares himself to be an exile from heaven. How strange, that he should have missed the essential point of the Hindu holy books he so admired, and of some of his own poetry, that the Many-Coloured Land is everywhere, all around us!

2. Bringing the Story to Life

Russell and his friends were members of the Irish Literary Revival, and were well known to each other. Young's book was beautifully illustrated by Maude Gonne, who was Yeats' lover for a time. They were probably familiar with the story of the *Cath Maigh Tuireadh*. ("Battle of Moytirra") That story records the arrival of the Gods in Ireland. I believe it was the original Celtic creation myth, edited and altered so as not to compete with the Christian creation myth that displaced it. With that story, and a firm grasp of the mys-

teries, it should not be difficult to assemble again a ceremonial structure that reenacts the story of the creation of the world and thus empowers and perpetuates your spiritual life and your community.

Here is an example of such a ceremony for groups, using a dovetailed interaction between the narrator of a story (the Bard) and the magical invoker of the figures, powers, and forces described by the story (the Druid). The full story is available in several published sources. The standard English translation of the original Irish text is Elizabeth A. Gray's *Cath Maigh Tuired* (Irish Texts Society, 1982). I also recommend Lady Gregory's telling of the story in *Gods and Fighting Men* (1904). I have used original text from both of these works to furnish the Bard's dialogue in this sample re-enactment of the origin story. Some parts of the Druid's speech comes from the *Carmina Gadelica*, the well-known collection of Scottish prayers.

Imagine now that your community, consisting in your circle of friends and a few not-too-distant acquaintances, are in a forest or a park somewhere. It is a festival, and at this moment, before it begins, people are still arriving, meeting one another, telling tales of their lives since the previous festival, setting up tents or trailers, or meditating on the land to feel its energy. A flag rises, and the blast of a horn fills the space, and everyone looks up. A ceremony is about to begin! And everyone starts to walk towards the center place. A circle is formed, the names of various gods are honored in the four cardinal directions and the three "realms" of land, sea, and sky. Then two cloaked figures stand in the center of the circle to recite the story of the creation of the world.

The Arrival of the Gods

The Chief Druid signals the community (with music, blast from a horn, a flag, or the like) that the ceremony is about to begin, and when everyone has gathered recites an announcement of the gathering. The re-enactment of the creation of the world may begin.

The Bard: "It was in a mist the Tuatha de Dannan came, through the sky to the Earth. It was from the north they came; and in the place they came from they had four cities, where they fought their battle for learning."

The Druid: "Ye who came from the North, and who now dwell within the lakes and hills, the sun and moon, the land, sea, and sky, and the hearts and minds of your people, we call upon you to be present with us for this rite. For behold, we are the People of the Earth. The land upholds us, the sea surrounds us, the sky enfolds us. And you are with us.

The Bard: "And the Tuatha de Dannan brought from those four cities their four treasures: From Falias was brought the Stone of Fál, which was located in Tara. It used to cry out beneath every king that would take Ireland."

The Druid: "O Gods of our people, the blessing of the Stone we request from you, that honor and truth be upon us as it was upon the great kings and queens of old."

The Bard: "From Gorias was brought the spear which Lugh had. No battle was ever sustained against it, or against the man who held it in his hand."

The Druid: "O Gods of our people, the blessing of the spear of Lugh we request from you, that it protect us from all danger in all the three worlds."

The Bard: "From Findias was brought the sword of Nuada. No one ever escaped from it once it was drawn from its deadly sheath, and no one could resist it."

The Druid: "O Gods of our people, the blessing of the sword of Nuada we request from you, that it shall oppose all those of baneful intent who stand in the way of our noble purpose."

The Bard: "From Murias was brought the Dagda's cauldron. No company ever went away from it unsatisfied."

The Druid: "O Gods of our people, the blessing of the Cauldron of Dagda we request from you, that we shall partake of its fertile bounty."

This sample ceremonial text essentially narrates the creation of the world and the arrival of the gods of the Tribe of Dana. It dramatically establishes the threshold between sacred and ordinary time, sacred and ordinary space. When this has finished, the tribe may proceed to the more specific purpose of the ceremony, which might be a seasonal celebration, divining of omens, initiations, or other business.

Let us imagine that on this occasion the specific purpose of the ceremony is to dramatize the full story of the creation of the world. The next major event in the narrative has to do with the rival tribe which was already present in Ireland (and who knows how they got there). These two competing groups of deities fought twice over possession of Ireland: or to be more specific, they fought over possession of a "great pillar." Dáithi Ó Hógáin, the professor of Irish at University College Dublin, speculated that the word for pillar (*tuir*) was confused with a place-name in county Sligo (Moytirra) and so the story's location

"Jupiter Column" in market square of Marburg, Germany.

was transferred there. The description of the pillar gives away the confusion. It is variously described as a tower of gold, silver, or crystal, which was typical early Irish imagery for the sun. The story of the Cath Maigh Tuireadh, therefore, is the story of the battle on the "plain of the pillar" (*magh tuir*). If the pillar is indeed the sun, then the plain of the pillar is the whole of that which is illuminated by the sun—it is the entire world. Moreover, the sun as "great pillar" is the *axis mundi* that stands at the center-place of the cosmos, uniting the three realms. I find it elegant that the battleground was the whole world, and the prize of the battle is the universal *axis mundi*, and yet at the same time the story is located on a certain mountain in the west of Ireland which can be visited. Indeed, almost all Irish storytelling is deeply rooted in actual locations around the country. For instance, the place "in the northwest of Connaught" where the Tuatha de Dannans landed is the mountain of Slieve Anierin, in county Leitrim.

The rival tribe which competes with the Tuatha de Dannan for possession of Ireland is called the Fomhoire, a name which means "under-spirits." They are also called Fir Bolg, roughly meaning "men of the bag." The Fomhoire come from out of the south of the world, led by their own sun-king, Balor of the Evil Eye. They are said to be darker and less virtuous than the Tuatha de Dannans. Because the gods are associated with the brighter other-world from across the sea or sky, whereas the Fomhoire are associated with the underworld and Neolithic mounds, and because the gods are generally portrayed in the stories as more wise, honorable, and generous, therefore the two tribes are natural opponents. The story of their war parallels the story of wars between two tribes of deities found in numerous legends around the world, such as the Norse gods who overthrow the Giants, or the Greek deities who defeat the Titans. In Babylonian mythology, the god Marduk fights and defeats Tiamat, and he shapes the world from her body. The Hindu god Indra battles and over-throws a serpentine creature named Vrtra. One finds this theme repeated in the image of St. George, the dragon-slaying patron saint of England. The Gauls of continental Europe used to erect great pillars called "Jupiter-columns" which were topped by the image of a horseman defeating a monster. In Ella Young's tale of the Earth Shapers, the gods descend to the Earth to clear away a race of monsters, by pushing them further underground or into the sea.

According to Mircae Eliade, the defeated powers represent chaos, and the victory over chaos makes the creation of the world possible. "The world was given existence through the sacrifice of a primordial monster, symbolizing chaos (Tiamat), or through that of a cosmic giant (Ymir, Pan-Ku, Purusa). To assure the reality and the enduring-ness of a construction, there is a repetition of the divine act of perfect construction: the Creation of the worlds and of man."[3] Such stories may also represent the folk-memory of the dynastic succession of one culture or tribe over another one, expressed in mythological form as the defeat of an older tribe of gods by a newer tribe. Indeed the association of the Fomhoire with certain pre-Celtic monuments is suggests this interpretation. However, in the Irish matter there are several deities who belong to both tribes at the same time. Lugh Lamh-Fada is one such deity, for he is the son of Balor's daughter. Manannan apparently pre-dates them all but remains apart from the major battles and is counted as a member of the Tuatha de Dannan af-terward. Moreover, we also know that the Celts took up many of the customs and practices of the pre-Celtic people they encountered in Ireland, including forms of art and of engineering. The important point here, however, is that by re-enacting the creation-story, we are brought closer to the gods and cosmic powers which feature in the story. Like the adventuring hero returning from the Otherworld with a treasure, we go back in history and retrieve the event of creation itself. This empowers us to renew or even re-create our world in our own life and time.

There was not one but two wars between these two tribes of divinities. The first one ended with a general amnesty.

The Tuatha de Dannan, as a token of their good-will, agreed to let a man who was born of both tribes rule as the high king of Ireland. His name was Bres (the beautiful), but he turned out to be a miserly, unjust, and inhospitable ruler. Bres was deposed by the first satire ever recited in Ireland, spoken by a travelling poet who castigated him for treating his guests poorly. Nuada argat-lamh, "silver-handed" or "silver-armed" is re-installed as the high king at Tara. Nuada lost his arm (and with it, the kingship) during the first battle, but Diancecht, the physician of the gods, fashioned an artificial arm for him and thus enabled him to reclaim the throne. Bres then went to the north part of the country to raise an army and recapture the kingship. His Fomhoir kinsman Balor was critical at first, saying "you should not take by force what you could not keep by justice." But Balor eventually gave his support.

In our imaginary community gathering, the two cloaked figures might continue the dramatization of the creation story with a dialogue like this one, in which the Fomorians are encountered and banished from the circle:

Encountering the Outsiders.

The Bard: *"It was on the first day of Beltaine, that is now called May Day, the Tuatha de Dannan came, and it was to the north-west of Connaught they landed. But the Firbolgs, the Men of the Bag, that were in Ireland before them, and that had come from the south, saw nothing but a mist, lying on a hill. And it was a long time before that that the Fomhoir came to Ireland, dreadful they were to look at, and maimed, having but one foot or one hand, and there never came to Ireland an army more horrible or more dreadful than the army of the Fomhoir. And their King was Balor of the Evil Eye, and anyone who looked into the eye, even if they were thousands in number, would fall dead."*

The Druid: *"Behold, People of the Tribe, that today is Beltaine itself, and the anniversary of the Coming of the Gods to Earth. Behold the four great treasures which they brought with them, to bless this land and to bless the people. And behold the Fomhoir, the Fir Bolge, the monsters and tempters of evil and corruption who were driven from the Earth by our Gods. Behold how they return every year, in the form of miserliness and greed, poverty and neglect, injustice and cruelty, avarice and vice. And let us now call upon our Gods to defeat them once again!"*

We are now about to introduce some new characters. If there is someone available to take the place of each deity called upon, he or she should not reveal him- or herself until after the invocation is done. He or she may be hidden behind a curtain or door, or if the ceremony is outdoors in a forest then hidden behind trees outside of the circle. Some chanting or singing of the name of the deity after the invocation might also add dramatic tension as well.

As the Bard mentions each of them in turn, the Druid recites a ritual speech calling for the god to be with us. The first new character to introduce is Ogma, who is the Dagda's brother, and Lugh Lamh-Fada's personal champion. They met at a place now known as Rathconrath (in present day county Westmeath); an interesting name, containing within it the words "rath," for a fortress, and "conradh," meaning an assembly or conference. Ogma's presence is important here because even in times of difficulty and strive, certain intellectual qualities are useful and necessary, such as clear thinking and good speech.

Invocation to Ogma

The Bard: *There were many great preparations which the Gods made in the final great fight with the Fomhoire. And the first task was to call a council to plan the battle. And it was Lugh Lamh-Fada, and the two brothers Dagda and Ogma, who conversed in secret on the hill of Grellach Dollaid, along with Goibhniu the Smith and Dian Cecht the Physician, and all the Druids of Ireland. They spent a full year at that secret conference, so that Grellach Dollaid is called the Amrún of the men of the Goddess.*

The Druid: *People of the Earth, I speak of the great god Ogma, the son of the goddess Etain, the brother of Dagda, the most eloquent speaker of all the gods, the teacher of writing and poetry, whose tongue is joined to the ears of his people by a golden chain. And during the reign of Bres, after the first battle of Maigh Tuireadh, Ogma was forced to carry wood from Clew Bay, of the Great Plain, to Tara, every day, and two-thirds of his bundle would be washed away by the tide. And yet under this indignity he kept his honour. And it was Oghma's great boast at the war council of the Tuatha de Dannan, that he would be a match for the king of the Fomhoir, holding his own against 27 others, and winning a third of the battle on his own for the people of Ireland. And for this great feat, Lugh Lamh-Fada made him his champion. At this place, as at Grellach Dollaid, the Amrún of the Men of the Goddess, your powers of speech and eloquence, your council and wisdom, and your champion's strength, lives on. Oghma, Son of Etain, God of writing, eloquence, wisdom, and Champion of the Tuatha de Dannan, forever.*

The next new character we meet is Lugh Lamh-Fada ("long-armed" or "long-handed"), a god of the sun, of light, of battle heroism, and the victor over the Fomhoire. He appears in the story while both sides are preparing for war: he brazenly walks up to the royal palace at Tara and demands to be admitted. The guards question him as to his worthiness. He lists his various skills, and the guards tell him that there is already someone present who has each of them. Finally he asks if there is anyone present who has all of the skills. The guards concede that they do not, and Lugh is admitted to the royal court. Thus he proves himself to be more skilful and multi-talented than anyone else there. Nuada, the reigning king at the time, immediately places him on the throne for nine days. He is then assigned the task of organizing the Tuatha de Dannan in the second battle against the Fomhoir.

Invocation to Lugh Lamh-Fada.

The Bard: The next choose is to select our battle chieftain, who was Lugh Lamh-Fada, the son of Ethne, the daughter of Balor of the Evil Eye.

The Druid: People of the Earth, I speak of the great God, Lugh Lamh-Fada, the son of the Sun, the bearer of the spear of light, and the master of all arts. On the day he arrived at the royal hill of Tara, he shone with the brilliance of the rising sun. And the gatekeeper challenged him and tried to turn him away, saying that they had a man for each of the skills that Lugh Lamh-Fada possessed. But Lugh was the Many Talented One, and the royal court had no one who could do all of them himself, and so he was admitted within the royal enclosure and placed on the throne of sovereignty for nine days. A wonder was upon the people of the royal court at Uisneach, where the King of Ireland hosted a great gathering of the Tuatha de Dannan, who saw him approaching from the west. For they thought he was the morning sun, although the sun rises in the east. And it was Lugh who stirred and inspired the armies of the Tuatha de Dannan to rise up against the Fomorians who were oppressing them. And it was Lugh whose casting spear took out the evil eye of his grandfather Balor, the chief of the Fomorians, and so made an end of him. And he was the only one who could do this, for he was descended from both tribes. At this time, as at the time of the festival named Lughnasad in his honor, his name and story lives forever. Lugh Lamh-Fada, son of the Sun, bearer of the spear of light, and the master of all arts.

There are many other characters who could be introduced here, for there were many who contributed something to the battle. It would also be appropriate, for instance, to recite the story of Dian Cecht, the physician of the gods, who created a magic healing well. Here I have the bard recite the story of how Lugh asked each of the gods to contribute something to the coming battle, and how at the end of the day he asked Dagda, who boasted that he could do everything himself.

Invocation to the Dagda

The Bard: The next task for preparation is to ask of each of the gods what they bring to the battle, to help defeat the Fomhoire. And Magthen, the great magician, promised to call down the mountains of the world to roll on the ground. The cup bearers promised to put a great thirst on the warriors of the Fomhoire, and to hold up the 12 great lakes of Ireland so that they would get no water from them. And Giobhniu the Smith promised that every sword that was broken and every spear lost from its shaft would be fixed, even if the battle should last seven years, and every spear made by his hand would find its mark. And Diancecht, the physician, promised that every man wounded there, unless his head was struck off, would be made whole and sound again the next day. And Dagda gave the greatest contribution of all.

***The Druid:** People of the Earth, I speak of the Dagda, the Good God, the Red Man of Knowledge. It was Dagda who lived in the great house on the River Boyne, that is known to us now as Newgrange, and with it he could make nine months pass as a single day. And he had a mighty club, so great that it took eight men to carry it, and it would drag a track on the ground deep enough for the boundary of a province of Ireland. It would bring instant death to anyone who was struck by the one end, and restore life to anyone struck by the other end. And he had a beautiful harp that would come to him when he called it, the music of which would put laughter, or tears, or sleep, on a whole assembly. And then Lugh was*

asking all the gods what they would bring to the battle, and each of them gave their offering, but it was Dagda who said that what each of them could do, he could do all of them with only himself. And so he was declared the good god, and all the gods gave a great shout of joy. Here at this place, as at the Magic House on the River Boyne, your name and story lives on. Dagda, the Good! The Red Man of Knowledge! Come Winter, come Summer, out of the mouths of harps and bags and pipes! You remain the God of our people forever.

The last of the preparatory tasks is to court the favor of the goddess of sovereignty, the goddess of the land, as the ancient kings used to do at their inaugurations. In the original tale, Lugh and Dagda and Ogma went to visit "the three gods of Danu" to collect some weapons for Lugh which they had been making for seven years. After that, the Dagda went to a house where he had arranged to meet the goddess Morrigan. The story says the two spoke for a short time, and then "united"— which is clearly to say, they had sex together, and that their lovemaking was a "Great Marriage." (Not that I'm suggesting the players of the re-enactment should do this!)

Because three male deities have been introduced, it may seem appropriate to introduce three female deities. In the presentation to follow, there is an invocation to only one Goddess, and that is the Morrigan. However, the

Morrigan, as we have seen, is actually three deities in one. In this imaginary re-dramatization of the creation of the world, the triple male god in the person of Lugh, Oghma, and Dagda, meet the triple goddess Morrigan. The Great Marriage between them makes possible the defeat of the Fomhoire. There are several ways in which the Great Marriage can be enacted. As we have seen earlier, one simple way is for the woman to offer to the man a drink from a cup. In Wiccan ceremonies, the Great Marriage (which they call the "Great Rite") is re-enacted by a priestess holding a chalice of wine and a priest who dips his ritual knife into the wine. Then the two drink from the chalice together and serve it to everyone else. For the purpose of re-enacting this battle, the three goddesses might offer chalices of mead to the three gods, or give them weapons with which to defeat the Fomhoir. However you choose to do it, it should be clear to other participants that the favor of the Goddess is given to the gods of the Tuatha de Dannan, and so they are empowered to defeat the Fomhoire and restore justice, prosperity, and peace to the world.

Invocation to the Morrigan

The Bard: The final task is to obtain the favor and the blessing of the Great Queen of the Land, the Goddess of the Sovereignty of Ireland, who we call the Morrigan. For the god Dagda went to his hidden house and met her there. When he arrived she was washing clothes in the water, with one foot at the north end of the lake and the other foot at the south end. She came to the Dagda and gave him her love, and they united.

The Druid: People of the Earth, I speak of the great Goddess who is called The Mhórrigan, the Great Queen, the Crow of Battle, the Queen of Phantoms, the Goddess of the many shapes and faces, and of the Sovereignty of Ireland. I speak of her sisters Macha, who cuts men down in battle, and Babh, who eats the heads of the slain. It is the Mhórrigan who is the bride of the true king of the land. It is she who must be respected and honored by us all, so that strong animals shall come to our hunters, and our crops grow tall in our fields. It was she who came to Cú Chullain and offered him her love, and for his refusal she hindered his fight against Ferdiad, and against the hosts of Maeve of Cruachan. And yet she loved him still, for at his death she came to him in the form of a raven, and perched on his shoulder, and kept his enemies at bay that he might die a noble death. And before that, on the eve of the second Battle of Maigh Tuireadh, she gave her love to the Dagda and so bestowed Her favor upon the Tuatha de Dannan. At this place, as at her sanctuary of Rath Maeve, on the Hill of Tara, and at Maeve's Cairn on the summit of the hill of Knock na Rae, her name and her story lives on. Mhórrigan, the Great Queen, the Goddess of the Sovereignty of Ireland forever.

If you have people representing the gods in the story, I strongly recommend against casting a person in the role of Balor. For Balor is the main source of fear and evil: he is the primordial scapegoat. He takes upon his shoulders the burden of the community's injustices and vices, and his defeat "purifies" the community. This burden should not be imposed on a friend or relation. In my experience it is best to use a mannequin, a puppet, or an effigy of some kind. Moreover, the effigy can be used to make "banishing magic" in your personal life: for instance by writing on a small slip of paper some situation or aspect of your life you want to be rid of, and slipping it into the effigy of Balor, to be destroyed.

During the battle, Lugh is assigned nine warriors to keep him out of the fighting, because the other gods regard him as too important to lose. But Lugh escapes their custody, and chants a curse upon the Fomhoire army using a technique called *corrghuinecht* ("crane magic"; chanting with the use of one hand, one eye, and one foot). A partial, paraphrased version of his poem is given here for Lugh to recite.

The Battle of Maigh Tuireadh

The Bard: *"Now when the time came for the great battle, the Fomhoire marched out of their encampment and formed themselves into strong indestructible battalions. There was not a chief nor a skilled warrior among them without armour against his skin, a helmet on his head, a spear in his hand, a sword in his belt, and a shield on his shoulder. To strike against the Fomhoire on that day was like striking a head against a cliff, a hand in a serpent's nest, a face in the fire. And Lugh Lamh-Fada broke into the battle, and fought fiercely so that none should be in bondage any longer. And Lugh chanted the spell which raised the spirits of the Tuatha de Dannan warriors, and put fear into the hearts of the Fomhoir.*

Lugh Lamh-Fada:

"Havoc and battle, strain and death upon the Fomhoir!

They shall be defeated by our host,

and birds of prey shall rain down on them.

Dark men are they! Roaring brightly are we!

Hurrah and Woe! Onward! O you my beautiful ones!

My fight will not relent until the end.

Courage be upon you,

Although our land of rushes be laid waste by fire

And the presence of death be among us.

Before the presence of all the gods,

before the sky and the earth and the sea,

before the sun and the moon and the stars.

O Band of warriors my promise here to you:

Our army is as mighty as the ocean

It shall be victorious upon the field of battle.

Strain and death, havoc and battle, upon the Fomhoir!"

If you have enough people to do it, this is the place to re-enact the whole battle, with Druids chanting, drummers drumming, and warriors fighting each other and dying everywhere.

Here we find another reason why it is important to use an effigy instead of an actor to play the role of Balor: for Lugh must throw a stone into Balor's eye! The story says that the eye was never opened except in battle, and four men had to lift the lid. At the moment he does so, Lugh casts a sling stone in to the eye, and it smashes through Balor's skull, destroying everyone standing behind him. The safest way to represent this in a re-enactment is if Balor is a puppet or an effigy, which is knocked over by the stone-throw or the spear-thrust of the person representing Lugh. This symbolizes the banishment of all that the Fomhoir represent, and to assert the sovereignty of all that the Tuatha de Dannan represent. You may want to consider letting everyone throw a stone at Balor!

Although the battle is a victory for the gods, the story makes it clear that it is still a terrible slaughter. Nuada of the Silver Hand, one of the important kings of the Tuatha de Dannan, is killed in the battle, for instance. And the enormous harvest of death on both sides cannot be regarded as worthy of much celebration. This is an important theme in Celtic heroic literature: even victories are tragedies. Furthermore, Lugh also captures Bres, but agrees to spare him in return for his knowledge of agriculture. Thus we find that the relationship of these two communities is complex. The one conquered the other, but simultaneously allowed a certain amount of intermarriage in the interest of peace, and also a sharing of some of their knowledge.

With the Gods victorious, Morrigan proclaims a special poem that has come to be known as "Morrigan's prophesy of peace." A paraphrased version is included here.

The Defeat of the Fomhoir

The Bard: Many beautiful men fell there in that stall of death. Great was the slaughter which took place there. Pride and shame were there side by side. Abundant were the streams of blood over the white skin of the young warriors, mangled by the rush into danger. Harsh was the noise made by the multitude of champions with their swords and spears. Harsh too the shouting and the clashing of bright shields. A gory, terrible, sharp, and bloody battle was upheaved, and many were the spear-heads reddened in the hands of foes. Then Lugh Lamh-Fada and Balor of the Piercing Eye met each other on the field. And Balor began to raise open his mighty poisonous eye. And Lugh Lamh-Fada cast a sling stone that struck Balor's eye and carried it through his head, and it was on Balor's own army that the eye looked, so that many of them fell dead. Immediately afterwards the battle broke, and the host of the

Fomhoir were driven into the sea. And as to the number of warriors who fell there: until the stars of heaven can be counted, and the sands of the sea, and flakes of snow, and dew on a lawn, and grass beneath the feet of horses, and all the horses of the son of Lir in a storm— they will not be counted at all. And after the battle was won and the slaughter cleared away, the Morrigan proclaimed the victory which had occurred there to the royal heights of Ireland, to its chief waters and to its rivermouths.

The Morrigan:

"Peace up to the sky!
Sky down to the earth,
Earth beneath heaven,
And strength to everyone!
A cup full of honey,
Summer in winter,
Fleece from the sheep
Forests filled with stags
Nuts on the trees
Warmth from the fire
Salmon in the rivers
Growth in the spring
The land held secure.
Peace up to the sky!
Be this nine times eternally."

Such a ceremony is likely to have been performed by Druids in and with their communities once each year. It is even possible that the drama was re-enacted only in parts: the story of the landing of the Gods on Beltaine, the battle and defeat of the Fomhoir at Lughnasad, for instance. One would have to attend all the ceremonies over the whole year to get the whole story.

At the center of the world, the primordial defeat of the dark powers is commemorated. We can imagine that the re-enactment of the battle and the defeat of the Fomhoir is necessary in order to prevent the Fomhoir from re-conquering the world again. After the Fomhoire are defeated, the establishment of a sacred Centre might be dramatized as follows:

Establishing the Center

The Bard: *"And the Tuatha de Dannans created a well below the sea where the nine hazels of wisdom were growing. And their leaves and their blossoms would break out in the same hour, and would fall on the well in a shower that raised a purple wave. And the five salmon that were waiting there would eat the nuts, and the colour would come out in the red spots on their skin, and any person that would eat one of those salmon would know all wisdom and poetry. And there were seven streams of wisdom that sprang from that well and turned back to it again; and the people of many arts have all drank from that well."*

The Druid: *"People of the Earth, behold the cauldron, which is the Well of Wisdom. A blessing I cast upon it and all who partake of it:*
Power of raven be thine,
Power of eagle be thine,
Power of the Fiann.

Power of storm be thine,
Power of moon be thine,
Power of sun.
Goodness of sea be thine,
Goodness of land be thine,
Goodness of heaven.[4]

The Bard: *"And the place called Uisneach, where the five provinces meet, was the first place where ever there was a fire kindled in Ireland. It was by Mide, son of Brath, it was kindled, for the sons of Nemed, and it was burning through six years, and it was from that fire every chief fire was kindled in Ireland."*

The Druid: *People of the tribe, behold this torch by which I kindle our sacred fire. A blessing I cast upon it and all who are warmed by it:*

"They shall not be slain,
They shall not be imprisoned,
They shall not be hewn,
They shall not be riven,
They shall not be anguished,
They shall not be wounded,
They shall not be ravaged,
They shall not be blinded,
They shall not be left bare,
Nor will the Gods of our people leave them forgotten."[5]

The assembled tribe may proceed to leap the fire kindled there, or walk or dance sunwise around it, with music and song. The Druid sprinkles each person with water from the Cauldron as they pass, using a leafy oak branch.

There are many ways in which the story can be understood. One interpretation of the story is purely environmental, because both Balor and Lugh are sun-deities. The story may represent the defeat of the "baneful" sun that might burn and scorch the earth as it rises higher in the sky from winter to summer, by the "beneficial" sun that warms and illuminates the earth gently and which decreases in power from summer to winter, allowing the land to rest. We could correspond this claim with the principle on the Coligny Calendar, in which the days, months, and the year alternate as "Mat" (favorable) and "Gia-mat" (unfavorable) times. Lugh is also associated with agriculture: his festival, called Lughnasad, is a harvest festival and indeed its name survives today as the modern Irish word for the month of August. This means that the timing of the defeat of Balor coincides with the post-midsummer period when the world is still warm and bright but the sun is measurably decreasing in power (that is, the total daylight time and the high-noon position of the sun is decreasing each day). As Lugh is also Balor's grandson, and the defeat of Balor thus an inter-generational succession in which youth defeats old age, the interpretation of the stories as mythological descriptions of environmental facts is quite elegant. The forces and powers of the sun, the wind, the sea, and the growth of plants, are all personified as divine beings with whom one can have a relationship. This anthropomorphic personification of natural forces is at the heart of "original" paganism. It is the human image projected outward and made divine.

It may therefore be said of Celtic Mysticism that it uses certain basic environmental facts as a symbolic vocabulary for the expression of spiritual experiences and aspirations. The exploration of nature through the spiritual attitude is thus a form of "knowing ourselves."

There is also a psychological interpretation. In recent popular pagan literature, this interpretation is obtained through the intellectual resources provided by the Austrian professor of psychology, Carl Jung. I am not a scholar of his thought (and neither are most recent writers on pagan spirituality either) so I will not explore his theory in great detail. But there is something very compelling about his claim that the characters, themes, and events of mythological storytelling are projections of the seeker's own internal life, her qualities of character and her deep subconscious drives and instincts, which are themselves shared with every other member of the human race. As internal experiences projected outwards on to the world, they can be internalized again to provide for the seeker a "spiritual path." In this respect, the Fomhoir are the parts of ourselves that Fomhoir-like, and the Tuatha de Dannan are those qualities in us which are closest to the divine. The myths are very specific about the qualities of character possessed by each: generosity, hospitality, and justice are the main qualities attributed to the Tuatha de Dannans, and the lack of the same is the mark of the Fomhoir.

Every year the Battle of Maigh Tuireadh is fought again, and every year the Tuatha de Dannan win. This should give us hope. Observe that the great battle to overcome the Fomhoir does not, as it were, end with a total annihilation of the "dark side." The worst of it is driven out, but some part of it remains. The dark side within us all must be acknowledged and recognized as still a part of ourselves, and its energy not so much suppressed as channeled into areas where it will bring benefit to oneself and one's world. Our Fomhoir nature is the seat of our primordial survival instinct. In some sense we cannot live without it, and yet we cannot allow it to consume the whole of our intentions. For survival is not an end-in-itself. If survival was our only guiding objective, then self-centred, miserly, aggressive, and destructive qualities would quickly rise to the surface. These qualities may enable one to succeed at competitively acquiring material resources. But because they also tend to lead to conflict, injustice, and misery, they are not in the long run conducive to the well-lived, worthwhile life, nor the sustaining of a functioning, healthy human community and culture. They must be coupled with the qualities of the Tuatha de Dannan. Our Tuatha de Dannan nature is the desire for culture, friendship, beauty, justice, and knowledge. It is the qualities which, when we act upon them, make us noble and bring us in touch with divinity.

Epilogue:
The Turning of the Wheel

The story of the creation of the world, it would seem, never really ends. But our re-enactment must come to a natural close somehow. The way to do this which has become standard in the pagan community is to release, dismiss, or banish any spirits, deities, or powers that were summoned at the beginning. Here I would like to close the ceremony a slightly different, not necessarily-incompatible way: by recounting the arrival of human beings in the world. This creates the continuity between the mythological events of the primordial battle and the present time. The race of humankind is referred to as the Sons of the Gael, or the Milesians after the name of Miled, an ancient king. They encounter the three goddesses Banba, Fodhla, and Eiru (remember them?) while making their way to Tara. When they arrive, the royal court is in an up-roar: three sons of the Dagda, one of whom is the king at that time, are argu-ing over how to divide their father's in-heritance. The Milesians find this surprising, as the land is so fruitful al-ready that there seems to be enough for all. So they demand to take the kingship right then and there, and they threaten to fight for it. Well, the king says he is not willing to give it up so easily, but is not ready to fight for it either, so he invites them to get back into their ships, retreat to the length of "nine waves" (that is, the horizon) and try to land again. He offers them a wa-ger: if they succeed, they can have Ire-land. The Milesians pile into their ships again, and the gods raise a magi-cal storm. Many people drown before Amergin finally calms the storm with a magic poem usually referred to as "The Invocation of Ireland." The poem essentially calls upon the Morrigan to favor him and his tribe. When the ships land, Amergin is the first off the boat, where he recites the famous Druidic poem known as Amergin's Song.

The Coming of the Human Race

The Bard: It is time now to bring this telling of the story of the world to an end. It is not known now how long the Tuatha de Dannan had Ireland, and it is likely it was a long time they had it, but they were put from it at last. The Sons of Miled, who were also called the Sons of the Gael, made a landing at Inver Sceine, in the west of Munster, and then made their way to Tara, and requested the right to stay in Ireland. They were told to withdraw their ships to the length of nine waves, and if they can make a landing again, they can have Ireland. This they did, and the Tuatha de Dannan raised a mighty storm to prevent them from landing. And Amergin, the great bard and Druid of the sons of the Gael, calmed the storm with a magical spell. And Amergin was the first to put his foot on the land, and when he stood on the shore of Ireland, it is what he said:

The Druid then recites the Song of Amergin: "I am the wind on the sea…"

***The Bard:** "This part of the story ends with the coming of our people, the human race, to the world. The Tuatha de Dannan retreated to the most beautiful of Ireland's hills and valleys to settle in, where they are protected by Manannan's hidden walls. There they eat the Feast of Age, and drink the ale of Goibhniu the Smith, that kept whoever tasted it from age and sickness and death. Behold, People of the Earth, that although the Old Gods have retreated, they remain among us, and live within us. In their special season, as at the times we call them, at the times we need them, they come again to us. And we shall assemble again to tell their story, which is indeed our own story. People of the Earth, the work of this place and time is ended. Go, and may the brightness of our gods go with you."*

From here, the Druid and Bard return to each of the four quarters, disbanding the circle and releasing the center, and thus resuming normal space and time.

There is, within Druidry, as we see in this part of the story, a extraordinary and unexpected humanism. For after the Milesians land on Ireland a second time, the Tuatha de Dannan meet them at the Battle of Taillten. The gods are defeated, and they are forced to retreat to hidden places under the hills, lakes, and mountains of Ireland. The implication is that the gods do not "rule" us. Because that is so, it is up to us, and us alone, to decide what to do with our lives, what to make of the world, and how to live. It is up to us to make the world into a realm of justice, prosperity, and peace, as the Tuatha de Dannan would have it, or let it decline into a bleak, impoverished, and rough world, as it was under the rule of the Fomhoir. Lady Gregory's telling of the tale ends by saying the gods retreated to the most beautiful of hills, lakes, and valleys of Ireland. Yet the tradition she was retelling also states that certain kinds of people are the descendants of the three races described in the stories. The Fomhoir, the Tuatha de Dannan, and the Milesians live on in the qualities of character possessed by living mortal men and women. Her exact words are:

> It is what the poets of Ireland used to be saying, that every brave man, good at fighting, and every man that could do great deeds and not be making much talk about them, was of the Sons of the Gael; and that every skilled man that had music and that did enchantments secretly, was of the Tuatha de Dannan. But they put a bad name on the Firbolgs...for lies and for big talk and injustice.[1]

The qualities of the gods, the heroes, and even the qualities of the Firbolgs and Fomhoire live on within us. The direction to "know yourself" leads to the divine image which is essentially human.

The Battle of Maigh Tuireadh, the war for the sovereignty of the land, can take place within each of our own hearts and minds. It is a struggle to overcome the propensity for self-centered corruption, which is how the Fomhoire now exist. It is a challenge to create the world in the image of what is noble. It is a struggle for the sovereignty of your own life. Every time you are faced with a situation that will change the direction of your life, like the choice the Morrigan offered to Setanta, the sovereignty of your life is gained or lost by your own choices. Battle and conflict is not the only metaphor of spiritual aspiration we find in the Celtic tradition. There is, most importantly, the metaphor of *love*, which is no metaphor at all, for we find it in our everyday lives as much as in the Great Marriage of the Sky God of the Tribe with the Earth Goddess of Sovereignty. There is also the metaphor of travelling on a path, as in the Otherworld journey of pagan Celtic heroes, the pilgrimages and exiles of Celtic Christian monks. The idea that spirituality is "walking a path" comes from the vocabulary of hunting, in which the seeker chases his or her spiritual attainments much as the hunter tracks the path of the animal. It appears also in stories that recount an *imramma*, a sea journey, which follows the same pattern as spirit-flight meditations. In the Middle Ages the same idea arises from the journey of the pilgrim following the long road to the great cathedrals. Christian and Pagan alike used all three of these metaphors.

If spirituality is following a path, then one may ask where you are going, and what might be the direction markers on the way? The original stage, before the spiritual journey begins, is a stage of receptivity and passivity, and also innocence and imagination and play, which are often regarded as the qualities of the most spiritually mature. But the innocence of the original state bears a subtle difference: it is *indistinguishable from ignorance.* Thus it is subject to fear, exploitation, and destruction as it is exposed to suffering. The original state lacks critical consciousness; that is to say, it has not yet formed questions about the world, and has not yet stood up to seek knowledge. It only stands back to passively receive knowledge. Thus it is often a kind of prison: a comfortable prison, and an invisible prison, but a prison nonetheless. This is the condition of someone whose word is "Yes," but it is not a positive, liberating Yes: rather, it is the affirmation of someone else's word.

The first spiritual season, which I call "the springtime," comes with the first inklings that there may be more to life than appearances and the beliefs impressed in one's mind by others. It is the season of awareness of the chimerical nature of much of what was once received as real, true, and good. Here, we discover that things are not what they seem, not what they ought to be, not what they were meant to be—and that the chimera one lives in may even be the deliberate design of others who benefit from its maintenance. I regard the springtime as the first legitimate season in the spiritual wheel because the first free and independent articulation of one's own word happens here: and the word is the sacred "No." This word *expresses the speaker's will to change her life,* and live differently than she has lived hitherto. It negates the chimera, and speaks of the will to tear down all fraudulent and cruel illusions, perhaps also to obtain justice for those who have been harmed by them. The quest to find the actuality, the true, the good, begins here, and the world begins to respond. But the trap at this stage, and which emerges occasionally in subsequent stages, is that one can make an occupation of negating the words of others, and thus never get to affirming anything.

The second is the stage of "high summer." A new reality is discovered and enjoyed, as the first inklings of sound from outside the prison that began in the springtime become here a full orchestra of music. The world opens up to the seeker in a way that had not happened before, and one discovers connections and bonds with others which, as most seekers who achieve high summer perceive it, always existed but were never previously realized. Instruments for obtaining energetic bliss and ecstasy are found here, which are more permanent and substantial than those of the pre-spiritual life: they rely on one's own capacities and are not dependant on the interventions of other forces. In the summertime, you do not merely hear the music, as in the spring: you begin performing it. Indeed the music of the spheres begins to play through you. One discovers that the sacred "No" from the springtime was spoken towards that which had to be negated before anything new could grow. It is transformed into a sacred "Yes," the affirmation of the beautiful, the just, the alive, and the true. Having said "no" to the stops, as it were, the word of high summer says "yes" to the fresh water that was thus enabled to flow. I wish to affirm that this stage is valuable but it too has its traps and dangers. It is a comfortable position, and therefore many seekers do not want to move on to discover more. Magical technologies such as Reiki, spirit flight, drumming, and the like, can have the addictive power of a chemical substance. A seeker may think he is constantly learning new things, when he is merely moving from one stimulus to another. There is also the urge to tell everyone about one's discoveries and become a great

teacher, which can quickly turn into an ego trip. At any rate, this stage is rarely surpassed because what follows after it can be discouraging, or even downright frightening.

The third stage, which comes after the first encompassing of spiritual bliss, is the first encompassing of spiritual pain: the stage of "autumn." It is normally triggered by confronting a reality that is hurtful, ugly, or even terrifying, but as much an immensity as any positive experience. It could be an experience of transience, old age, or death, facing you directly, or a close friend. The opening of the world to the spiritual consciousness of the seeker, which began during summer, tends at this stage to reveal realities that are difficult, unpleasant, frightening, and repugnant. One becomes more sensitive to the suffering of others, by means of the same knowledge-expanding consciousness that brought happiness in the previous stage. Depression may set in, or anger against the sources of the suffering. Therefore we speak again the sacred "No," but this time not to the illusions of the world that prevent spiritual knowledge, but to the realities of the world that enable such knowledge: it is a No spoken to the Path itself. For how could a path be called *spiritual* if it makes life *harder* to live? Is life rendered meaningless by the transience of everything in it, including the spiritual path, and the inevitability of death? Hence the Poet laments "all that's beautiful drifts away, like the waters," therefore he spits into the face of time. But the path is functioning properly when its manifestations reveal ever more widening ranges of reality, even if what it reveals is uncomfortable or ungratifying. The trap here is that we may invent new illusions to protect ourselves from such realities. Due to these hidden self-deceptions, this is a stage people rarely explore to its final end.

If we learn to eventually transform the second sacred "No" into a second sacred "Yes," a yes that affirms the autumn, that affirms the transience and suffering of others, a yes that refuses to ignore suffering but fully accepts it and takes possession of it, and works to overcome it, then we are admitted into the fourth season. This is the stage of "winter," of darkness and the Great Silence. This season is what life feels like for someone able to experience the stillness and peace that lies "beneath" or "behind" the world. This is the most private part of the spiritual path. Social titles and responsibilities like being a Druid matter very little here, or even not at all. It has an element of loneliness in it because it affords not only a sense of unity and connectivity with the whole of the universe, but also the knowledge that the universe is all that there is, the universe has nothing "other" than itself. Beyond the world there is silence. A fundamental *emptiness* within both the good and the bad is opened to you: *the possibility that things might have no value at all, neither good nor bad,* is opened to you. Here you confront the prospect that there is nothing in the world that is beautiful and also eternal. The spiritual realms which were discovered in the spring, which flooded the seeker with love in the summer, and which in the autumn shared its pain, now ceases to respond at all. One loves, hopes, prays, and gives as before. Only now there is no echo, nothing responds: *silence* is the response. This season is the most subtle and thus the most difficult challenge, where the path ceases to lead by holding out sweets to reach for, or by offering sores on lepers for would-be saints to kiss. Now the path is teaching how to do one's work for the sake of the work itself, not for the sake of results or consequences. Now the path teaches how to love without interest in getting anything back for it, without attachment to a return, nor even attachment to success. Now one learns to love for the sake of loving, now one begins to learn something really valuable. But this stage is hard, for it is here we doubt not the path but the seeker who walks it. Here we doubt ourselves. Loneliness may set in as one finds fewer and fewer other people who could understand one's thoughts and feelings, and as even the spirit world itself ceases to respond. We progress when we see the winter of darkness, stillness, and silence as the *original* season. It is the season of the unfertilized seed still hidden in the soil, the season where the darkness of the buried coffin is indistinguishable from that of the mother's womb, and the empty is indistinguishable from the infinite. One begins to *leave behind the self,* that one may do more than simply *know* the world: one may *achieve* it. It is a stage of total receptivity, like the spring, but unlike the spring there are no illusions. They too have been dissolved, and thus there is no ignorance concerning what they hide. This discovery transports the seeker into a new spring.

What is beyond here, I do not know, for I have not travelled that far. From what I read in the accounts of the worlds greatest mystics, I anticipate a recycling of the seasons on the wheel, until one settles into a spiral, feeding into itself so that each repetition is more intense than the last. Perhaps this lasts indefinitely, or perhaps until the cycle is interrupted by a breakthrough into the center. The places I described as "winter" and "summer" may be mere rehearsals for events yet to come, which are far worse and far better: the *Dark Night of the Soul*, and then the final *Great Marriage with the Beloved*.

I believe the ancient Druids knew this, but I can only speculate about that. It was certainly known to the Irish monk who, just as the Celtic Heroic age was ending and the Christian period was beginning, wrote this short but deeply profound poem:

> To go to Rome,
> Is great trouble, small profit.
> The King that you seek there,
> You will not find unless you take Him with you.[2]

The urgency to "Know Yourself," the first imperative of every form of Mysticism, is reaffirmed here. Searching within ourselves we find the wisdom and beauty of the Tuatha de Dannan, the honour and bravery of the Milesians, the peace and love of the Celtic Christ. Similarly we find the malice and miserliness of the Fomhoir. The heroic quest to "know yourself" takes us to the gods and the monsters who are immanent: that is, they are part of us and part of the world, and are inseparable from our own way of life in and with the world. Perhaps this discovery is what enabled the ancient Druids to claim "we created the world." It is what enabled Blake to say that the divine image is essentially human. It is what enabled Amergin to identify himself with the wind from across the sea, the flash of the sun, and ultimately the whole of the world. It is this discovery which drives the turning of the wheel, enables the defeat of the

Fomhoir, and carries the seeker on a spiral path closer to the Well of Wisdom at the center. There we find that all of us are Sacred Kings and Great Queens, connected to the landscape of the world in which we live. Thus, if your meditation is on anger and resentment then the world will be full of hardship and frustration. If your meditation is on courage and compassion, then you will manifest the gods in your life, and you will recreate Tir Na n-Og here on Earth.

Put out the candle now, and close the window. For a moment before doing anything, be still and at rest. In your sleep tonight, let these thoughts drift in your dreams. And when the morning comes and the sun awakens, follow the adventure of your life.

Notes

Introduction

1. This is the version of the story as it appears in Lady Gregory's *Cuchullain of Muirthemney* and Kinsella's translation of *The Táin*. Quoted text here is from Kinsella's *The Táin*, pg. 84-85.

Chapter 1

1. Strabo, *Geographica*, IV, 4.
2. Thomas Kinsella (trans.) *The Táin* (Oxford UK: Oxford University Press, 1969) pg. 84.
3. Julius Caesar, *De Bello Gallico,* VI:14.
4. Julius Caesar, *De Bello Gallico,* VI:14.
5. As cited by Dáithí Ó hÓgáin, *The Sacred Isle*, pg. 82.
6. Ó h-Ógáin, *The Sacred Isle*, pg. 96.
7. Two books I recommend to learn more about the Celtic festival calendar are Kondratiev, A. *The Apple Branch*, and Hutton, R. *The Stations of the Sun*. A good book which describes the meaning of these festivals for modern Wiccans is Farrar, J & S. *A Witch's Bible*.
8. See Hutton, *The Stations of the Sun*, pp. 360-380.
9. See Ann Ross, *The Life and Death of a Druid Prince* (New York, USA: Touchstone, 1989) for the complete account.
10. Frazer, *The Golden Bough*, pp. 312-313
11. See R. Nichols, *The Book of Druidry*. (Aquarian Press, 1990) pg. 10, for reference to the Apple Tree Tavern.
12. See C. Knight & R. Lomas, *The Second Messiah*, pg. 72. A Freemason connection is also discussed by R. Nichols in *The Book of Druidry*, although Nichols says "they were similar to, but not identical with, the Lodge of Freemasons." [pg. 100.]

Chapter 2

1. "Fath-fith" (prayer #133), in Alexander Carmichael, *Carmina Gadelica*, pg. 131. According to the translator's footnote, a *scan* is "probably some animal."

2. Gregory, *Gods and Fighting Men*, pg. 105.

3. Fergus Kelly (trans.) *Audacht Morainn* (Dublin: Institute for Advanced Studies, 1976) pg. 5-7. [6-21]

4. 84, *Caith Maigh Tuireadh*, Elisabeth Gray, trans. (Dublin: Irish Texts Society, 1982) [pg. 45]

5. Julius Caesar, *De Bello Gallico*, VI, 18.

6. Mircea Eliade, *The Myth of the Eternal Return*, pg. 25-26.

7. Eliade, *The Myth of the Eternal Return*, pg. 13.

8. Gray, trans. *Caith Maigh Tuireadh* § 1-7, pg. 25. (Irish Texts Society, 1982)

9. J. Campbell, *The Hero with a Thousand Faces*, 2nd edn. (Princeton University Press, N.J. USA, 1968) pp. 30, 40.

10. Ó h-Ógáin, *The Sacred Isle*, pp. 160-161.

11. Pliny, *Natural History*.

12. See Erynn Laurie, *A Circle of Stones* (Eschaton, 1998); see also her article *The Cauldron of Poesy* which appeared in Obsidian Magazine No.2, Spring 1996.

13. Dáithí Ó h-Ógáin, *The Sacred Isle*, pg. 80.

14. Kuno Meyer, *Sanas Cormac* (Halle, 1912) pg. 40.

15. Yeats, *Folk and Faerie Tales of the Irish Peasantry*.

16. Yeats, *Autobiography*, (London: MacMillan, 1955) pg. 189.

17. Tolkien, "On Fairy Stories", lecture delivered in 1938; here quoted from a published version in *Tree and Leaf* (Allen and Unwin, 1964) pg. 1.

18. R. Ellmann, *Yeats: The Man and the Masks* (Macmillan, 1949) pg. 116.

19. At the risk of blowing my own horn, this definition comes from my previous book: *Dangerous Religion: Environmental Spirituality and its Activist Dimension*.

20. Mela, *De Situ Orbis* IV, IV, 4; see also Kendrick *The Druids* (London, 1927) pg. 87-8.

21. Diodorus, *Bibliotheca*, V, 28.

22. Lady Gregory, *Gods and Fighting Men* pg. 74.

Chapter 3

1. Lady Gregory, *Gods and Fighting Men*, pg. 145.
2. 166, *Caith Magh Tuireadh* [pg. 71.] I have rendered a different English translation of the Old Irish text supplied by Gray.
3. Harris, *Our Kind*, pg. 415.

Chapter 4

1. Dáithí Ó h-Ógáin, *The Sacred Isle*, pg. 172.
2. Ó h-Ógáin, *The Sacred Isle*, pg. 71.
3. Kinsella (trans.) *The Táin* pg. 60.
4. 245, Carmina Gadelica, pg. 217.
5. 216, Carmina Gadelica, pg. 187.
6. Mircea Eliade, *The Myth of the Eternal Return*, pg. 35.
7. Virtuvius, *The Ten Books of Architecture* book 2, ch. 1,1. Trans. Morris Hickey Morgan (New York: Dover, 1960), pg. 38. Quoted in Karsten Harries, *The Ethical Function of Architecture* pg. 137.
8. Carmina Gadelica §83, "Kindling the Fire," pg. 94.
9. See Brennan, *The Stones of Time*
10. Aaron Wilson, "The sounds of transformation", in Neil S. Price (ed.), *The Archaeology of Shamanism* (London: Routledge, 2001) pg. 188.
11. See Dronfield, "Entering Alternative Realities: Cognition, Art, and Architecture in Irish Passage-Tombs" *Cambridge Archaeological Journal* Vol. 6 No. 1 (1996) pp. 37-72; "Subjective vision and the source of Irish megalithic art" *Antiquity* 69 (1995) pp. 539-549; "Migrane, Light, and Hallucinogens: The Neurocognitive Basis of Irish Megalithic Art" *Oxford Journal of Archaeology* Vol. 14 No. 3 (1995) pp. 261-275. I am grateful to Ken Lymer for supplying me with copies of these papers.
12. William Blake, "The Divine Image" and "A Divine Image", *Poems and Prose* (Fount Classics, 1997) pp. 16 & 56.

Chapter 5

1. George Russell "A.E.," *The Candle of Vision* (London: MacMillan and Co., Ltd. 1931) pp. 10-12.
2. As cited in Ó h-Ógáin, *The Sacred Isle*, pg. 157.

Chapter 6

1. Harris, *Our Kind*, pg. 190.
2. Harris, *Our Kind*, pg. 191.

3. 31, *Testament of Morann*.

4. Campbell, *Myths to Live By* (London: Palladin, 1985) pg. 15.

5. Campbell, *Myths to Live By*, pg. 34.

6. 55, *Testament of Morann*.

7. 62, *Testament of Morann*.

8. See Alfred P. Smyth, *Warlords and Holy Men: Scotland AD 80-1000* (Edinburgh University Press, 1989)

9. Mircae Eliade, *The myth of the Eternal Return*, pg. 23.

10. For more detailed information, see Fergus Kelly, *A Guide to Early Irish Law*

11. 22, *Instructions of Cormac*

12. Julius Caesar, *De Bello Gallico*, VI: 14.

13. *Pharsalia*, 1, 450-458.

14. I would also like to say, with some hesitation, that the shape of this initiation came to me in a dream. It was revealed to me over three nights after my first visit to the Hill of Uisneach, in early October of 2003. I was left with a great feeling of the weight of history, and yet also a great sense of peace, and it stayed with me for the whole of the following month. What I have presented here differs from my dream in several respects, mainly concerning personal matters.

15. A.E. *The Candle of Vision*, pp. 15-17.

Chapter 7

1. O'Donovan *The Ancient Laws of Ireland* (Dublin: 1865) 1,22.

2. Ella Young, *Celtic Wonder Tales* (New York USA: Dover, 1995 [first published 1910]) pp. 1-11.

3. Eliade, *The Myth of the Eternal Return*, pg. 20.

4. Carmina Gadelica, §282, "Good Wish".

5. Carmina Gadelica, §264, "Blessing of Brigid."

Epilogue

1. Gregory, *Gods and Fighting Men*, pg. 76.

2. Anonymous, "To Find God", in Ruth P.M. Lehmann, *Early Irish Verse* (Austin: U. of Texas Press, 1982) pg. 30.

Index

About the Author

Brendan **Cathbad Myers** is originally from a small town in rural Ontario. His father emigrated to Canada from Ireland, and thus Celtic culture and folklore has been a part of his life since childhood. This influence eventually inspired him to study and practice Celtic spirituality, which he has done for many years. In the Pagan community his writings have appeared on the Internet and in numerous printed magazines and journals in four countries, including *Oak Leaves*, *An Tribhis Mor* (USA), *Imramma* (Ireland), *Pentacle* Magazine, *Comhairli Cairde* (UK), *Pagan's Wake*, and *Wiccan Candles* (Canada).

Cathbad is one of the founding members of the Order of the White Oak (a Druidic society) and of Conradh Draoithe na h-treann/Convocation of Irish Druids. For three years he served as CDEs secretary. He holds a B.A. and an M.A from the University of Guelph, and a Ph.D in philosophy from the National University of Ireland, Galway. He also studied folklore at Memorial University of Newfoundland.

Presently, Cathbad continues to practice Celtic spirituality, and continues to research the philosophical foundations of environmental spirituality. *The Mysteries of Druidry* is his second book; his first, *Dangerous Religion: Environmental Spirituality and its Activist Dimension*, is published by Dubsar House/Earth Religions Press, and available at *Amazon.com*.

CPSIA information can be obtained at www.ICGtesting.com
Printed in the USA
LVOW01s1912061015

457159LV00013B/310/P